HISTORY OF LITERATURE SERIES
General Editor: A. NORMAN JEFFARES

HISTORY OF LITERATURE SERIES

General editor: A. Norman Jeffares

SIXTEENTH-CENTURY ENGLISH LITERATURE
Murray Roston

SEVENTEENTH-CENTURY ENGLISH LITERATURE
Bruce King

TWENTIETH-CENTURY ENGLISH LITERATURE
Harry Blamires

ANGLO-IRISH LITERATURE
A. Norman Jeffares

HISTORY OF LITERATURE SERIES

SEVENTEENTH-CENTURY ENGLISH LITERATURE

Bruce King

Schocken Books · New York

First American edition published by Schocken Books 1982

10 9 8 7 6 5 4 3 2 1 82 83 84 85

Published by agreement with The Macmillan Press Ltd., London

Printed in Hong Kong

ISBN 0-8052-3826-3

Contents

Acknowledgements

The author and publishers wish to acknowledge, with thanks, the following illustration sources:

B. T. Batsford Ltd (Doreen Yarwood: The English House) 4a
Belton House, Lincolnshire 15, 16
Bodleian Library 6
D. E. Bower Collection, Chiddingstone Castle 8
British Tourist Authority 12b
J. Allan Cash Ltd 13
Devonshire Collection: by permission of the Trustees of the Chatsworth Settlement 2, 4b
Greater London Council Photograph Library 12a
Huntingdon Libraries 7
National Portrait Gallery 5, 14
Victoria and Albert Museum 9, 11

List of Plates

1. Garden of Plenty. Design for triumphal arch in Cheapside for Royal Entry of James I into London, 1604. Drawn by chief architect Stephen Harrison; texts for the pageant written by Thomas Dekker and Ben Jonson.
2. Oberon's Palace. Inigo Jones's design for Scene II of Jonson's *The Masque of Oberon* (1611).
3. Preaching at St Paul's Cross. Unknown Jacobean artist (*c*. 1616).
4(a) Gilt Jacobean wine-cup (1616–17).
4(b) A Dwarf Postillion from Hell. Costume design by Inigo Jones for an antimasque to Jonson's *Chloridia* (1631).
5. Five Children of Charles I, painted by Antony Van Dyck, 1638.
6. Emblematic title page to Henry Vaughan's *Silex Scintillans*, 1650. Within the heart a face can be seen.
7. Portrait of Oliver Cromwell's daughter Bridget, attributed to Sir Peter Lely.
8. Nell Gwyn, actress and mistress of Charles II, painted by Sir Peter Lely.
9. Gilt Restoration cup and cover (1669).
10. From Act V of Settle's *The Empress of Morocco* (1673), the first play to be published with illustrations of its scenes.
11. *An Owl Mocked by Small Birds*, painted by Francis Barlow, 1673.
12(a) St Laurence Jewry (1671–77), one of the churches restored by Christopher Wren after the Great Fire.
12(b) St Paul's Cathedral (1695–1710), also restored by Wren.
13. Abingdon Town House (1680), built and probably

Also by Bruce King

Books
The New English Literatures (Macmillan, 1980)
Marvell's Allegorical Poetry (Oleander Press, 1977)
Dryden's Major Plays (Oliver & Boyd, 1966)

Books Edited
West Indian Literature (Macmillan, 1979)
A Celebration of Black and African Writing (with Kolawole Ogungbesan; Ahmadu Bello University Press and Oxford University Press, 1976)
Literatures of the World in English (Routledge and Kegan Paul, 1974)
Introduction to Nigerian Literature (University of Lagos Press and Evans Brothers, 1971)
Dryden's Mind and Art (Oliver & Boyd, 1969)
Twentieth-Century Interpretations of All for Love: a collection of critical essays (Prentice-Hall, 1968)

General Editor (with Adele King), 'The Macmillan Modern Dramatists'

Study Guides
York Notes to *G. B. Shaw's Arms and the Man* (Longmans, 1980)
York Notes to *Ibsen's A Doll's House* (Longmans, 1980)
York Notes to *Fielding's Joseph Andrews* (Longmans, 1981)

Editor's Preface

THE study of literature requires knowledge of contexts as well as of texts. What kind of person wrote the poem, the play, the novel, the essay? What forces acted upon them as they wrote? What was the historical, the political, the philosophical, the economic, the cultural background? Was the writer accepting or rejecting the literary conventions of the time, or developing them, or creating entirely new kinds of literary expression? Are there interactions between literature and the art, music or architecture of its period? Was the writer affected by contemporaries or isolated?

Such questions stress the need for students to go beyond the reading of set texts, to extend their knowledge by developing a sense of chronology, of action and reaction, and of the varying relationships between writers and society.

Histories of literature can encourage students to make comparisons, can aid in understanding the purposes of individual authors and in assessing the totality of their achievements. Their development can be better understood and appreciated with some knowledge of the background of their time. And histories of literature, apart from their valuable function as reference books, can demonstrate the great wealth of writing in English that there is to be enjoyed. They can guide the reader who wishes to explore it more fully and to gain in the process deeper insights into the rich diversity not only of literature but of human life itself.

A. NORMAN JEFFARES

TO LILLIAN, ADELE AND NICOLE

Preface

THE seventeenth century was probably the greatest century of English poetry and drama and, while the novel was still in its infancy, has left us such prose classics as Bacon's *Essays*, Browne's *Religio Medici* and Bunyan's *Pilgrim's Progress*. Although by the conventions of literary history Shakespeare belongs to the sixteenth century, his greatest tragedies, tragicomedies and romances are contemporary, and share characteristics, with the writings of Jonson, Donne, Marston and Fletcher. In an ideal world, not governed by the economics of book publishing, I would have written on how Shakespeare's late plays are influenced by and yet dissimilar to the other Jacobean dramas. I would also have written at more length of George Herbert, Marvell and Crashaw — three poets with claims to greatness. But then there would also need to be fuller discussions of such interesting and now neglected authors as Oldham, Carew, Shirley, Ravenscroft and Behn. The good literature of the seventeenth century sometimes seems as endless as modern discussions of the Puritans, the causes of the Civil War, the influence of the new science on literary style and what is meant by the Baroque.

I thank the following for help with this book, ranging from organisation and style, Denis Walker, David Gunby; manuscript assistance, Ian Richards and Elizabeth Crayford; answers to queries, Max Novak, David Vieth, William Frost, Douglas Canfield, Haskell Hinnant and Howard McNaughton; and the University of Canterbury for a research grant. The further reading list indicates other debts. Some reading was done while I held a fellowship at the William Andrews Clark Library.

BRUCE KING

1
The background:
1600-25

I Causes of political instability

AFTER the weakening of the feudal barons, many countries in Europe developed in the direction of nation-states, with power centralised into the hands of a monarch, Court and administrative bureaucracy. In a few countries, such as England and Holland, there were successful struggles with the monarchy for control of the nation. The clashes between King and Parliament in England during the seventeenth century were a struggle within a small ruling class for dominant power. Over the decades the conflict crystallised in the matter of royal prerogative: had the King the right to dispense with laws as he saw fit for the benefit of the nation, or was he bound to act as desired by the House of Commons, the representative of the largest propertied interests?

The ruling establishment consisted of perhaps 4 per cent of the population. The number of peers at one time or another ranged from fifty-five at the end of Elizabeth's reign to about one hundred and twenty. As the Tudors had weakened the peerage, few families could trace their title before the sixteenth century and there was continual strife for prestige among the newly created peers and those who were titled a generation or two previously. Land, although remaining the most significant source of power and prestige, changed hands, with the newly wealthy buying estates and titles. Unlike the titled nobility of the Continent, no landed warrior class in England saw its fate linked to that of monarchy. There were, however, twenty-six bishops who, until 1688, viewed their interests as similar to those of the throne, and who in asserting their rights helped to destroy the rule of both Charles I and James II. Next in precedence were some 300 baronets and Englishmen with Irish or Scottish titles. There were, early in the century, perhaps 1700 knights, 8000 'esquires' and 12,000 'gentlemen' (the lesser landed gentry, traders, lawyers, merchants and Crown officers). Although the 'gentlemen' played a significant role in the century's politics they were not powerful on their own; more powerful was the squirearchy who, along with the gentlemen, claimed to represent the nation through the House of Commons. They claimed their rights not in terms of universal freedom, which they were against, but as the supposed traditional privileges of the propertied.

As there was no standing army or national police force and as England lacked the administrative bureaucracy common to European countries, the Crown depended on the peerage and squirearchy to control the countryside. The upper 4 per cent of society traditionally were responsible for law and order; they raised the army from their tenants when one was needed, they acted as justices of the peace, controlled elections and provided jobs — in return for economic and social advantages.

A major cause of social and political unrest was the instability of the peerage. In destroying the power of the feudal barons the Tudors had undermined a source of local authority; Elizabeth even refused to create new peers to replace those who died. The rapid giving of titles by James I, many of which were sold to the highest bidder, resulted in the dissatisfaction of the older nobility and charges of corruption; the creation of such new orders as the baronets meant that the new nobility often did not take upon themselves traditional social responsibilities. Another cause of the instability of the peerage was the long period of inflation from the mid-sixteenth to the mid-seventeenth century, which reduced income from land and ruined many of the older families, causing them to sell their estates. Some peers, however, grew rich by enclosing communal lands, applying more efficient methods of agriculture and steeply raising the rents of their tenants. Traditional local social relationships were disturbed and many rural labourers were driven from the land to the cities. The peerage was also weakened by its obsession with displays of magnificence. Possibly because of the sudden emergence of wealth during the sixteenth century and the rapid social mobility that followed, personal honour became associated with visibly lavish expenditure. Extravagant houses were built and weddings, royal visits and other social occasions were celebrated at great cost with immense sums of money spent on masques and other entertainments. Even dowries became magnificent. The Court and peerage were usually heavily in debt.

Because of rising prices and wealth gained through trade, industry and modern farming, the late sixteenth and early seventeenth centuries saw a rapid shift in those holding economic power from the Lords to the House of Commons; it was said that the members in the House of Commons had three times the wealth of those in the House of Lords. As the Stuart kings were perpetually short of money, for which they necessarily turned to Parliament, the Commons increasingly challenged the Lords, Church and Crown for ultimate power.

While England was still mostly an agricultural country, by the end of the sixteenth century London had become a large city, continually increasing in population, a centre of wealth, finance and entertainments. It drew rural labourers in search of new jobs, attracted the peerage and landed gentry in search of pleasure, and became a place for rapid social and economic advancement. In the rush by the nobility to London and the Court, the responsibilities of the peerage were often neglected. Whereas the older manors were centres for local government, estates were now left in the hands of managers who were required to obtain high rents and profits. The social and political effects were destabilising and the monarchy wanted the nobility to return to the country to ensure social control. While the country peerage preferred urban life instead of attending to their farms and duties as justices of the peace, London was also increasingly a centre of opposition to the Court. It was the only place in England where the Presbyterians were in the majority, and its militia was the basis of the Parliamentary army at the start of the Civil War; throughout the century opposition leaders could raise city mobs to besiege Parliament. As more and more rural labourers, university graduates, students at the Inns of Court and peers came to London seeking opportunities and found their advancement frustrated, dissatisfactions increased and the basis was laid of a political opposition.

Although the demarcation between Court and opposition was seldom as clear as it is sometimes represented, there was a tendency for the English ruling class to split between those with Court interests and those whose advancement, security, property or religious preferences seemed threatened by the monarchy; the opposing interests were often identified with two distinct cultures. The Stuart monarchs supported the arts and were far more European in their tastes than Elizabeth. Under James the Court masque became a costly high art, using recent Italian innovations in movable scenery and perspective staging; the presence of women actresses in the masques outraged the Puritans. Inigo Jones introduced classicism into Court architecture, while a few peers began collecting the 'papist' art of Italy and Spain. As can be seen from the poetry of Ben Jonson and Robert Herrick, the classical revival often made use of pagan and Roman motifs and used mythology to celebrate the royal family; it associated the classical pagan world with a merry old England of maypoles, festivals and other ceremonies now distasteful to those who wanted church reform. Even the style of Donne and the metaphysical poets was strongly influenced by the literature and taste of Italy and Spain and can be seen as an English adaptation of continental Mannerist and Baroque poetic techniques. (Sixteenth and early-seventeenth-century Mannerism in art, music and architecture implied a sophisticated manner, elegance and wit; the Baroque was ornamental, irregular, dynamic and strongly rhythmic, with oratorical tendencies.) The witty metaphysical style, which is sometimes said to have first developed in continental Catholic sermons, is a high- rather than low-church style in seventeenth-century England. The Puritans were against witty, learned sermons. At the start of the Civil War almost every writer of significance, except Milton, took the side of the King.

The continental, Catholic culture of the Court was made more distasteful to the opposition because each of the Stuarts had a Catholic queen and there were Catholics at Court, often in high positions. Elizabeth by force of circumstance had been anti-Spanish, and her foreign policy was supported by those merchants and traders who saw Spain as a rival for the wealth that could be obtained through command of the seas. By the early seventeenth century Spain had become a minor sea power and the Protestant Dutch were England's new rival. Essex and Ralegh could dream of daring raids by Protestant ships to steal Spanish gold, but the seventeenth century was no longer a time for buccaneers; it was a time for colonisation and developing overseas trade. The country wanted England to lead a Protestant alliance against the Catholic nations of Europe, but the kings could not afford such wars, Parliament would not pay for them, and there was often no economic advantage to be gained. Cromwell in power spoke of defending continental Protestants, but he carried on naval wars against the Dutch.

While the Court sympathised with the persecuted English Catholics (perhaps one-third of the population at the beginning of the century), and hoped to become free of Parliamentary restraint by forming a grand alliance through marriage with France or Spain, the opposition focused on seeming pro-Catholic characteristics of the Court as a means of rallying the country against the King. Much of the religious controversy of the century was political in origin. The opposition to the Court increasingly put on Puritan warpaint as a means of raising support in what was essentially a conflict over power. Even such seemingly pure religious matters as Sunday observance were coloured by politics. Since the Tudors used church homilies as a means of creating propaganda for the monarchy and the established social order, it seemed necessary to control preaching. As Sunday dancing, games and drinking provided an outlet for the workers, then if such recreations were forbidden, the masses would gather to discuss politics and attend unlicensed, Puritan sermons which were likely to be subversive to Church and State.

For the main European powers in competition for dominance of the Continent, England was a side show. Its monarchy was poor, it had a weak administration and no standing army, its rich were undertaxed, its nobility were no longer warriors, and its ruling class was divided. The heart of the problem was the struggle over who would rule the country. The nation could have no role in Europe as long as it was divided and its government was impoverished. The French kings earned more from just the salt tax than all the revenues of the King of England.

II   Queen Elizabeth and James I

Some events of the last years of Queen Elizabeth's reign fore-shadow the political and religious strife which plagued England during the new century. The founding of the East India Company in 1600 indicated the growing significance of foreign trade and companies to capitalise such ventures. Although Parliament's criticism of monopolies in 1601 was softened by Elizabeth revoking patents, she continued to claim the right of monarchy to license trades, to collect fees for doing so, and, since there was no government bureaucracy, the right to rent the privilege of licensing and collecting fees and taxes to whom she chose. As licences were a major means of the monarchy raising money, and as the monopolies were resented by those unable to obtain permits, such practices would remain a central conflict between the House of Commons and the throne. The two main directions English Protestantism was to take, which split the Church and con-tributed to the Civil War, were represented by Richard Hooker (*d.* 1600) and William Perkins (*d.* 1602). Hooker's *The Ecclesiastical Polity* had laid down the intellectual foundations for the Anglican Church and its place within the national community. The English was a reformed church continuing the traditions of the primitive church. In contrast to Hooker's ceremonial, sacramental, hierarchical vision (a source of the Arminian high-church movement under Laud during the Caroline period), Perkins brought the extreme Calvinism of Theodore Beza to England. The Puritans, who by the 1560s were already strong in the House of Commons, were suppressed by Elizabeth throughout the 1580s and 90s, but during the last years of her reign were once again becom-ing troublesome in Parliament and tried to influence church and foreign policy. Elizabeth, as would James I and Charles I, regarded attempts to change the doctrine and organisation of the national church as part of a political struggle for power: who controlled the Church would control the nation.

A year after the accession of James I (1603) to the throne of England, a conference was held at Hampton Court between the leaders of the Church of England and some Puritan divines who objected to parts of the Prayer Book, church ritual and such ceremonies as the sign of the cross during baptism. The only compromise reached was to co-operate on a translation of the Bible, the Authorised Version which appeared in 1611. Calvinist doctrine was perhaps held by the majority of the clergy in contrast to those who believed in free will. Under the Calvinist system as developed in Geneva and Scotland, the state did not control the Church, which was ruled by an elaborate system of elected officers. While James I was himself generally Calvinist in theology, he was determined to uphold the existing system of episcopacy in which the monarch was supreme governor of the Church, and by 1607 James had forced bishops upon the Scottish Church. The Puritan demand for church reform was closely bound to the developing conflict for supremacy between the House of Commons and the Crown. Part of the King's power was asserted through his appointment of high-church officers who controlled the lower clergy. In any political conflict the bishops could be counted upon to support the King in the House of Lords, to raise revenue and to have sermons read supporting the divine right of kings. The ecclesiastical courts could be used to suppress many forms of political and social dissent. It is not surprising that the House of Commons was strongly Puritan.

Early in the century there was no distinction between the government and the household staff of the King. The Privy Council, the Secretaries of State, and the judges were part of the Court which, with various hangers-on, totalled thousands. The great nobles still travelled with hundreds of personal officers and servants in attendance. Elizabeth, to avoid becoming dependent on revenue from Parliament, lived frugally and sold Crown lands. James by comparison was extravagant and could not support his Court through traditional sources of revenue. He also inherited large debts from Elizabeth. Both by enlarging the peerage and leasing or selling monopolies and the collection of taxes to others, James contributed to the resentment of those outside the Court's favours. The House of Commons complained against monopolies, the selling of the peerages, the ecclesiastical courts and the Crown's raising of money without Parliamentary permission. From 1606 onwards common-law judges and lawyers appealed to Parliament for support against the ecclesiastical courts. It was largely through common law that

Sir Edward Coke developed his many precedents and claims of historical right against the power of the King and Church. Common law was seen as a defence of property. In 1611 Coke and the common-law judges tried to limit jurisdiction of the highest ecclesiastical court, the Court of High Commission, by issuing prohibitions. The creation and sale of the order of baronets began the same year.

Another area of conflict was foreign policy. Whereas James, who could not afford a foreign war, hoped to be a peace-maker between the rival European Catholic and Protestant powers, many longed for the old days when war with Spain offered opportunities of piracy. The anti-Spanish policy of the merchants and traders was associated with defence of the Protestant cause on the Continent. As the Stuarts were usually attempting to form alliances with Spain or France, the Commons increasingly began to demand a say in foreign policy, which previously had been solely within the King's rights. The death of Prince Henry (1612) was a blow to those who associated him with Protestantism and an anti-Spanish policy. The celebration of the marriage (1631) of Princess Elizabeth to Frederick V, the Elector Palatine, while pleasing to those who wanted an anti-Catholic foreign policy, brought the King even more deeply in debt. In 1619 the Bohemians rebelled and invited Frederick to the throne. When Catholic powers occupied Bohemia, James's prestige was lowered by his inability to aid his daughter and son-in-law.

Besides the selling of peerages, administrative positions and monopolies, and James's extravagant infatuation with favourites, the atmosphere of corruption was furthered by an elaborate scandal which developed around the divorce of the Countess of Essex and her marriage to the favourite Somerset. When the bishops were unwilling to annul the Countess's first marriage, the King intervened and appointed additional judges. Sir Thomas Overbury, who opposed the marriage, was imprisoned in the Tower by Somerset, and poisoned in 1613. At their trial in 1615 the murderers confessed that they had been hired by the Earl's new wife; further evidence linked Somerset to the murder. Although he and his wife were tried and found guilty in 1616, the King pardoned them.

Meanwhile a previously unknown gentleman, George Villiers, replaced Somerset as the King's favourite, and rapidly became the Duke of Buckingham. All his family, relations and in-laws were given high positions and the King forced wealthy nobles to marry their children into the Villiers family. A good administrator, but ruthless and corrupt, Buckingham had absolute control over the King, to whom he referred as 'Dad'. With a social upstart now the King's chief minister and in total control of Court patronage, a 'Country' opposition began to form between the landed families and those who had previously challenged the King.

In 1621 James called his first Parliament since 1614. In trying to break the powers of the monopolies, parliamentary committees began investigating patents; government ministers and royal officers, including Francis Bacon, were impeached for bribery and malversion. Parliament claimed the right to advise the King on foreign affairs and the Church; it wanted to declare war on Spain and marry Charles to a Protestant. When Parliament was dissolved, several of the leading opposition members were arrested. The rise of an opposition was aided by the long and eventually unsuccessful negotiations (1617–24) to marry Prince Charles to the Infanta of Spain. When Charles and Buckingham went in person to Madrid in 1623 to court the Infanta, James hoped the dowry would pay off his debts and free him from depending on Parliament for money.

After the breakdown of negotiations for the Spanish marriage, James called a new Parliament, which met in 1624. He died the next year. Although his reign saw the House of Commons beginning to challenge the King's supremacy, the Court became the centre of English life. Attendance at Court meant the chance of titles, offices, monopolies and sophisticated entertainments. Both the King and the Queen supported the theatre companies, and the drama of the period mirrors the ruthlessness and corruption which had become a feature of Court life.

III Literature and society

As government had become more complex there was an increasing need for graduates of the universities and Inns of

Court as administrators, secretaries and clergy. While the Tudor expansion of grammar schools and colleges enabled many to rise to significant positions, a new class dependent upon patronage for advancement was created, which included many of the writers, intellectuals and discontented of the early part of the century. Under Elizabeth and James the social status of literature depended upon whether it was an accomplishment or a trade. Poetry was an expected talent of a courtier which led to preferment, and for the university graduate writing was a means of attracting attention, patronage and a position as clergyman or secretary to one of the peers. Gentlemen did not publish books, although their works might be printed after their death; their writings circulated in manuscript at Court or among friends. Those who wrote for money were usually of plebian origin and either earned their living from the stage or lived precariously from what they were given by patrons. Ben Jonson was one of the very few professional writers who managed to attract noble patrons who were themselves scholars, intellectuals and amateur writers and who treated him as an equal. Occasionally the younger son of the gentry, such as Francis Beaumont, or an impoverished gentleman, such as John Fletcher, became professional dramatists, but they were still rather the exception than the rule. There were literary coteries at Court, the universities, and in London, some patrons among the nobility, and a somewhat larger popular readership among the small middle class; but there was an insufficient readership for serious literature to enable professional writers to do without patronage. Those who wrote for a popular audience of tradesmen and apprentices were treated with contempt.

Perhaps even more influential on the late Elizabethan and Jacobean literary scene than the universities and the Court were the four London law schools known collectively as the Inns of Court. Usually the sons of the gentry who were being educated in the legal profession, their residents formed the largest literate and cultured group in London. They attended the playhouses, wrote verse and drama, created literary fashions, and saw themselves as the intelligentsia of the day. Their tastes were reflected in the new verse satire of the late 1590s by Hall, Marston, Gilpin and Davies, the satiric drama of Marston and Jonson which followed the banning of verse satire, and the use of the malcontent as a satiric character in the plays of Middleton and Webster; they were also an influence on the fashion for obscure, witty, epigrammatic, learned verse, which bred Donne and metaphysical poetry. The sophisticated intellectual tastes of the Inns of Court were catered for by the new private theatres in which companies of boy actors brought an increase of artifice to the stage.

The Inns of Court became significant during the Elizabethan period because the increase in litigation, brought about by the re-emergence of common law, provided opportunities for wealth and because the landed and merchants thought such an education useful to their sons. Many nobles lived at the Inns although they never planned to practise. As the courts under the Stuarts challenged the rights of the kings, the legal profession became more significant, and formed what was essentially an opposition party in Parliament. They provided the leadership against Charles I and later against Cromwell.

Writers who are at one time or other lived at the Inns of Court include Marston, Overbury, Ford, Sandys, Donne, Francis Beaumont, Bacon, Campion, Lodge, Gilpin, Harington and probably Webster. Later, many of the Restoration dramatists also attended the Inns of Court. During 1590–1600 there was a close circle of friends at the Middle Temple which included the poets John Davies, Henry Wotton and John Hoskyns, and which overlapped with Jonson's Mermaid Tavern circle. The Middle Temple wits had a reputation as troublemakers, rakes and satirists; they were intellectual, sarcastic, sophisticated, disrespectful and enjoyed literary parody. Donne's early poems, especially his elegies, were written with such an audience in mind, while the 'Gulling Sonnets' of Sir John Davies (1569–1626), which mock Petrarchanism (deriving from the early Italian humanist Petrarch (1304–74) whose love sonnets were very influential in England) and Elizabethan poetic metaphor by carrying them to extremes, show the context in which Jonson, Marston and Donne thrived. Another side of the Inns is shown by Davies's philosophical poem, *Nosce Teipsum* ('Know Thyself', 1599), written in a plain style, which uses scholastic reasoning to argue for the immortality of the soul. The practice of legal disputation, thorough mastery of rhetoric and the logical proving of an argument undoubtedly contributed to the analytical, forceful, oral style of Donne and other poets.

Meditative and contemplative practices influenced the religious poetry and prose of the first half of the century. While both the Reformation and Counter-Reformation emphasised individual devotion, the English Protestants necessarily made use of the older Catholic mystical tradition and the devotional practices which had become common on the Continent. The most influential method during the first decades of the century was the *Spiritual Exercises* of St Ignatius Loyola (1491–1556), the founder of the Society of Jesus (the Jesuit Order). Using the three 'powers of the soul' — memory, understanding and will — the Ignatian meditation consists of a short preparatory prayer and two preludes (an imagined 'composition of place' followed by the appropriate emotion) which exercise the memory in recollecting images. The meditation proper usually consists of three or more points to be considered which make use of reason, followed by the exercise of will in a colloquy. While the poems of Donne, Herbert and Quarles show familiarity with such a devotional pattern, there were other popular forms of meditation. The Salesian method was less rigid and encouraged the mind to dart back and forth between points, placed emphasis on the mutual love between man and God (which ran contrary to Presbyterian notions of man's sinful helplessness), and urged abandonment of the self to divine love. The middle decades of the century were a time when writers turned increasingly towards Augustinian contemplation, deriving from St Augustine (354–430), the most famous of the Church Fathers, the author of *Confessions*, *City of God* and *On Christian Doctrine*. They were also influenced by such mystics as St Bernard (1090–1153), the famous theologian and founder of the Abbey of Clairvaux, and St Bonaventura (1221–74), the Italian Church Father and author of *The Mind's Road to God*, a classic of meditation in which the mind moves by various steps to mystical communion with the divine. Marvell, Vaughan and Traherne are among the poets whose work shows a nostalgia for paradisial innocence, and a familiarity with the various stages of ascent through recollection, purification and illumination towards spiritual communion. Such poetry is sometimes tinged with Hermeticism, Neo-Platonism and other modes of mysticism which offered a refuge from the political uncertainties of the time. During the first half of the century there were somewhat more women writers than previously. The poems of Lucy Harington Russell, Countess of Bedford (1581–1627?) were unpublished; Elizabeth Cary, Viscountess, Falkland (1585?–1639) wrote *The Tragedie of Mariam* (1613), the first play by an English woman. A prose romance, interspersed with Elizabethan-style poetry, *The Countess of Montgomeries Urania* (1621) by Mary Sidney Wroth (1586?–1640?) was withdrawn after publication because it included thinly disguised parallels to scandals of Jacobean high life. During the 1620s Rachel Speght wrote several defences of women, including *Moralities Memorandum, with a Dreame Prefixed*, a rather dull, didactic, argumentative poem. The most powerful woman writer of the period was Elizabeth Melvill, Lady Culross, whose *Ane Godlie Dreame* might be described as a versified Calvinist *Pilgrim's Progress*; it was extremely popular and soon translated from Scottish into English. Diana Primrose wrote *Chaine of Pearle* (1630), a verse allegory of the virtues of Queen Elizabeth, while Eleanor Davies (*c*. 1590–1652), wife of the poet Sir John Davies, was inspired to write *Strange and Wonderfull Prophesies* (1649). Most women writers, however, still did not publish. Margaret Hoby (1571–1633) left a record of the years 1599–1605, the earliest extant diary by an Englishwoman; there are letters by Brilliana, Lady Harley (1600?–43) for the years 1625–43, a diary by Grace Mildmay, and correspondence by Katherine Paston (1578?–1629).

IV Staging

The performance of plays by professional companies for the public followed Elizabethan conventions of staging until the close of the theatre with the Civil War. Staging in the professional theatre was fairly simple. An open, raised stage extended into the gallery, which was the playing area, the stage jutted out from the theatre building or house, which provided entrances and other playing areas in its windows and balconies. There were trap doors in the floor of the stage and in the permanent theatres there was some machinery such as winches for lowering and raising devices from the room; but, while there was little scenery, costuming and pageantry were elaborate. The effect of such a theatre is unlike that which we know today. As there were no curtains, no changes in scene, no dimmed lighting of the auditorium or stage and no illusion of a real life seen in perspective within an enclosed frame, there was also no rigid separation of audience and actors. The Elizabethan and Jacobean theatre provided an auditorium for speeches, dialogue, gestures, movement and pageantry, the style was static and the audience was addressed directly; an act and play ended when the performers left the stage. In such a theatre communication was verbal; the audience heard, rather than saw, a play. Drama was poetry and oratory.

In contrast to the professional stage, Court entertainments early began using movable scenery in the form of clouds and other simple mechanical devices. Throughout Europe during the sixteenth and seventeenth centuries there were extravagantly expensive entertainments using machinery, curtains, screens and perspective to create marvellous, spectacular visual effects; by the early seventeenth century the Court masque in England was transformed by such techniques from masquerades and dancing to a high theatrical art somewhat similar to the allegorical pageants and plays performed in Italy and France. A major difference between the masque and the professional theatre was in its audience; the Court entertainments were performed for the King and the nobility who usually took part in the play. Often the King and Queen had roles and the masque celebrated the heroic ideals which formed part of the ideology of the aristocracy. The masque allegorically or symbolically celebrated the King and ended in dancing and revels, which included both the masqueraders and the spectators.

From about 1605 onward the Court masques began using a different stage from that of the professional theatre. At first plays performed at Court did not use masque staging, but by the 1630s they did. The radical change began with Inigo Jones's use for masques of a proscenium arch to enclose the stage. While a curtain was raised at the beginning and lowered at the conclusion of a play, it was not dropped between acts as in the modern theatre; but during the century various other curtains and screens were added to mark changes in acts and scenes. The stage was raked and had grooves in which to insert scenery on the sides. Although the scenery was at first left in place, later in the century it was changed during the course of the play. Further back on stage there were shutters which opened and closed to present other scenes and to create a further impression of depth, while behind this there was a permanent, unchanging scene which could be varied by drop curtains. The masque and Court stage did not aim at realistic perspective. Although the action was enclosed by a picture frame within receding planes, the scenery itself was part of the action; it visibly changed in front of the audience with the curtain open. The frame itself was covered with symbolic and allegorical designs. Properties were pulled off and on stage with strings and wires. The backscreen was usually not related to the play but was part of the spectacle as a background to the stage. In several plays the texts indicate that scenery changed while people were speaking. The scenery was somewhat independent of the action and was a show in itself; the visual effects were magnificent to the delight of the audience, which was sometimes more interested in them than in the plot. As the century progressed, the shutters, side wings and drop screens became more complex, allowing many changes in scenery, entrances from between shutters and other illusions. After the Restoration Sir William Davenant built the first professional theatre with such a stage and, with greater complexity, this was the usual theatrical mode until the mid-nineteenth century when lighting and three-dimensional scenery brought about another change in the theatre.

V Art, music and science

A major form of Elizabethan art carried over into the Court of James I was the miniature portrait which was particularly suitable for the idealising, stylised, hierarchical taste at the turn of the century. Elizabethan and Jacobean painting emphasised jewels, regally embroidered clothing and elaborate head-dress at the expense of background and spatial relationship. Portraits were studies in intricate patterning and contained emblematic symbols or allusions. The miniaturist Nicholas Hilliard (1547–1619) painted elegant, detailed portraits in watercolour on vellum which could be worn, similar to jewellery; he treated lacework, hair and jewellery with exquisite precision. Isaac Oliver (1560?–1617) is the best-known portraitist of the reign of James I; his subjects are drawn in profile and occasionally portrayed in a natural landscape. While his use of light, shade and modelling in the round was more European than the Elizabethan miniatures, there is, however, a stiffness and awkwardness in the poses.

The arrival in London between 1616 and 1620 of Paul Van Somer, Daniel Mytens and Anthony Van Dyck from the Netherlands brought English taste more in line with that of the Continent; instead of the miniature portraits and symbolic art of the Elizabethans, Jacobean painting became more classical with subjects treated at full length in everyday contexts.

The major English artist of the reigns of James I and Charles I was Inigo Jones (1573–1652), whose attempts to naturalise continental classical Renaissance painting and architecture have similarities to Ben Jonson's verse. While visiting Italy he studied Renaissance art, theatre and acquired a copy of *I Quattro Libri del' Architettura* by Palladio (1518–80), the influential late Renaissance Italian architect who followed Greek and Roman models. Working with Jonson, Jones became the principal set designer and producer of Jacobean and Caroline masques. Jones's sketches and colour washes for costumes and scenery reveal an ingenious, fertile, fantastic imagination; in the Queen's House at Greenwich and the Whitehall Banqueting House (completed 1622) Jones introduced a classical harmony to English building in contrast to the Dutch Mannerism favoured by other architects. A similar Italian-influenced classicism is seen in the church sculpture of Nicholas Stone (1586–1647).

A proliferation of ornamentation is, however, characteristically Jacobean and reflects the arrival of Northern European, German and Dutch Mannerism, along with the employment of Flemish carvers. While the homes of merchants were exceptionally large by earlier standards, a sign of their new social standing, there are more notable for their elaborately carved, timbered fronts than for the Neo-Classicism Inigo Jones was introducing into Court architecture. Intricate patterns decorations, contortions and arabesques give the ornamentation of a Jacobean house a theatrical appearance. Along with such conspicuous architecture, there was a change from buildings with medieval great halls towards the new importance of galleries, suites and apartments. As the kitchens and servants' quarters were located in other parts of the building, the new houses permitted more privacy, but reinforced class distinctions and especially affected traditions of communal dining. Instead of the open hospitality of the past when all classes, tenants and strangers, ate the same food at the lord's great table, feudal generosity was becoming less frequent. When writers contrast the values of the past with those of the present, they often use hospitality and feasts in the great halls as illustrations of the relationship of established noble families to local communities, whereas the newly rich build large vulgar houses but neglect their responsibilities to society. Poems which celebrate the old families and the well-ordered life supposedly to be found in their houses and on their estates include Jonson's 'To Penshurst' and 'To Sir Robert Wroth', Herrick's 'Panegerick to Sir Lewis Pemberton', Carew's 'To My Friend G. N.' and Marvell's 'Upon Appleton House'.

   William Byrd (1543–1623), Queen Elizabeth's favourite composer, remained a Catholic writing masses to be used at the private chapels of Catholic families. A master of the contrapuntal and fugal style in which each line is independent, he is progressive in his expressive chromatic cadences and use of dissonance to reflect the words in the text; he was also the first in England to compose madrigals. The English madrigal mixes the old modal style with new chromatic harmonies and modulations and shows that music at the time was moving towards the use of scale. Among the famous madrigal composers included in Thomas Morley's (1558–1602) *The Triumphes of Oriana* (1601) in honour of the Queen, were John Wilbye (1574–1638), Thomas Weelkes (1575–1623) and Orlando Gibbons (1583–1625). John Dowland (1563–1626), a famous lute player and the best song writer, published his first ayres in 1597; the influence of the expressive, declamatory solo voice and the new scalar harmony, introduced from Italy, can be seen in his songs, which evolve from a mixture of the declamatory and contrapuntal to homophonic part song in which the parts move together. As the Elizabethans were generally more interested in the voice than in instruments, instrumental music often consisted of little more than the rapid playing of scales. Although this was the great period of madrigals and ayres, when lords and ladies were expected to read their parts on sight, such musical forms were beyond the abilities of most of the population, who continued to be entertained by drums, pipes and bagpipes.

The Jacobean period saw the older musical tradition beginning to disintegrate and be replaced by new fashions, as dance rhythms became more prominent and such instrumental forms as the suite were created by the alternation of dances. English instrumental chamber music started with Orlando Gibbons's *Fantasies of three parts* (1610), Byrd's six-part *Fantasia for Viols* (1613) and the publication in 1611 of a collection for virginal (harpsichord) by Byrd, Gibbons and John Bull (1562?–1628). While Gibbons was famous for his anthems, he also composed for violins, an instrument that did not become popular in England until the Interregnum.

During the first third of the century England was not in the mainstream of the new scientific thought which was soon to change the way the world was viewed. Sir Walter Ralegh was interested in the new ideas, Donne occasionally referred to other worlds in his poetry, and Bacon, although not a significant scientist, became a famous propagandist for an experimental, empirical approach to knowledge; but, in general, the English view of the world remained pre-Copernican. There were, however, exceptions. The rich merchant Sir Thomas Gresham founded Gresham's College, London, in 1596; among its seven established professorships were three in the sciences. After Giordano Bruno (1548–1600) visited England and published *On the Infinite Universe and its Worlds* (1584), the philosophical notion that the earth circled around a moving sun in a universe of many solar systems became a subject of speculation. The one early contribution to modern science was *On the Magnet* (1600) by William Gilbert (1544–1603), who through experimental investigation showed that the earth was a giant magnet with its poles near the geographical poles. Long after Gilbert's death, the publication of his *On our Sublunary World, a New Philosophy* (1651), showed that he had been influenced by Bruno's speculation that the universe was infinite with stars at the centre of planetary systems. Thomas Harriot (1560–1621) put algebra into a modern form, used telescopes to observe Jupiter's satellites and by 1606 had made a map of the moon. William Harvey (1578–1657), who had studied modern methods at Padua, applied the new experimental and mechanical approach to anatomy and physiology to explain the circulation of the blood in *On the Motion of the Heart* (1628). Medical science had little understanding of diseases and most people still died young. When Prince Henry was dying in 1612, probably of typhoid fever, the doctors bled him and applied rhubarb, 'unicorn's horn', powdered pearl and the 'bone' of 'stagges heart' as medicines. In an attempt to cure his delirium, the doctors shaved his head and applied the warm bodies of freshly killed roosters and pigeons.

As the *Dialogues* (1632) and *Mathematical Discourses* (1638) by Galileo (1564–1642) were not published until the third decade of the century, it is perhaps not surprising that English science under James I remained entangled with alchemy and the occult. Even the propagandists for experimental method were rather concerned with the utilitarian gains to be made in navigation, mining and manufacture than with the new radical cosmology which was developing on the Continent. It was not until the middle of the century that the explanation of the universe as centred on the sun, put forward by Copernicus (1473–1543), became widely accepted in England.

2
Late Elizabethan literature

I The new styles and forms

IN the late 1590s the most lively development in poetry was the emergence of a group of satirists among the members of the Inns of Court. Attempting to imitate what they understood as the vituperation, allusiveness, topicality and purposeful obscurity of classical satire, Hall, Marston and Middleton created ironic personae in which to attack vice, mostly as represented by contemporary types. Like many other writers at the turn of the century, and anticipating major themes of Jacobean drama, the satirists were particularly concerned with lust and showed a corrupt world in moral disorder. The techniques and conventions of the new satire were to have both an immediate and a lasting effect on seventeenth-century literature. The close-textured, tight-knit but colloquial language and the ironic, often sardonic, highly educated speaker were rapidly assimilated to the developing metaphysical or 'strong lines' style of poetry of Donne, based on Ovidian wit (Ovid (43BC—AD17), the Latin poet, author of the *Metamorphoses*, the *Art of Love*, and *Remedies for Love*, was a favourite poet of the Renaissance), the contemporary European fashion for unlikely metaphors or conceits, and an argumentative, logical structure. In contrast to leisurely Elizabethan narrative, the new style was compressed and dramatic. The metaphysical lyric was to be a major literary form of the first half of the century as such poets as Donne and Carew moved beyond the conventions of the Petrarchan sonnet to an apparently more immediate personal expression of feelings and to a more complex and subtle treatment of such themes as courtship and love. The inventiveness and expressiveness of the new subjective but intellectual lyric mode was imitated by Herbert, Vaughan and

Crashaw in religious poetry which used the characteristics of secular verse to analyse feelings of guilt, sinfulness, hope, or for purposes of meditation and contemplation.

Developing alongside the metaphysical style, and increasingly influencing its articulation, there was a more classical manner which Ben Jonson had created from the study of oratory and rhetoric, mostly for such conversational genres as the epistle, elegy and panegyric. Jonson, and such poets as Edward Fairfax and Sir John Beaumont (1583?- 1627), contributed to the early development of the heroic couplet which eventually ousted stanzaic verse. The genres and oratorical organisation were retained while Jonson's 'plain style' subsequently became more ornamented and elevated as it developed into the conscious Neo-Classicism of Waller and, later, Dryden.

The conventions of satire in the early years of the century influenced drama, through the plays of Jonson, Marston and Middleton, both creating a new kind of satiric comedy, concerned with avarice and social pretentions, and, by merging with such older genres as the morality and revenge play, creating an ironic and ambiguous form of tragedy, which often treated of lust and corruption. Under the influence of Jonson and Marston drama became filled with multiple perspectives, such framing conventions as characters who operate both inside and outside the play, and other techniques which distance, stylise and parody the action and actors. Beaumont and Fletcher introduced the providential design of tragicomedy, intricate plot patterns and quirky character psychology. The enriched dramatic texture and complex psychology brought about by such experiments can be seen in Shakespeare's great plays of this period, including *Measure for Measure* and *The Tempest*, which share in the new developments.

The complex, intellectual poetry and drama of the early decades of the century were part of a larger change of literary sensibility in which the dominant sixteenth-century fashion of elegant, rhetorical expression was replaced by a more immediate, colloquial manner expressive of the movements of the writer's mind. In prose the balanced, sonorous, rhetorical, Ciceronian (after Cicero, the Roman orator and politician of the first century BC) style of the high Renaissance was ousted by a concise, antithetical, aphoristic, epigrammatical style associated with the Roman Stoic author Seneca (c. 4 BC—AD 65) and the Roman historian Tacitus (c. 55–120).

> I mean the stile, being pure, and strong, and round,
> Not long but Pythy: being short breath'd, but sound.
> Such as the grave, acute, wise Seneca sings,
> That best of Tutors to the worst of Kings.
> Not long and empty; lofty but not proud;
> Subtile but sweet, high but without a cloud,
> Well setled, full of nerves, in briefe 'tis such
> That in a little hath comprized much.

The curt Senecan manner was especially used in such new prose genres as the essay, 'resolve', and 'character'. The modern essay began in France with the French moralist Montaigne (1533–92) whose *Essays* were based on his observations and experiences. In England Bacon's *Essayes. Religious Meditations* (1597) were followed by Sir William Cornwallis's *Essayes* (1600), Robert Johnson's *Essaies* (1601), and Daniel Tuvill's *Essaies Politicke, and Morall* (1608) and *Essaies, Morall and Theologicall* (1609). During the next decade the essay was mixed with the character. The new prose style also influenced sermons, where metaphysical and Senecan wit was the preferred Anglican manner until the mid-century when it was ousted by those who wanted a plain, clear style of preaching.

II Towards a new poetry: from Campion to Drayton and Hall

At the beginning of the seventeenth century, many writers, such as Daniel and Greville, either continued developing the Elizabethan styles of Spenser, Sidney and Gascoigne, or, in the case of Chapman, evolved a manner of their own with some similiarities to the new poetic fashions, or, like Drayton, having been criticised as out of date, revised their diction and attitudes to accommodate contemporary tastes. Often Elizabethan, Renaissance literary attitudes continued in the first decade of the seventeenth century. Elizabethan experiments with quantitative verse were continued by

Thomas Campion (1567–1620), whose *Observations in the Art of English Poesy* (1602) uses the precedent of Latin to argue for the writing of rhymeless, quantitative verse in English. He wrote in English and Latin; many of his poems appear in both languages and were meant to be sung. Writing for musical compositions, it seemed natural that English stress should be treated as the equivalent of long vowels and have musical duration. Campion's sensitivity to cadence and duration produced such fine songs as 'My Sweetest Lesbia', 'When to her lute Corrinna sings', 'Rose-cheekt Lawra', 'What if a day' and 'Follow your Saint'. They are rhythmically inventive, move more lightly and musically than most Elizabethan verse, but are of slight content. A student of the classics, influenced by the Latin lyric poet Catullus (*c*. 84– *c*. 54 BC), the Roman poet, satirist and critic Horace (65– 8 BC), the Roman elegaic poet Propertius (*c*. 48–*c*. 15 BC) and the Latin poet and epigrammatist Martial (*c*.40–*c*.104AD), Campion is a delicate, rather subdued poet. While he demonstrated that rhyme is not necessary to English, his quantitative poetry succeeds because it is also accentual. His four books of *Ayres*, published between 1601 and 1617, are representative of the movement begun in England with Dowland away from the complex madrigal of two or more unaccompanied voices to the solo voice accompanied by the lute or other instruments.

A member of the Pembroke–Spenser circle, Samuel Daniel (1562–1619), who wrote one of the earliest Elizabethan Petrarchan sonnet sequences, *Delia* (1592), was involved in the period's controversies concerning classical and vernacular literature. The Countess of Pembroke's translation from the French of Robert Garnier's *Marc Antoine* (1578, trans. 1590) and Daniel's verse plays, *The Tragedy of Cleopatra* (1594) and *Philotas* (1605), were meant to demonstrate that English drama was capable of developing along classical lines, with long speeches, monologues and chorus; they were intended as a counterpart to Spenser's poetry and Sidney's *Apologie for Poetry*. *Musophilus* ('A Lover of the Muses', 1599) is Daniel's own elevated, long-winded, versified defence of literature. His *Defence of Ryme* (1603) is an answer to Campion's advocacy of classical metres for English poetry. Daniel argues that 'ryme is the fittest harmonie of words', that accent in English is 'the chiefe Lord and grave Governour of Numbers', and that Campion's poems only succeed because they in fact use English accentual metres. In 1603 Daniel published some plain but stately Horatian verse epistles which in their Christian stoicism and ethical concern anticipate Jonson.

The continuity between Elizabethan and early-seventeenth-century verse is further illustrated by the poetry of Fulke Greville, first Lord Brooke (1554–1628), whose work has both the formality of the Elizabethans and the dark, pessimistic tones of the Jacobeans. A close friend of Sir Philip Sidney and the Pembroke circle, a courtier, knighted in 1603, Chancellor of the Exchequer (1614–22), elevated to the peerage in 1621, loyal to Essex, and a friend of Bacon, Greville was involved with those who during the 1570s and 80s attempted to give English poetry elevation and dignity. The early *Caelica* poems show a concern with the resources of oratory, rhetoric and ornamentation, but Greville's model is rather Sidney's attempt to create an improved plain style than the sugared sonnet or the Spenserian sublime. Greville approached love poetry with scepticism. The imagery of sighs and devotion seems ironic; the general tone and attitude is less adoring than negative: 'Time hath made free of teares, sighs, and despaire, / Writing in furrowes deep; *she once was faire*'. The awareness of time, mutability, the transitory nature of earthly pleasures makes such poems more than conventional anti-Petrarchan exercises. Greville brought to the Platonic vocabulary of Renaissance love poetry scepticism which is both wordly ('While that fine soyle, which all these joyes did yeeld, / By broken fence is prov'd a common field'), and which views all experience as vain: 'As neither partie satisfying other, / *Repentance still becomes desires mother*'. The bitter psychology of the love poems ('Faire Nymphs, if I wooe *Cynthia* not to leave me, / You know 'tis I my selfe, not she deceaves me') finds its resolution in divine love.

Greville takes an austere, even stark view of the world. Self-aware, self-distrustful, he views man and the world as fallen, treacherous and lacking 'delight'. The many political poems refer to corruption, injustice, falsity. The formal diction, regular metres, slow, stately rhythm, dense sound patterns, close reasoning, precise control of emotion and aphoristic statements are fatiguing; but the careful manipulation of rhetoric, the logical exposition, the measured cadences and the seriousness of tone can rise to excellent poetry.

Caelica was followed by two Senecan verse dramas, *Mustapha* and *Alaham*, designed 'to show the high ways of ambitious governors' and how they contribute to their own fall. Meant rather for declamation than acting, the plays contain such powerful verses as the final chorus of *Mustapha*:

> Oh wearisome Condition of Humanity!
> Borne under one Law, to another bound:
> Vainely begot, and yet forbidden vanity,
> Created sicke, commanded to be sound:
> What meaneth Nature by these diverse Lawes?
> Passion and Reason, selfe-division cause:
> Is it the marke, or Majesty of Power
> To make offences that it may forgive?

There is a Machiavellian, cynical attitude towards politics in Greville's writing, which sits uneasily alongside deep religious feelings. All churches are corrupt; only Christ can enable man to be saved. The feeling of hopelessness and the self-examination of motives suggest the influence of Calvinism on the literature of the period.

The poetry of Michael Drayton (1563—1631) shows how some writers were changing their style under pressure from the new fashions provided by the satirists. Drayton, rather than attending university, followed an older social tradition, seeking advancement through becoming a household page of Sir Henry Goodere, a minor poet, who encouraged him to write. Drayton's early publications include *The Harmonie of the Church* (1591) and *Idea The Shepheards Garland, Fashioned in nine Eglogs* (1593). The early Drayton was struggling to be an Elizabethan poet. His versified psalms, long narrative stanzas, pastorals and Petrarchan sonnets belong to the world of Daniel, Sidney and Spenser. *The Owle* (1604), a satire, was influenced by Spenser's *Mother Hubbard's Tale*. Although Drayton generally avoided Spenser's archaic diction, he otherwise followed Spenserian notions of decorum and style; he was one of the first of Spenser's followers to create a nostalgic world of a pastoral Merry England, patriotism, national legends, fairyland, and vague, abstract ideals. Such attitudes can be found in the immense, longwinded *Poly-Olbion or A Chorographicall Description of . . . Tracts, Rivers, Mountains, Forests, and other Parts of this renowned Isle* (1613, expanded 1622), a tour through the nation, surveying local legends, monuments and landscape, written in Alexandrine couplets ('heroic' lines of twelve syllables with regular mid-line caesuras). In *England's Heroical Epistles* (1597), with their Ovidian brevity and antithesis, however, Drayton showed his awareness of the newer literary fashions.

In *Idea The Shepheards Garland* (1593) Drayton used the eclogue for eulogy. Henry Goodere's daughter Anne is the 'Idea' of it and the sonnets in *Ideas Mirrour, Amours* (1594). After such wits of the Inns of Court as Joseph Hall, John Marston and Sir John Davies parodied his mannerisms and ridiculous emotional extremes, Drayton began revising *Ideas* in subsequent editions, creating a libertine persona for the speaker, removing the excessive Petrarchisms, tightening up the syntax, and using a more vigorous language:

> No farre-fetched Sigh shall ever wound my Brest
> Love from mine Eye a Teare shall never wring,
> Nor in *Ah-mees* my whyning Sonnets drest,
> (A libertine) fantastickly I sing:
> My Verse is the true image of my Mind,
> Ever in motion, still desiring change;
> And as thus to Varietie inclin'd,
> So in all Humors sportively I range.

He rearranged the order and added new sonnets with the result that by the 1619 edition of *Poems* the sixty-three sonnets progress from libertine, cynical poems sceptical of romantic love to a conclusion in which love of Anne is affirmed by a man of experience.

The *Poems* also include *Odes*, one of the earliest attempts to bring the varied form of the ode into English. Drayton surprisingly went back to Skelton's short staccato lines and rhymes to find a vigorous alternative to Elizabethan prettiness and patterned rhetoric. The odes, written in various rhyme schemes and sometimes influenced by the older ballads, allowed Drayton to find his own voice and express his own personality. The first ode, 'To Himselfe', is a declaration of his new aims: 'And why not I ... Th'old *Lyrick* kind revive? ... Who shall oppose my way?' The ode 'To His Valentine', the praise of poets drinking to their muse in 'The Sacrifice to Apollo', the Cavalier-like pose of 'To His Rivall' and the canzonet 'To His Coy Love' are unfortunately not as well known as the ode 'To the Virginian Voyage'. Some of Drayton's elegies, including 'Of His Ladies Not Coming to London', have the energy, personality and irony of Donne, Jonson and the newer poetic style. Drayton, who was earlier ill at ease with logical exposition, learned how to work his thought throughout a stanza with the syntax driving forward over the end of the line. There is also a pleasing variety in the placement of the caesura. *Nimphidia, The Court of Fayrie* (1627) is a satire on romance and extra-marital love.

One of the generation of the 1590s who seemed deter-mined to 'make it new', Joseph Hall (1574–1656) was among the earliest English satirists to use classical models and perhaps the first to adapt the Theophrastan character. (Theophrastus (*c*. 372–287 BC) was the author of *Characters*, descriptions of types of behaviour.) Besides contributing to the movement away from a Ciceronian to a Senecan prose style, Hall participated in the attempt to harness Stoicism to Christianity. Hall's *Virgidemiarum*, 'the gathering of rods' (1597), modelled on the satires of the first-century AD Roman poet Juvenal, is written in iambic pentameter couplets and, because the satirist is supposedly in danger of revenge, is filled with obscure allusions. The style is purposely crabbed, disorderly, and seems a profusion of disjointed epigrams. For a satiric mask Hall created a foul-mouthed and caustic persona of a railing cynic. It was this manner which remained an influence on English satire until the late 1670s, when Rochester and Dryden created finer, sophisticated methods of mockery. Hall, however, wrote more clearly than he intended; much of the ranting seems worked up. Hall, along with Marston, Davies and Everard Gilpin, satirised the Elizabethan fashion for love sonnets. In the first book of *Virgidemiarum*, Satire VII mocks the 'love-sicke Poet, who importune prayer / Repulsed' turns to 'patched Sonettings / His love, his lust, and loathsome flatterings'. 'Careth the world, thou love, thou live, or die? / Careth the world how fayre thy fayre one bee?'

Hall's Senecan prose, with its plain language, short phrases and sentences, familiar similes, aphoristic antithesis and rapid staccato movement, enlivens his *Characters of Virtues and Vices* (1608) and *Epistles* (1608). The first collection of characters in English, Hall's are longer, more generalised and serious than their Greek prototypes. Where Theophrastus is amusing, Hall is a moralist; he praises virtue and satirises evil. Besides such moral types as Honesty, Justice, the Happy Man, the characters include the Good Magistrate, the first of what was to become the English tradition of social character sketches. *Heaven Upon Earth* (1606) explains Seneca's philosophy and is an example of the Neo-Stoicism of the time; Hall, however, argues that tranquillity is impossible without Christianity and the promise of salvation. *The Arte of Divine Meditation* (1606) helped make Catholic devotional practices acceptable to English Protestants and influenced Richard Baxter's *Saints' Everlasting Rest*.

One of the Middle Temple wits of the late 1580s and early 1590s, John Hoskyns (1566—1638) was part of the Donne— Jonson circle. He acted in and wrote part of *Le Prince d'Amour* (1598, published 1660), a revel presented at the Middle Temple, to which he contributed a 'fustian' speech, one of the many parodies of contemporary style and literary manners in the entertainment. While the *Directions for Speech and Style*, written for the benefit of a young Templar, includes the usual Renaissance instruction on rhetoric, figures for 'varying' and 'Amplification', its tendency is towards brevity and the plain style, 'a kind of diligent negligence'. Although Hoskyns warns against far-fetched metaphors and an extremely aphoristic style, the *Directions* are part of the period's anti-Ciceronianism. Hoskyns wrote poems in Latin and English. 'Absence' for many years was thought to be by Donne because of its analytical logic, psychology and wit:

> By absence this good means I gaine
> That I can catch her
> Where none can watch her
> In some close corner of my braine:
> There I embrace and there kiss her,
> And so enjoye her, and so misse her.

III Towards a new drama: Marston and Chapman

If Jacobean and Caroline dramas by Middleton, Webster and Ford bear a resemblance to our drama of the Absurd, they show the influence of John Marston (1576–1634), one of the many interesting writers associated with the Inns of Court. The cynical *Metamorphosis of Pigmalions Image* (1598), an Ovidian mythological poem, satirises the Petrarchan lover and (what was to become one of Marston's main themes) the discrepancy between the idea and the actual object of love. The long, exaggerated similes suggest the absurdity of the possibilities inherent in rhetoric and the way people deceive themselves with words. While the poems in *Certaine Satyres* (1598) and *The Scourge of Villainie* (1598) are obscure, violent, allusive and abrupt in style, the manner, along with the diffuse, almost arbitrary succession of satiric topics and character types, was imitated from the Roman satirist Persius (AD 34–62), from Juvenal and the epigrams of Martial. The new satire of the late 1590s, besides being ruthless, raucous and obscure, uses an unreliable, malcontent narrator, who claims no other attitude is honest in such a society, and who while a mouthpiece is also an object of the author's sense of mockery. Although Marston's verse suggests a universe in which man is predestined to fall and unable to rise above vice without divine grace, its Calvinism seems mostly a reflection of the intellectual mood of the day; Puritans, especially in their supposed self-righteousness and hypocrisy, are among Marston's satiric targets. But his main concern is with lust, especially when dressed in romantic clichés. Satire VIII in *The Scourge of Villainie* expresses Marston's attitude:

> Lust hath confounded all,
> The bright glosse of our intellectuall
> Is fouly soyl'd. The wanton wallowing
> In fond delights, and amorous dallying,
> Hath dusk'd the fairest splendour of our soule:
> Nothing now left, but carkas, lothsome, foule.

After the Bishop of London in 1599 banned the printing of verse satire, Marston turned to the theatre, and set a social precedent for Beaumont, Fletcher and Ford among the sons of the gentry who later became professional dramatists. *Jack*

Drum's Entertainment (1600), written for the Children of Paul's, includes parody of the romantic love drama of the 1590s. The conscious absurdities form a link between the ironic rant in such early Tudor plays as *King Cambises*, the stylised, almost farcical extreme emotions of many Jacobean tragedies and the often humorous bombast of the Restoration heroic play:

> Oh how a kisse inflames a Lovers thought,
> With such a fewell let me burne and die,
> And like to *Hercules* so mount the skie.

The child actors undoubtedly made the representation seem even closer to stylised burlesque. Marston wrote three more plays for Paul's boys (1600–1?). *Antonio and Mellida* is a tragicomic *Romeo and Juliet* with a ranting, almost farcical, villainous duke, a weak hero disguised in woman's clothing, and a happy ending in which all is forgiven. In *Antonio's Revenge*, the comedy of the previous play becomes serious and bloody. Piero Sforza, the Duke, is an amusingly treacherous, cold-blooded murderer, but also a very deadly one. Spurred on by the ghost of his murdered father, Antonio turns into a revenger and learns that he lives in a world in which all must become guilty. *What You Will* (1601?) is a play of mistaken identities, love-sick fools, libertines and adulterers, set in a Venice where appearance is of prime significance and where it is necessary to be vile to be successful. The play is filled with satirical characters, including a satirist who bitterly and unsuccessfully complains.

Influenced by the anonymous 1602 translation of Guarini's *Pastor Fido* ('The Faithful Shepherd'), *The Malcontent* (1604) is a tragicomedy which ends in regeneration and restoration. It begins with out-of-tune music and presents a world turned upside down in which Altofronto, the usurped duke, is disguised as Malevole. Malevole is both a satirist and a revenger; he can also be seen as a God-like figure who, as Altofronto, apparently withdraws from the world, but through surprising means overthrows sin and guides the characters to the play's last judgement in which compassion triumphs over rigid justice: 'Who doubts of providence / That sees this change? A hearty faith to all!' The scenes are active, detailed, yet broken, and shift to the various characters involved in corrupt or amoral plots. The language, especially of Malevole, is notable for rapid changes in tone and sentiment. The play involves elaborate staging and has similarities to a Court masque in its use of dancing, music and costumes. With at one time four characters in disguise and multiple roles for actors, *The Malcontent* is excellent theatre.

After collaborating with Jonson and Chapman in *Eastward Ho!* (1605), Marston wrote *Parasitaster, or The Fawn*, followed by *The Dutch Courtesan*. In the former, since 'Vice is now term'd fashion', Hercules, the Duke of Ferrara, disguises himself as Faunus and begins

> flattering all
> In all of their extremest viciousness,
> Till in their own lov'd race they fall most lame,
> And meet full butt the close of vice's shame.

The prominence of flattery at the Court, the sexual vices and the foolish Duke Gonzago, who claims to be a great poet, philosopher, linguist, rhetorician and orator, suggest that *The Fawn* was a satiric mirror for the Court of James I. Although irony, disjunctive contrasts, the distancing of characters, satire, a variety of registers of language and the use of disguises are characteristic of Marston's plays, each is unlike the others. Marston restlessly experimented with new dramatic conventions to illustrate the need both for common sense and for higher ideals in an unsatisfactory world.

Believing poetry to be a divine art which expressed high philosophical truth to the learned few, George Chapman (1559?–1634) wrote tough, knotted verses. While his gnarled, conceited, dark style is a somewhat analogous development to the strong lines of Donne and the satirists, the themes of his poetry have little in common with the metaphysicals; its tradition is Renaissance esoteric mythology and allegorisation of philosophical, ethical, religious and political ideals. His high notion of a poet, his frame of reference, the complexity of his aims and many characteristics of his style are a link between Spenser and early Milton. Although the predominant themes and presentation change from work to work, Chapman's ideas change little. The world of man is chaotic, ruled by passions and chance; if man is to approach heavenly wisdom, the soul must govern the body, the ethical must control the passions and morality must rule the state. The alternative is degeneration into the bestial.

Desiring order, form, self-governance, Chapman blends Stoicism with Platonism to make up a typical Renaissance eclectic Christianity, owing more to Ficino (Renaissance Italian Neo-Platonist and scholar (1433–99), author of an influential commentary on Plato's *Banquet*) and Epictetus (Roman Stoic philosopher, first century AD) than to any church. Through grace the poet is divinely inspired, but Chapman's inspiration is Homer, especially the Homer of the allegorical commentators. From the two obscure allegorical poems, *Hymnus in Noctem* ('A Hymn to Night') and *Hymnus in Cynthiam* ('A Hymn to Cynthia'), included in *The Shadow of Night* (1594), through *Ovid's Banquet of Sense*, published with *A Coronet for His Mistress Philosophy* (1595), the continuation of Marlowe's *Hero and Leander* (1598), the exposition of his philosophy in *Tears of Peace* (1609), the Neo-Platonic celebration of marriage in *Andromeda Liberata* ('Andromeda Freed'), written for Somerset's marriage (1614), to the translation of *The Whole Works of Homer* (1616), Chapman's verse is symbolic, orphic, allegorical and concerned with spiritual order and regeneration. The style is uneven and often suffers from unnatural word order, neologism, mixed metaphors, and the piling up of subordinate clauses, but it can be fiery and strong in its long, complex sentences, rich metaphors and elevation.

Chapman's plays examine the relationship of his philosophical concerns to the realities of politics and society. Bussy, the great-spirited, natural man who follows virtue as his guide, is a hero of epic proportions who rises quickly at court as a reformer, but soon becomes a braggart, an adulterer and a murderer. *The Tragedy of Bussy d'Ambois* (1604?) shows that in the real world of relative values, the individualism of the hero is inappropriate or soon corrupted. In Bussy, the Marlovian superman becomes an ambiguous figure. The two-part *Conspiracy and Tragedy of Charles Duke of Byron* (1608) is a study in the disintegration of the self-sufficient individual. Byron is a hollow Bussy, used and mocked by others, who after becoming a traitor is forgiven by the king in the first play. In the second, Byron progresses from individualism and Stoic self-assertion to a megalomaniac lust for power and hysterical self-deceit. In *The Revenge of Bussy d'Ambois* (1610?), Bussy remains a confused figure and it is his brother Clermont, moderate, self-disciplined and private, who provides a moral centre. Similarly in *Caesar and Pompey* (1612?) victory and worldly power are shown to be useless; heroism is private, the stoical triumph over the self. Using the old conventions of revenge and melodrama, along with the new fashionable malcontents, experimenting with dramatic and tonal ironies, Chapman created uneven but powerful plays.

IV   Popular writers and translators: Heywood, Dekker, Breton and Fairfax

Of the over 220 plays which Thomas Heywood wrote (1574?–1641) co-authored, altered or patched, only sixteen were printed with his name on the title page; the problem of his authorship is a messy, unrewarding task for scholars. Heywood wrote daily, acted on stage almost as frequently in the plays of others, and somehow found time to dash off a 13,000-line heroic poem, *Troia Britannica; or, Great Britain's Troy* (1609) — which in the Elizabethan manner retells the Trojan wars and concludes with a history of England from Brute to the present — *An Apology for Actors* (1612) — a defence against Puritan attacks on the stage — the verse *Hierarchy of the Blessed Angels* (1635) and numerous other works including city pageants and masques. His writings reflect a growing taste among the aristocracy and middle classes for patriotism, myths of English origins, and Spenserian narrative, especially of mythology:

> Her weapons are the Iavelin, and the Bow,
> Her garments *Angell-like*, of Virgin white,
> And tuckt aloft, her falling skirt below
> Her Buskin meetes: buckled with silver bright:
> Her Haire behind her, like a Cloake doth flow,
> Some tuckt in roules, some loose with Flowers bedight:
>   Her silken vailes play round about her slacke,
>   Her golden Quiver fals athwart her backe.

A Woman Killed with Kindness (1603) is perhaps his best play. Influenced by such middle-class domestic tragedies as *Arden of Feversham*, it treats of friendship, virtue and honour in a realistic setting, to show the blessings of family life and the need for contrition through repentance, atonement and forgiveness. If it suffers from a lack of psychological depth, its barren language and diction seem right for the social environment, and the total effect is dramatic. Although it is impossible to date accurately the first performance of the two parts of *The Fair Maid of the West* (published 1631), it is probable that the plays are separated by two or three decades. Exciting adventure stories, they appear to reflect two different audiences and moral climates; part one is moralistic and middle-class, part two is influenced by the more sophisticated, even cynical attitudes of the late Jacobean and Caroline Courts.

Thomas Dekker (1572?–1632) wrote for the less sophisticated who liked racy, direct language, obvious ironies, and who were interested in literature that treated of London life, its artisans, rogues, plagues, and which could range from the sensational and horrific to the tender, while offering a simple morality in which there are clear virtues and vices. He draws upon the popular inheritance from earlier ages with his devils, scenes of hell, seven deadly sins, saints' legends and such traditional character types as Patient Griselda. His earliest plays, dating from 1594, are lost, but it seems he already had become a competent hack; during the year 1598 he appears to have had a hand in fifteen plays. Later he worked with such playwrights as Ford, Middleton and Webster. His one individual achievement for the stage is *The Shoemaker's Holiday* (1599), a mixture of romantic love (two princes disguised as shoemakers), London tradesmen, and corrupt courtiers. Also of interest are *Old Fortunatus* (1599), a folk-tale adapted into a morality play, *Satiromastix* ('Satirical Whip', 1601), a romantic tragicomedy which lampoons Ben Jonson, *The Honest Whore* (1604), a mixture of realism and romance written with Middleton, and *The Witch of Edmonton* (1621), written with William Rowley and John Ford, showing that mistreatment of old women makes them turn to witchcraft.

Dekker's prose continues the Elizabethan line of pamphleteering made popular by Nashe and Greene; while influenced by their vigorous, racy, vivid language, he is more urbane and has a lighter touch. His pamphlets include the still readable *The Wonderful Year* (1603) recounting the death of Elizabeth, the accession of James and the plague that devastated London and which he saw as God's warning to reform. *The Seven Deadly Sins of London* (1606) is satiric and moralistic. *News from Hell* (1606), revised as *A Knight's Conjuring* (1607), continues the theme of Nashe's *Pierce Penniless's Supplication to the Devil* (1592). *The Bellman of London* (1608), its continuation, *Lanthorn and Candlelight* (1608), and several later revisions and continuations, are part of the rogue literature of the period and are rich in underworld slang. *The Gull's Hornbook* (1609) offers ironic advice to a young man from the country, how he can make himself foolish (a gull) by attracting attention in London while attempting to act like a gentleman:

> which wonders you may publish, when you returne into the country, to the great amazement of all Farmers Daughters, that will almost swound at the report, and neuer recouer till their banes bee asked twice in the Church.

Dekker contributed six 'Prison Characters' to the ninth edition (1616) of Overbury's *Characters* and some essays and characters to Geffray Mynshul's (1594?–1668) *Certaine Characters and Essayes of Prison and Prisoners* (1618).

If the popular literature of Elizabethan and Jacobean England seems endless, Nicholas Breton (1555?–1626?) contributed more than his fair share. Prolific at producing essays, fiction, characters, dialogues, satires, pastorals and meditations, Breton's prose includes a romance, *The Strange Fortunes of Two Excellent Princes* (1600), the schoolboy humour of *A Poste with a Packet of Mad Letters* (1603, 1637), and *A Dialogue full of pithe and pleasure: between three Phylosophers . . . Upon the Dignitie, or Indignitie of Man. Partly Translated out of Italian* (1603). Breton tries to be entertaining and sometimes succeeds but, because he is writing for a middle-class audience, his work is moral, didactic or religious. *Characters upon Essaies Morall and Divine, Written For those good Spirits, that will take them in*

good part, And Make use of them to good purpose (1615)
and *The Good and The Badde, or Descriptions of the
Worthies and Unworthies of this Age. Where the Best may see
their Graces, and the Worst discerne their Basenesse* (1616)
are typical of later Breton. The style is brief, aphoristic in
the new Senecan manner, but without energy. The contents
are stereotypes:

> A Reprobate is the childe of sinne, who being borne for the service
> of the devill, cares not what villany he does in the world. His wit is
> alwaies in a maze, for his courses are ever out of order, and while
> his will stands for his wisedome, the best that fals out of him, is a
> foole. Hee betrayes the trust of the simple and sucks out the blood
> of the innocent.

Breton's verse is sixteenth-century in manner and shows the
continuing influence of George Gascoigne's plain style and
of Sidney's experiments with Petrarchan rhetoric, in contrast
to the more classical plain style being created by Jonson. He
wrote some good pastoral love lyrics, including 'In the Merry
Moneth of May', published in *England's Helicon* (1600).

Towards the end of the sixteenth century, translation was
becoming an art. During the early seventeenth century, which
saw such still widely read classics as John Florio's (1553–
1625?) Montaigne's *Essays* (1603), John Healey's Saint
Augustine's *The City of God* (1610), Thomas Shelton's *Don
Quixote* (1612–20), and Sir Tobie Matthew's Augustine's
Confessions (1620), Philemon Holland (1552–1637) was
famous for the quality and scholarship of his translations.
A school teacher in Coventry, he somehow found time to
turn into English an immense number of such long works
as Livy's (59 BC–AD 17) *Romane Historie* (1600), Pliny's
(AD 23–79) *Historie of the World* (1601), Plutarch's (*c.* AD 46
–*c.* 120) *Morals* (1603) and Suetonius' (AD 75–160) *Historie
of the Twelve Caesars* (1606). Holland compared editions of
the original and often used material from commentaries and
foreign translations to clarify and adorn his versions.
Although he purposefully wrote in a 'mean and popular
style', he had eloquence, vitality and a mixture of the idiomatic and majestic.

Another classic translation, *Godfrey of Bulloigne or the
Recoverie of Jerusalem done into English heroicall verse*

(1600) influenced Waller, Dryden and others, who acknow-
ledged Edward Fairfax's (1580?–1635) role in the reformation of versification. As a translator of Torquato Tasso's
Jerusalem Delivered (*Gerusalemme Liberata*, 1575), a
Counter-Reformation mixture of the chivalric romance with
the epic, Fairfax was faced with the problem of imitating the
'Ottava rima' (an eight-line stanza rhyming a b a b a b c c,
used by the Italian poets Ariosto (1474–1533), author of
Orlando Furioso, a romantic poem, and Tasso (1544–95)
in English, which is a more compact language than Italian. He
expanded his source by additional biblical and classical
allusions, epithets and sententious sayings: 'They drink
deceived; and so deceiv'd they live.' In particular he seized
upon the stylised couplets which concluded Tasso's stanzas:
'Down fell the Duke, his joints dissolv'd assunder, / Blind
with the light, and stricken dead with wonder.' Fairfax's
neat, balanced, antithetical closed couplets anticipate what
was to become the Restoration Neo-Classical manner, as does
his slightly elevated and harmonious diction in which
archaisms are used sparingly.

V Bacon

Francis Bacon (1561–1626) was a significant influence on
the intellectual and literary developments of the new
century; besides leading the reaction against a Ciceronian
prose style, he argued for an experimental approach to
knowledge. He was a public figure who was aided in his
advancement at Court by Lord Essex, whom he later
prosecuted for rebellion against Queen Elizabeth. Knighted
in 1603, during the next two decades Bacon rapidly advanced
to become Lord Chancellor in 1618. Made Viscount in 1621,
shortly afterwards he was tried, imprisoned and heavily fined
for receiving bribes.

The early years of the century, when there was a conscious
reaction to Ciceronianism, were a time when the curt
Senecan style was most pronounced. Although Bacon's essays
are known for their striking beginnings, easy transitions and
good conclusions, the ten essays in the 1597 edition are
aphoristic, abstract and rather discontinuous, somewhat like

clever, loosely related notes on a topic. Bacon revised and enlarged his collection of essays to thirty-eight in 1612; his collection of fifty-eight essays appeared in 1625. As he revised his essays he expanded them by adding quotations, examples, analogies, anecdotal imagery and longer sentences. The revised essays are concise, clear and highly persuasive, but remain rather loosely organised. Themes are restated by division rather than developed. The essays are a wisdom literature concerned with public life. Whereas Montaigne is concerned with himself and his thought, Bacon is practical and worldly. He is more a realist who observes life than a moralist. 'Of Marriage and Single Life' opens:

> He that hath wife and children hath given hostages to fortune; for they are impediments to great enterprises, either of virtue or mischief. Certainly the best works, and of greatest merit for the public, have proceeded from the unmarried or childless men, which, both in affection and means, have married and endowed the public.

While Bacon was not himself a good scientist, he popularised the case for a scientific method based on experiment, and argued for a divorce between theology and the study of nature. The reform of language and style was associated with the transformation of philosophy from a concern with words to a concern with the objective world of things which would make knowledge of practical relevance. In *The Advancement of Learning* (1605) the Ciceronian style is seen as a reaction by the church reformers and the Renaissance humanists to scholasticism; but the Ciceronian style, based on Latin, became excessively eloquent:

> men began to hunt more after wordes than matter, and more after the choisenesse of the Phrase, and the round and cleane composition of the Sentence, and the sweet falling of the clauses, and the varying and illustration of their works with tropes and figures, then after the weight of matter, worth of subject, soundnesse of argument, life of invention, or depth of judgement.

The 'first distemper of learning' is when men study words and not matter.

In *Novum Organum*, or *New Instrument* (1620), Bacon defined four '*idols*', which misdirect man from the truth. The idols of the 'tribe', 'cave', 'market-place' and 'theatre' are the result of our human nature, individual circumstances, language and philosophy. It is necessary to recognise the causes of superstitions and errors before true ideas can be 'delivered and reduced' to the 'understanding'. The unfinished fable *New Atlantis* (1626), influenced by More's *Utopia* and Plato's *Republic*, concerns the ideal society. Solomon's House, or the College of the Six Days' Works is dedicated to 'the Study of the Works and Creatures of God'. Scientific experiments are performed and models are exhibited of excellent inventions. Solomon's House was the ideal behind the various attempts during the century to form a comprehensive academy of modern knowledge, and indirectly the inspiration for the Royal Society after the Restoration.

3
Donne and Jonson

I Introduction to metaphysical poetry and Donne's life

JOHN DONNE (1572–1631) was, along with Ben Jonson, the main influence on the poetry of the first half of the century. He brought to lyric poetry the colloquial language, irony, immediacy and intellectual pressures of late Elizabethan satire; he made the witty conceits of European Mannerist verse adaptable to English through a personal voice which expressed experience, feeling and thought. Carew's praise of Donne as the monarch of wit points to his influence on contemporaries and the next generation; wit meant ingenuity and especially intellectual cleverness. Its basic method was the conceit, an extended metaphor or extreme analogy, in which dissimilar concepts, objects or ideas are used to express thoughts and feelings. Because ideas from all realms, but especially from religion, science and philosophy, were used in such poetry it was termed metaphysical by Dryden, and later by Samuel Johnson. The contemporary description was 'strong lines', an indication of the extreme compression of ideas and purposeful harshness of style. Strong lines could not be read superficially for conventional ideas and pretty, rhetorical patterns; thought, intelligence, learning and a sense of the ironic are required from the reader. If the metaphysical style in its later followers declined to mere playful cleverness, at its height it extended the range of techniques and articulation of emotion in the short poem. Along with Jacobean drama, the metaphysical poem was supreme in English literature, until challenged by the novel, for its expression of psychology and experience. It was particularly suitable to the early seventeenth century when rapid social change, the expansion of education, the diffusion of new ideas, and the focusing of religion upon the individual, created a new intense sense of the self as unique.

Donne came from a London merchant family. After a time at Oxford and Cambridge, where as a Catholic he could not take a degree, Donne entered Lincoln's Inn, 1592, to study law. Although no longer a Catholic, he had not become an Anglican; for many years he was a Christian of no particular church. After joining naval expeditions to Cadiz (1596) and the Azores (1597) Donne entered the service of Sir Thomas Egerton. In 1601 he secretly married Anne More, daughter of Egerton's brother-in-law. As a consequence he was dismissed by Egerton and for many years lost his chances of advancement to a government appointment. Tom Morton, whom he had assisted, was made Dean of Gloucester in 1607 and urged him to take holy orders; but Donne, perhaps still hoping for a court career, replied that he was unworthy. It was probably during the next few years that Donne wrote *La Corona* ('The Crown'), *A Litany* and most of his Holy Sonnets. It was after writing 'A Funeral Elegy' and the two *Anniversaries* on the death of Elizabeth Drury that Donne's life took a new turn. He became attached to Sir Robert Drury, travelled with him to the Continent, and in 1614 became Member of Parliament for Taunton. In 1615 he was ordained deacon and priest at St Paul's. He preached at Court and was appointed Divinity Reader at Lincoln's Inn. In 1617 his wife died. Four years later he was made Dean of St Paul's.

II Donne's secular poetry

Except for the *Anniversaries* and a few minor pieces, Donne's poems were not published during his lifetime; as was then usual, they circulated in manuscript among friends and few can be dated with any accuracy. The elegies, satires and many of the *Songs and Sonnets* appear the work of the 1590s and the first decade of the seventeenth century. Although his satires are more urbane, somewhat less crabbed and obscure, they are similar to other late Elizabethan attempts to castigate vice and fashion. They work up outrage and take a shotgun approach with too many targets vaguely in sight. Even the most interesting, Satire III, begins with the Satyr's fustian 'Kinde pitty chokes my spleene' and 'I must not laugh, nor weepe sinnes' before contrasting trust in God with the confusing variety of Christian churches and doctrines. The satires make explicit the persona of many of the lyrics, a cynical, educated young man of the world, familiar with London and the Court, experienced in love, somewhat libertine, but as willing to judge others as any moralist.

The elegies are more successful. Whereas elegy now usually means a poem written for a funeral, Donne's elegies are Ovidian in their urbane wit, sexual frankness, elegance, vigour, amorality and satiric touches. The persona is similar to that found in the Satires; but the subject matter is more unified and the situations involve the love and sexual life of two people. There is intellectual vigour and knowledge in the speech:

> Natures lay Ideot, I taught thee to love
> And in that sophistrie, Oh, thou dost prove
> Too subtile: Foole, thou didst not understand
> The mystique language of the eye nor hand.

Although 'To his Mistress Going to Bed' is filled with rapid allusions and analogies to Neo-Platonism, religion, mysticism, explorations and political theory, they are assimilated to a humorous celebration of the erotic:

> Licence my roving hands, and let them go
> Before, behind, between, above, below.
> O My America! my new-found-land,
> My kingdome, safeliest when with one man man'd,
> My Myne of precious stones, My Emperie,
> How blest am I in this discovering thee!

Exercises in wit, consciously written within a classical sub-genre to express the libertinism of the late sixteenth and early seventeenth centuries, the elegies have a zest for life and an intelligent worldiness which is always contemporary.

The elegies, satires, *Anniversaries* and many verse letters are in couplets; Donne's great *Songs and Sonnets*, however, use a variety of stanzas, each of which is created for the specific work. The rhythms are extremely colloquial with elided and slurred vowels and many stresses. They are both intimate and filled with the real world. The range of tones as each poem develops is remarkable. 'The Canonization' opens with the exasperated 'For Godsake hold your tongue, and let me love'. The second stanza begins less assertively: 'Alas, alas, who's injur'd by my love?' In the next two stanzas the voice becomes introspective, then mysterious: 'Call us what you will, wee are made such by love'; 'Wee can dye by it, if not live by love'. There are satiric touches ('Soldiers finde warres, and Lawyers find out still / Litigious men, which quarrels move') and witty double entendres:

> So to one neutrall thing both sexes fit,
> Wee dye and rise the same, and prove
> Mysterious by this love.

Many of the poems treat of the psychology of love. In 'Air and Angels' and 'The Good Morrow' Neo-Platonic ideas are used to express nuances of emotions. The great 'A Nocturnal Upon S. Lucies Day' uses alchemical, seasonal and zodiacal analogies to the dark side of passion. The relationship of physical to spiritual love is explored in 'The Ecstasy', 'The Expiration' and 'A Valediction: Forbidding Mourning'. Although the poems sensitively and precisely use analogies to express complex emotions, there is no consistent philosophy of love; some poems are cynical, brutal, or humorously worldly. 'The Blossom' makes fun of spiritual love. The speaker in 'Love's Alchemy' complains:

> Oh, 'tis imposture all:
> And as no chymique yet th'Elixar got,
> But glorifies his pregnant pot,
> If by the way to him befall
> Some odoriferous thing, or medicinall,
> So, lovers dreame a rich and long delight,
> But get a winter-seeming summers night.

Donne's poems are recognisable by their striking openings with their colloquial rhythms, immediacy and situations:

> Who ever comes to shroud me, do not harme
>   Nor question much
> That subtile wreath of haire, which crowns my arme.

Situations are developed or explored through what appears to be a logical argument in which conceits, metaphors and other forms of analogy bring a wide range of relationships to bear on the progressive revelation of feelings. Often the tone and perspective move from an assertive rejection of the external world towards sensitive introspection. Then the poem concludes with a gesture of defiance. 'The Relic' begins 'When my grave is broke up againe / Some second ghest to entertaine', uses the analogy of the lovers' bones to relics in time of 'mis-devotion', becomes introspective ('First, we lov'd well and faithfully,') and concludes: 'All measure, and all language, I should passe, / Should I tell what a miracle shee was'.

While extending the range of the love lyric, Donne relies on the conventions of Renaissance poetry. 'The Apparition', with its sexual taunts at a cruel mistress, is a more fantastic, tougher version of the Renaissance lover's ' threat to take revenge upon his mistress after he dies from her scorn. 'The Bait' is an urbane, sophisticated, psychologically aware variation on a theme already treated by Marlowe and Ralegh. 'The Blossom' has behind it both the traditional body and soul debate and poems in which flowers are used as examples of why it is necessary to live fully. 'Break of Day' is an aubade, or morning lyric. 'The Damp', 'The Dissolution', 'Farewell to Love' and 'A Fever' are among the many *Songs and Sonnets* which develop a situation used by Petrarch. 'Confined Love', 'The Dream' and 'The Flea' belong to the Ovidian tradition. The bringing together, often in a single poem, of previously dissimilar kinds of poetry, and bringing to them a more realistic and intelligent evaluation of experience and a more colloquial voice, is part of Donne's originality. The feelings are deep and the mind without illusions. Donne's voice, attitudes and poses were to be echoed in English poetry throughout the following decades.

The Epithalamia, or marriage songs, show Donne's consciously off-key use of poetic genre. The early 'Epithalamion made at Lincolnes Inne', written before 1598, has a wry relationship to Spenser's great 'Epithalamion'. Whereas previous epithalamists sometimes used the genre as a rhetorical game, the tone of Donne's poem teases with its farcical and satirical notes: 'Put forth, put forth that warme balme-breathing thigh'; 'Then may thy leane and hunger-starved wombe'; 'The priest comes on his knees t'embowell her'. The tone of the 'St Valentines Day Epithalamion', written for the marriage of Princess Elizabeth to Frederick, Elector Palatine, is less puzzling, as might be expected for a celebration which united the Stuarts to one of the hopes of Protestantism. Donne, however, does treat the contrast between the social festivities and the wedding night with good-natured humour:

> But oh, what ailes the Sunne, that here he staies,
>   Longer to day, then other daies? . . .
>   And why doe you two walke,
> So slowly pac'd in this procession?
> Is all your care but to be look'd upon,
> And be to others spectacle, and talke?
>   The feast, with gluttonous delaies,
> Is eaten, and too long their meat they praise,
> The masquers come too late, and'I thinke, will stay.

The two *Anniversaries*, written to commemorate the death of Elizabeth Drury, are unusual funeral elegies. The *First Anniversarie* (1611) is entitled 'An Anatomy of the World' and is a powerful intellectual exercise in surveying the fallen world. Elizabeth is treated figuratively as an ideal 'shee'. The famous passages on the impossibility of health, on marriage ('For that first marriage was our funerall: / One woman at one blow, then kill'd us all') and the 'new Philosophy' ('Tis all in pieces, all cohaerence gone; / All just supply, and all Relation:') offer examples of a corrupted world 'Quite out of joynt, almost created lame'. The *Second Anniversarie* (1612), 'Of the Progres of the Soule', is in length and structure similar to the earlier poem and implicitly contrasts this life with the next. The meditation in lines 85–120 points to the soul's future liberation from the fallen world:

> Thinke then, my soule, that death is but a Groome,
> Which brings a Taper to the outward roome,
> Whence thou spiest first a little glimmering light,
> And after brings it nearer to thy sight:
> For such approches doth Heaven make in death.

'Shee' is a 'patterne' for the Christian life and death; and her joys in heaven anticipate those which will follow the general resurrection at the end of time: 'When earthly bodies more celestiall / Shalbe, then Angels were'.

III Donne's religious poetry

The use of secular lyric forms, especially the sonnet, for devotional practices was pioneered in English by the two Jesuits Robert Southwell (1561–95) and William Alabaster (1567–1640). Donne's religious poetry consists of nineteen Holy Sonnets, the seven linked sonnets in *La Corona*, three hymns, 'A Litanie', and a few occasional pieces. *La Corona*, recalling the main events of Christ's life and the mysteries of the faith within the Christian scheme of redemption, is a crown of prayer and praise woven from liturgical phrases. The Holy Sonnets dramatise Donne's sense of unworthiness in contrast to divine power and mercy. Their intense immediacy is influenced by Ignatian meditational practice with its use of memory, the 'composition of place', the stimulation of emotions and the progression through under-standing, will, the cry of wonder, the colloquy and the asking of God's mercy. Six of the sonnets focus on Last Things; 'This is my playes last scene' and 'At the round earths imagin'd corners, blow/ Your trumpets, Angells, and arise, arise / From death' begin by imagining the moment of death and the last judgement. Six are colloquies on divine love:

> Batter my heart, three person'd God; for, you
> As yet but knocke, breathe, shine, and seeke to mend; . . .
> Take mee to you, imprison mee, for I
> Except you'enthrall mee, never shall be free,
> Nor ever chast, except you ravish mee.

The sonnets show a soul here and now in fear and trembling. The voice is idiomatic, impatient, tense, exclamatory, stress-ful, often monosyllabic. Both the octaves and sestets are dramatic. The twelve sonnets can be read as a linked sequence beginning with the prelude 'As due by many titles I resigne/ My selfe to thee, O God' and concluding with reconciliation: 'Thy lawes abridgement, and thy last com-mand / Is all but love; Oh let that last Will stand!'

The other sonnets comprise four penitential meditations

('Thou has made me, And shall thy worke decay?/ Repaire me *now*, for mine end doth haste'), and some miscellaneous pieces including the resigned poem on the death of his wife ('Since she whome I lovd, hath payd her last debt'). Although the occasional poems contain striking images, word play, conceits and paradoxes, they are less urgent and immediate than the twelve Holy Sonnets. 'Goodfriday, 1613. Riding Westward' begins as a scholastic debate ('Let mans Soule be a Spheare'), and through paradox ('There I should see a Sunne, by rising set') and typology the argument proceeds to the plea:

> O thinke mee worth thine anger, punish mee,
> Burne off my rusts, and my deformity,
> Restore thine Image, so much, by thy grace,
> That thou may'st know mee, and I'll turne my face.

A similar concern with sin and grace is a feature of 'A Hymne to God the Father' with its puns on son and done:

> Sweare by thy selfe, that at my death thy Sunne
> Shall shine as it shines now, and heretofore;
> And, having done that, Thou has done,
> I have no more.

While Donne's religious poems are part of the early-seven-teenth-century attempt to use secular verse forms for spiritual purposes, they are stanzaically less inventive than the poems of Herbert or Donne's own secular songs. Their power partly results from the personal application of the drama of sin and grace. The conceits, analogies, puns, paradoxes and other forms of wit are means of bringing intelligence to bear on the articulation of emotions.

IV Donne's prose

The use of wit, word play, ideas and conceits found in Donne's poetry is also characteristic of his prose. His colloquial, witty, often antithetical prose is part of the reaction against Ciceronianism towards a manner associated with Seneca. *Paradoxes and Problemes* are trivial but clever prose exercises within a recognised Renaissance genre. Satire, humour and playfulness are used for such topics as 'A Defence of Womens Inconstancy', 'That Women ought to paint', 'That Nature is our worst Guide', and 'That only Cowards dare dye'. The paradoxes reveal the same love of argumentation that appears in the poems:

> That Women are *Inconstant*, I with any man confesse, but that *Inconstancy* is a bad quality, I against any man will maintaine. . . . so in Men, they that have the most reason are the most alterable in their designes, and the darkest or most ignorant, do seldomest change; therefore Women changing more than Men, have also more *Reason*. . . . I would you had your *Mistresses* so constant, that they would never change, no not so much as their *smocks*, then should you see what sluttish vertue, *Constancy* were. . . . In mine Opinion such men are happy that Women are *Inconstant*, for so may they chance to bee beloved of some excellent Women (when it comes to their turne) out of their *Inconstancy* and mutability, though not out of their owne desert. . . . To conclude therefore; this name of *Inconstancy*, which hath so much beene poysoned with slaunders, ought to bee changed into *variety*, for the which the world is so delightful, *and a Woman for that the most delightfull thing in this world.*

Pseudo-Martyr (1610) criticises Catholics, especially Jesuits, who after the Gunpowder Plot refused to take the Oath of Allegiance. *Ignatius his Conclave* (1610) is a lively satire; in Hell Ignatius Loyola debates with Copernicus, Columbus and Machiavelli as to who is the most troublesome innovator. Lucifer is so impressed by Ignatius that he sends him to the moon to start a 'Lunatique Church' and create a 'Hell in that world also'. While having fun with contemporary ideas, Donne satirises Jesuit interference in politics; at the conclusion Ignatius creates a riot in Hell by attempting to depose Pope Boniface. The *Essays in Divinity* (1611?), rigorously subdivided into topics and influenced by Augustine's blending of philosophy with exegesis and meditation, consist of 'Disquisitions, Interwoven with Meditations and Prayers' on verses from Genesis and Exodus.

Devotions Upon Emergent Occasions (1624) are divided into twenty-three sections (each containing a meditation, 'expostulation' and prayer) tracing the stages of the serious illness from which Donne was then suffering. The prose has the intensity, introspection, passion, wit, visual imagery and display of learning found in the Holy Sonnets. Donne repents his sins, his sinful feelings, fears God's justice, entreats compassion, sees his illness as God's means of correction, and asks divine mercy through Christ. The most famous passage was occasioned by Donne's hearing the tolling of church bells:

> No man is an *Iland*, intire of it selfe; every man is a peece of the *Continent*, a part of the *maine*; if a *Clod* bee washed away by the *Sea*, *Europe* is the lesse, as well as if a *Promontorie* were, as well as if a *Mannor* of thy *friends* or of *thine owne* were; any mans *death* diminishes *me*, because I am involved in *Mankinde*; And therefore never send to know for whom the *bell* tolls; It tolls for *thee*.

Donne was the most famous preacher of his time. Vigorous, immediate, dramatic, intense, his sermons reflect the Augustinian tradition of moving back and forth between prayer, meditation, exposition and analysis. The style is varied, ranging from short memorable sentences, balanced antithesis and asymmetrical constructions to long sentences built from cumulative clauses. The organisation is clear, although in local detail the relationship of passages to each other seems more by association and effect than by logic. Donne begins by introducing his text and the occasion, announces the various divisions (usually two or three) which his sermon will follow and proceeds to the divisions, sub-dividing them into many smaller sections. Similar to other Anglican preachers of the time he shows his respect for Church tradition and authority by incorporating in his text quotations from Church Fathers and the Bible. The sermons are, however, less orderly than those of Laud and Andrewes; they are more personal, impassioned. Although the 'I' of the sermons is the Christian, Donne often alludes to himself and his calling as a priest. The sermons are Augustinian in their emphasis on the self, sin, love, mercy, death and resurrection, and in recalling, through intellect and emotion, what the Christian is supposed already to know about doctrine. Instead of dogma and the Bible as history, Donne is concerned with the Bible, and its language, as symbolic. Similar to St Bernard, Donne uses metaphors and analogies to recollect spiritual mysteries and bring them into relation with the self. The sentences accordingly are restless, broken, repetitive, rhythmic and musical as they follow the progress of the mind. As a topic is elaborated both intellectually and emotionally, there are parentheses, quotations, irony, repeated words, word play and a disregard for strict grammar. Donne is self-conscious, urgent, sometimes humorous, and unusually vivid as he plays on the emotions of his audience. As in his poetry, metaphors explain the spiritual through analogy with the physical:

> If you looke upon this world in a Map, you find two Hemisphears, two half worlds. If you crush heaven into a Map, you may find two Hemisphears too, two half heavens; Halfe will be Joy, and halfe will be Glory; for in these two, the joy of heaven, and the glory of heaven, is all heaven often represented unto us. And as of those two Hemisphears of the world, the first hath been knowne long before, but the other, (that of America, which is the richer in treasure) God reserved for later Discoveries; So though he reserve that Hemisphear of heaven, which is the Glory thereof, to the Resurrection, yet the other Hemisphear, the Joy of heaven, God opens to our Discovery, and delivers for our habitation even whilst we dwell in this world. As God hath cast upon the unrepentant sinner two deaths, a temporall, and a spirituall death, so hath he breathed into us two lives.

V Jonson's classicism and poetry

If Donne and the metaphysical poets exemplify the wit and fantasy of the early Baroque, Ben Jonson (1572–1637) emphasises its classical tendencies. Jonson began his career in the late Elizabethan theatre and dominated the London literary world during the early decades of the century when he was a favourite of James I, who appointed him Poet Laureate in 1616. Through sheer will, personality and learning he advanced in society from bricklayer, soldier and actor to friendship with the peerage, and attracted his own circle of literary followers known as the 'sons' or 'Tribe of Ben'. Jonson's literary ideas and practice influenced the work of lesser writers of his time and continued to be explored and developed by later generations. He transformed the Court masquerades from entertainments into an artistic genre; his comedies of 'humours' and the structure of his serious plays remained a model for dramatists through the century. Jonson's rediscovery of Greek 'new comedy' provided the century with its many plots in which youth outwits and takes possession from its elders. His *Workes* (1616) were the first published collection of plays by an English author.

Jonson's most influential contribution to literature was the adaptation to English of many classical literary genres, the conscious development of a plain style in contrast to the Elizabethan and metaphysical, and the creation of an accompanying persona which expressed values as accepted social norms. Jonson's methods influenced the poetry of the Cavaliers and was one source of the Neo-Classicism that ran parallel to, and often blended with, the metaphysical style, until a larger version of Neo-Classicism triumphed at the Restoration. The plain, like the metaphysical, style was a reaction against the florid, flowery, artificial Petrarchism and Euphuism that had characterised Elizabethan verse. Whereas both Donne and Jonson wrote poetry in a colloquial language without the studied ornamentation, elegance and mythological decoration of the preceding generation, Jonson turned to the clearness and classicism of Catullus, Horace, and Martial as models rather than the wit of Ovid or the conceits of European Baroque poetry. Just as Erasmus (1466–1536) the Dutch Humanist scholar and satirist (who advocated simple piety, criticised Church abuses, and took a moderate position between Luther and the Catholic Church), Lipsius (1547–1606) the French Humanist (whose edition of Tacitus contributed to the new fashion for a plain 'Senecan' prose style) and Bacon rejected the elaborate, rhetorical Ciceronian prose often prized by the Renaissance, so Jonson aimed at writing verse in which the meaning was unambiguous and in which the seeming absence of rhetoric suggested a natural voice.

Addressed to the élite who can discriminate, the style is essentially rational, in contrast to fanciful; Jonson supposedly wrote his poems first in prose before turning them into verse. He avoided figurative language, such stylistic graces as elaborate word play, symmetry, bold metaphors, repetitions, sensory imagery, and such formal devices as the regular placement of the caesura, consistently end-stopped lines and elaborate stanzas. By avoiding unusual words, he aimed at an idiomatic, current speech. The style depends on energetic syntax; while the number of syllables and stresses is controlled, the syntax does not conform to a pattern and usually breaks the rhythmic unity of the line. Jonson makes free use of the caesura, commas and other means of varying rhythm. He sometimes uses an odd word order to separate elements of a sentence and create roughness. The effect is abrupt, staccato, sharp, somewhat like the curt style of Senecan prose, except that Jonson purposefully dislocates balance, parallels and symmetry to create an illusion of an absence of rhetoric. Although he usually preferred the couplet to stanzaic poetry, he experimented with both the Horatian and Pindaric odes. In his couplets he only lightly end-stopped the line; however, the syntax seldom runs over into the next line as he wanted to keep the regular stress and tension of the syllabic line as a means of preventing his verse from having the slackness of prose. The resulting style is sinewy, tense, epigrammatic, compressed, rich in generalisation, maxims and movement but sometimes overloaded and crabbed. As Milton was also to show, by crowding the line with words, by using active verbs, by controlling enjambement and the energy which results from elision, it is possible to write strong lines without using the conceits, word play and allusions found in Donne and the metaphysical style.

Jonson aims at a decorum in which images and words are appropriate to a logical, persuasive, restrained manner of speaking. It defines his attitudes and creates intimacy between the poet and the person addressed. Whereas Donne appears to inhabit a private world, concerned with personal anxieties, emotions and beliefs, Jonson's world seems larger, more populated with friends, if less public than that of Dryden. The Cavalier poets learned from Jonson this intimate but urbane manner in which feelings are placed within a social context. In contrast to the introversion and artificiality of the Renaissance sonnet, the plain style can also give poetry a greater intimacy. Jonson's love poems express little passion, but they reveal personalities engaged in the various psychological and social relationships which courtship involves. By assimilating the plain style to such genres as the epigram, epistle, ode and satire, Jonson created a poetry which expresses character, personality, social relationships and responsibilities. His verse discriminates and celebrates; it offers a sense of standards, self-sufficiency, and character in an actual world.

The focus on friendship, family and marriage results from Jonson's desire for a harmonious society in which tradition, long-established great families and ordered lives centred upon country houses represent civilisation; the poems celebrate a hierarchy in which the responsibilities of the aristocracy towards the land, the community and the state are implicitly contrasted to the destructive energies of the city, individualism, ambition and glory. The implied comparison of English manorial life to a classical golden age with pastoral scenes peopled by Pan and other rustic deities, nymphs and satyrs, influenced Herrick's vision of the English countryside continuing the rites and customs of classical civilisations. In praising, even idealising, friends and the aristocracy, Jonson attempts to create models for conduct: 'I Doe but name thee *Pembroke*, and I find / It is an *Epigramme*, on all man-kind; / Against the bad, but of, and to the good'. Such poems as 'To Penshurst' ('Thou art not, *Penshurst*, built to envious show') and the Pindaric ode 'To the Immortall Memorie, and Friendship of That Noble Paire, Sir Lucius Cary, and Sir H. Morison' summarise a way of life which integrates behaviour and virtue. Jonson addressed the great men directly. There is, however, a stoicism in Jonson's view of life. It is necessary to be self-centred; the evils of the world must be ignored; virtue is its own reward.

Jonson's career as a professional man of letters and his vision of a good society as including the arts, philosophy, learning, friendship and urbanity, along with monarchy and the responsibilities of nobility, reflected the social changes of the early part of the century. His praise of the noble families, their way of life and their estates soothed anxieties during a time when the peerage was rapidly changing, estates were being sold, and the recently created Elizabethan nobility strove to distinguish their supposedly long lineage from the newcomers advanced by riches or influence under James I. The idealising of the country house in Jonson's 'To Penshurst' with its Horatian ideal of retirement to the country was useful to the Stuarts if the peerage were to continue their local responsibilities and remain a force of stability throughout the nation.

Jonson published in his 1616 *Workes* a book of *Epigrammes*, short occasional poems 'To my Booke-Seller', 'To King James', 'To Alchymists' and to various friends. They included such social subjects as 'To a Fine Lady Would-Bee' and 'Inviting a Friend to Supper'. The poems in *The*

Forrest (also 1616) are longer, more varied in form and include such innovations in English as the Horatian epistle and topographical verses. *The Forrest* begins with 'Why I write not of love' ('*Love* is fled, and I grow old') and the celebration 'To Penshurst':

> Each morne, and even, they are taught to pray,
>   With the whole houshold, and may, every day,
> Reade, in their vertuous parents noble parts,
>   The mysteries of manners, armes, and arts.
> Now *Penshurst*, they that will proportion thee
>   With other edifices, when they see
> Those proud, ambitious heaps, and nothing else,
>   May say, their lords have built, but thy lord dwells.

Although there are a few sixteenth-century predecessors, Jonson laid the foundations for the many Caroline and Interregnum poets who built their lyrics, odes and epistles by imitating classical models. The magnificent 'Come my *Celia*, let us prove' and 'Drinke to me onely, with thine eyes' show the uses of imitation, as they are assemblages of passages from classical poets. Jonson's renewal of poetic conventions through mockery can be seen in 'And must I sing? what subject shall I chuse?' The epistle 'To Elizabeth Countesse of Rutland' is remarkable for its opening sentence of nineteen lines, an experiment in remodelling the couplet unit into a verse paragraph. The 'Ode: To Sir William Sydney, on his birth-day' shows Jonson bringing the plain style to other stanzaic forms and making poetry of social occasions.

The Underwood (1640), published from Jonson's manu-scripts by his friend Sir Kenelm Digby, includes examples of the plain style used for religious poetry, epistles, elegies, odes, translations of Horatian odes, 'ten lyric pieces' to 'Charis' (Jonson's humorous, sociable equivalent to a sonnet sequence), and excellent poems in which women defend 'their Inconstancie':

> Hang up those dull, and envious fooles
>   That talke abroad of Womans change,
> We were not bred to sit on stooles,
>   Our proper vertue is to range:
>   Take that away, you take our lives,
>   We are no women then, but wives.

There is the humorous psychology of 'A Nymphs Passion' ('Yet if it be not knowne, / The pleasure is as good as none'), the self-mockery of 'My Picture Left in Scotland' ('My mountaine belly, and my rockie face'), and the comic invective and literary satire of 'An Execration Upon Vulcan' and 'A Fit of Rime against Rime'. In the epistles Jonson expresses his code of civility:

> Your Booke, my *Selden*, I have read, and much
> Was trusted, that you thought my judgement such
> To aske it.

VI Jonson's criticism

Although Jonson did not write a critical treatise or essays, literary criticism is scattered among his writing. Besides his literal verse translation of Horace's *Ars Poetica* ('Art of Poetry'), there is *Timber, or Discoveries* (a collection of notes, many of which are adapted or translated from other writers), the prefaces, prologues and epilogues to his plays and masques, many scenes in the plays, and the not necessarily accurate conversations reported by William Drummond of Hawthorden. The criticism is that of a practising writer attempting to learn from and adapt what had been learned in the past. Jonson is less concerned with rules than with the logical methods by which practice and discipline can improve native abilities. English literature needed to be improved through study and method. Believing English writing of his time to be undisciplined and addressed to the uneducated multitude, he wanted to find methods which would satisfy those men of taste and education who govern society and to whom he felt literature is addressed. Art offers moral instructions to its patrons. Jonson is influenced by classical oratory. The style, diction, topics, and manners are the clothing of thought, and are meant to persuade or win the listener to your side. Jonson chooses the plain style because it is suitable for rational discourse without being inelegant and flat; it is therefore appropriate · for addressing intelligent readers. Jonson is not what is usually meant by a Neo-Classical critic. He does not follow precedents and authority. Starting from the assumption that the purpose of art is to elevate and instruct, he attempted rationally, using previous critics as a guide, to distinguish what was suitable for his purposes in poetry and drama.

His theory of dramatic structure provided a method by which the sprawling Elizabethan play could be shaped into five acts having logical movement. The *protasis* or introduction of the characters and plot in the first and second acts, is followed by the *epitasis*, or complication in the third act; the *catastasis*, or crisis, occurs in the fourth or early in the fifth act and is followed by the *catastrophe* or conclusion. The difference between *catastasis* and the *catastrophe* is that the former appears to conclude the action, but it is a false resolution followed by an unexpected, more satisfactory, ending. Jonson wants a plot constructed to delight the audience and to have an artistically pleasing shape; his formula was followed by Dryden and others.

VII Jonson's plays

His first successful play, *Every Man in His Humour* (1598), introduces many of the themes, situations and character types found in the later dramas. A satire on social climbing and snobbery, it shows middle- and lower-class characters being duped by those who prey on gullibility. Set in Italy, it was later revised for the 1616 Folio and the action placed in London. Jonson's classicism is seen in his respect for the unities of time and place; the action lasts twelve hours and takes place in and around one city. Jonson uses neither the single story of classical drama, nor the multiple plots of the Renaissance; he attempts to integrate several stories into a single, unified plot. *Every Man out of His Humour* (1599) brings the methods of formal verse satire to the stage through a play within a play which allows characters to observe and comment. Rather than a story, *Every Man out of His Humour* presents a variety of types, like those of the verse satires, who are brought forward for inspection. Jonson says his characters are 'humours'; each is obsessed by a monomania. Although the notion of humours was part of Elizabethan psychology, based on medical theory, Jonson's humours are moral and spiritual aberrations. The use of an 'induction' explaining the satiric humour, the play within a

play, and the various commentators, create a complex perspective which draws attention to the play as artifice. Such
sophistication of the art of drama creates both an immediacy
with the audience (the commentators having the relationship
that the speakers of Jonson's and Donne's poems have with
the reader) and a distancing of the events on stage which, we
are reminded, are being displayed for our inspection.

Cynthia's Revels (1600) combines satire on the Court with
the glorification of Queen Elizabeth. *Poetaster* ('Worthless
Poet', 1601), for the Children of Chapel Royal, appears to
have begun the feud with Marston and Dekker known as the
War of the Theatres, in which the dramatists included slightly
disguised caricatures of each other in their plays. The first
of Jonson's classical Roman tragedies, *Sejanus His Fall*
(1603) — the second is *Catiline* (1611) — is a portrayal of
the rise and fall of ambition unmotivated by any moral
conscience. The play shows a struggle for power among a
tyrant's favourites, in which the cleverest villain wins while
the good men of society are unable to resist evil. Although
Sejanus can be seen as part of Jonson's concern with the
effect of unbridled individualism on community, its conclusion is pessimistic. As communal values flow from the ruler,
tyranny breeds greater tyranny. Jonson's scholarly use of
historical sources did not prevent the Court from seeing
contemporary analogies to the Earl of Essex and the use of
informers; Jonson was accused of treason before the Privy
Council. Although the debt to Senecan drama in the monologues, political debates, epigrammatical sentences and
narration of off-stage events makes *Sejanus* similar to
Elizabethan poetic closet drama, the play provided Jonson
with the techniques and discipline of the great comedies
which follow. Sejanus's ecstasy at his power and cunning,
while derived from Senecan bombast, is shaped by the same
satiric attitude which will create the ironic speeches of
Volpone and Sir Epicure Mammon:

> Swell, swell, my joys: and faint not to declare
> Your selves, as ample, as your causes are.
> I did not live, till now; this my first hower:
> Wherein I see my thoughts reach'd by my power.
> But this, and gripe my wishes. Great, and high,
> The world knowes only two, that's *Rome*, and I.

> My roofe receives me not; 'tis aire I tread:
> And, at each step, I feele my 'advanced head
> Knocke out a starre in heav'n! Rear'd to this height,
> All my desires seeme modest, poore and sleight,
> That did before sound impudent: 'Tis place,
> Not bloud, discernes the noble, and the base.

After collaborating with Chapman and Marston on *Eastward Ho!* (1605) for the Children of the Queen's Revel, for which the authors were imprisoned for their satire on Scottish Court favourites, Jonson wrote *Volpone* (1606), the first of his great comedies in which the clever outwit the foolish by playing on their vanity and greed, until the clever fall through pride in their own cunning. Although Jonson draws his characters in simple outlines, Volpone and Mosca have a magnificence which results both from their passion for deceit and from their use of language. Besides the grand opening speech in which Volpone's praise of gold perverts all accepted cultural values, there is the comedy of Volpone in love:

> Those blowes were nothing: I could beare them ever.
> But angry *Cupid*, bolting from her eyes,
> Hath shot himselfe into me, like a flame;
> Where, now, he flings about his burning heat,
> As in a fornace, some ambitious fire,
> Whose vent is stopt

and the grotesque romantic grandeur of Volpone's imagination:

> If thou hast wisdome, heare me *Celia*.
> Thy bathes shall be the juyce of *July*-flowres,
> Spirit of roses, and of violets,
> The milke of unicornes, and panthers breath
> Gather'd in bagges, and mixt with *Cretan* wines.
> Our drinke shal be prepared gold, and amber;
> Which we will take, untill my roofe whirle round
> With the *vertigo*: and my *Dwarfe* shall dance,
> My *Eunuch* sing, my *Foole* make up the *antique*.
> Whil'st, we, in changed shapes, act *Ovids* tales,
> Thou, like *Europa* now, and I like *Jove*,
> Then I like *Mars*, and thou like *Erycine*,
> So of the rest, till we have quite run through
> And weary'd all the *fables* of the *Gods*.

Volpone and Mosca have similarities to the speakers in late Elizabethan verse satires. Although we enjoy their derision of and superiority to others, the only aesthetically and morally suitable conclusion is their downfall. In a play of grotesque relationships, in which all social values are perverted (even the characters' names are those of animals and insects) and almost everyone is corrupted by temptations of wealth, the worst vanity and greed is that of Volpone, the superior man who falls through pride in his own cunning.

Epicoene, or The Silent Woman (1609) has a clarity of exposition and theme rare to English comedy. Following the New Comedy of Terence and Plautus, Jonson devised a plot in which youth overcomes the obstacles of the old to inherit the family possessions. Despite its happy ending, *Epicoene* is a cynical comedy which satirises the private lives of the upper classes, the sexual mores of the time, what Jonson felt to be a confusion of sexual roles, the law, legal jargon, and even common sense. If Morose is ridiculed for his misanthropic withdrawal from society, society behaves in a manner worthy of his disdain.

A similar disillusioned view of society can be seen in *The Alchemist* (1610). Although the play is more genial than the earlier comedies, there are no virtuous characters; everyone is either a deceiver or a self-deluding victim, greedy for wealth and power. The characters, whether tricksters or victims, live in a fantasy world of disguises, self-deception and dangerous imaginations. There is no final reconciliation between characters or reassertion of morality; when Lovewit returns to his house, which in his absence has been turned by his housekeeper into a nest for confidence tricksters, the play fizzles to an end with both the rogues and their victims disappointed and disillusioned. Before Lovewit's return, however, *The Alchemist* is a play of great activity. The various stories interrupt each other in an excellent display of Jonson's ability to unify a variety of actions into a homogeneous plot. The tight time scheme and restriction of the action to the house also contribute to the intensity. *The Alchemist* is notable for its excellent blank verse, which is varied to express Tribulation's fluency as a preacher, Drugger's nervousness and Sir Epicure Mammon's grandiose fantasies.

Bartholomew Fair (1614) shows Jonson's mature mastery of weaving many strands into a unified plot while using the swirl of activity of the many characters to express social disorder. Although there is no dominant character, the thirty scenes are held together by the Fair and each of the acts builds towards a crescendo before concluding in an anti-climax. The Fair is similar to the alchemical laboratory, being a place where swindlers stimulate the imaginations and desires of society and, as a by-product, strip their victims of their pretences to respectability. The play's main themes concern the acquisitive and hypocritical puritanical attitudes of the middle classes especially in regard to marriage. The rogues, cheats and pimps seem more honest and likeable than their supposedly respectable victims. Respectability and pretence are deflated by the absurdity of Rabbi Zeal-of-the-Land Busy arguing with a puppet about the immorality of the theatre and being defeated when the puppet reveals it has no sexual organs. The play concludes with a call for the restoration of a community spirit; the justice of the peace is reminded that 'You are but Adam, Flesh, and blood! You have your frailty, forget your other name of Overdo, and invite us all to supper.'

Turning his talents increasingly to collaborations with Inigo Jones on Court masques, Jonson avoided the public stage until after the death of James I when, with the accession of Charles I to the throne, he found himself out of fashion with the Court. He returned to playwriting with *The Staple of News* (1626), *The New Inn* (1629), *The Magnetic Lady* (1632) and a revision of his early *A Tale of a Tub* (1633). Jonson's long involvement with the masque is largely lost to the reader as this curious and unstable blend of dance, music, spectacle and poetry depends upon performance. Originally an entertainment of the nobility in which the Court and King were praised, the masque consisted of masked courtiers who danced, celebrated the King and joined with the audience in the final dances or 'revels'. By the turn of the century the masque had developed into a series of dances and spectacles formally linked by poetic speeches which explained the plot. Jonson and Jones transformed the masque, integrating its varied elements into a whole, developing its significance and, finally, extending the realistic illusionism until the inherent tension between poetry and theatre led to the dramatist's quarrel with his accomplice and, under Charles I, the domination of the masque by spectacle.

The emergence of the masque as a distinctive art form followed similar developments on the Continent where, in Italy and France, elaborate Court and civil pageants used dance, song, and newly devised theatre machinery to present complex allegories in emblematic and symbolic displays. The delight in lighting, dance, song, moveable and spectacular stage effects rapidly changed the arts and soon gave birth to ballet, opera and the modern perspective stage with change-able scenery and realistic illusionism. With *The Masque of Blacknesse* (1605) Jonson and Jones created for England an equivalent of the elaborate continental allegorical entertain-ments; besides combining spectacular theatre machinery, scenic emblems, symbolism, and poetry, the masque stunned its audience by breaking social decorum in having courtiers painted black like 'Moors'. As the masque form developed towards realism and it became inappropriate for the courtiers to act, professional actors were used for the new anti-masque sections in which the bizarre, grotesque and vulgar are seen in symbolic contrast to the ideal represented by the Court and King. *The Golden Age Restored* (1615), *The Vision of Delight* (1617) and *Pleasure Reconciled to Virtue* (1618) moved away from emblems and mere spectacle towards a realistic illusionism. As the anti-masque expanded and spectacle became less important, the masques became more dramatic. The final collaborations between Jonson and Jones, *Chloridia* (1631) and *Love's Triumph* (1631), reflect, how-ever, the new direction of the Caroline masque in which the meaning of allegory is rather shown visually than told through poetic language.

4
Jacobean literature

I Drama: Fletcher, Middleton and Webster

The plays of John Fletcher (1579–1625) and Francis Beaumont (1584?–1616), both gentlemen's younger sons who became professional dramatists, set a new direction for Jacobean drama which remained influential throughout the century. Jonson and Marston brought to the stage the energies, conventions, urban realism, situational ironies and ambiguous attitudes of the satiric verse of the late 1590s; Beaumont and Fletcher brought to English drama the elegance, nervous movement, dazzling effects, wit and aristocratic tastes of mid-sixteenth-century Italian Mannerism, as represented by such writers as Ariosto and Guarini (1538–1612). It was Guarini in particular who influenced Fletcher's notion of tragicomedy, expressed in the preface to *The Faithful Shepherdess* (1608), as a distinct and superior literary kind in which a delightful, intricate plot hovering on the brink of tragedy would conclude with a surprising, happy reversal, thus supposedly conforming to the Christian providential scheme. This theory gave unusual prominence to the design of the plot as itself of interest. It also raises the question whether the many plays during the century which conclude with the restoration of social and moral order are illustrations of divine providence or merely follow a successful dramatic formula.

It was possible for Beaumont and Fletcher to bring continental Court tastes to the English stage because of the new coterie theatres, sponsored by royalty, which had also given support to the satirists. This was drama for the nobles, the refined, the jades, the sophisticated and the intelligent and educated who had attended the Inns of Court. Its characters are usually noble, in contrast to city comedy, and speak with courtly manners; the plots, involving love and war, rival lovers, rival kings and usurpers, are set against a background involving the fate of the nation. The characters form a pattern of types, hero and villain, heroine and villainness. There is much movement, a striving after effect, reversals of attitudes, and strangely vacillating, passive heroes, who are often faced, because they believe in the divine right of kings, by irresolvable conflicts of love and honour.

As there are over fifty plays associated with Beaumont and Fletcher, a few of the more famous must be representative. Beaumont's *The Knight of the Burning Pestle* (1607), probably acted by the Children of the Queen's Revels, is a burlesque of chivalric romances and middle-class drama and tastes. Using the device of unsophisticated, rather stupid spectators watching and commenting upon a play, Beaumont ridicules both chivalry and middle-class values. *Philaster* (1609), probably written in collaboration, uses the conventions of prose romance, with its remote world and intricate, improbable but highly patterned plot to dramatise problems of love and honour in the setting of a usurped kingdom. The play ends happily with a popular revolution in favour of Philaster.

The Maid's Tragedy (1610) also concerns love and honour in a world of romance, but ends more bleakly. The evil is also more convincing. A lustful tyrant abuses the royal prerogative in preventing Amintor from marrying Aspatia, and forcing him to marry Evadne. Evadne, the tyrant's mistress, refuses to sleep with Amintor, who mistakes her behaviour for virginity and is mocked: 'A maidenhead *Amintor* at my yeares!' When he threatens to kill her lover and she torments him '' 'tis the King', he immediately wilts:

> Oh thou hast nam'd a word that wipes away
> All thoughts revengefull; in that sacred name,
> The King, there lies a terror, what fraile man
> Dares lift his hand against it? let the Gods
> Speake to him when they please, till when let us
> Suffer and waite.

Although Amintor's mistaken notions of honour seem contrasted with Melantius's revenge on the king, the play ends with the moral: 'for on lustfull Kings / Unlookt for suddaine deaths from God are sent, / But curst is he that is their instrument'. The tragicomedy *A King and No King* (1611) concerns a king who loves and commits incest with his sister, but ends happily when it is discovered that he is not after all related to her. The ending is a remarkable reversal as during the course of the play the king's passion is shown as sinful and evil; but such teasing and playing with emotions made the drama of Beaumont and Fletcher attractive to the sophisticated.

One of the satirists who contributed to the new drama, Thomas Middleton (1580–1627) began publishing poetry while still a student at Queen's College, Oxford. *The Wisdom of Solomon Paraphrased*, published when he was seventeen, was followed by *Micro-Cynicon* ('A Small Cynicism'), six short 'Snarling Satyres'. The satires use the common techniques of the 1590s, an angry commentator who rants in an energetic but clotted style about character types representative of such vices as greed, lust and cheating; following the new conventions, the satirist himself becomes an object of satire. Using the stanzaic form of Shakespeare's *Rape of Lucrece, The Ghost of Lucrece* (1600) condemns sexuality. By 1602 Middleton was involved with the theatre, and while the canon and dates of his work are controversial, he appears to have written or had a share in at least twenty-five plays, including probably *The Revenger's Tragedy*, one of the best plays of the century.

If Elizabethan comedy can be characterised as romantic, celebratory and aristocratic, Middleton, along with Jonson and Marston, after the banning of verse satire in 1599 made comedy of contemporary London life. His plays evolve from the explicitly satiric to the indirectly satiric (in which the moralist finds expression through an ironic presentation of character and events) and a detached, unheroic view of life in which both comedy and tragedy are mixed with the satiric. Because of complex, compressed plots and rapid dramatic exposition the stories jump ahead without expected preparation and transitions, causing often paradoxical and ironic juxtapositions. It is often unclear whether Middleton's attitude is moral or cynical. His plays treat sexual appetites unromantically and as the prime cause of moral disintegration. The richly metaphoric, vigorous, yet stylised verse suggests comic absurdity. Man is either a brutal, lustful, incompetent animal, or a clever dissembler who will over-reach himself.

The influence of satire on Middleton's early plays can be seen in *The Phoenix* (1603?), a survey of sins brought before a commentator. Although *Michaelmas Term* (1605) also uses the structural device of a commentator, it is more lifelike than the earlier plays. Set in the streets of London, it portrays the city as a place of deception, intrigue, dupes and cunning; it is fast, vigorous and funny. While Middleton seems amused by the manipulation and craft with which people deceive others and are themselves deceived in *A Mad World, My Masters* (1606?), the effect is of a world in disorder where people do not understand each other or them-selves, and in which all conduct seems ironic. *A Trick to Catch the Old One* (1606?) continues the portrayal of shabby practices and cunning; youth is disadvantaged by the old, but through unscrupulous wit and cleverness the young overcome the apparently solid, but equally unscrupulous aged. In *The Mayor of Queenborough, or Hengist*, (1616–20?) Vortiger, a ludicrous brutal tyrant, is treated with a mixture of awe and amusement. The ironies are dry, but the play is tinged with destructive comedy. Despite Middleton's reputation as a realist, based on the naturalistic detail and settings of his plays, his plots and characters are fantastic; often the charac-ters do not seem to take themselves seriously. The early plays were written for the Children of Paul's and the Children of the Revels.

Although *A Chaste Maid in Cheapside* (1613?) shows the new influence of Beaumont and Fletcher in its sentimentality and sensationalism, it is filled with Middletonian paradox, irony and mirrored or juxtaposed relationships. Each of its four stories involves a triangular situation between two men and a woman. *Women Beware Women* (1621?) is similar to *The Revenger's Tragedy* in portraying a society of manipula-tors and victims and in its atmosphere of corruption and sexual depravity. In a world of moral disintegration, innocence is quickly corrupted; the psychology of the characters, especially Livia, is complex. The many asides and soliloquies contribute to the feeling of stylised, purposeful deception; there is no centre, no character has a total view of the plot.

At the conclusion, when everyone becomes a revenger and there is a general slaughter, it is difficult to decide whether the play is an assertion of justice or is ironically comic:

> Vengeance met vengeance
> Like a set match; as if the plagues of sin
> Had been agreed to meet here all together.

The Changeling (1622), written with the actor and some-time dramatist William Rowley (*c.* 1585–1626), continues Middleton's study in lust. Beatrice still thinks of herself as innocent after being directly responsible for two murders; she is less concerned with guilt than with her sexual honour:

> BEATRICE: Why, 'tis impossible thou canst be so wicked,
>   Or shelter such a cunning cruelty,
>   To make his death the murderer of my honour!
>   Thy language is so bold and vicious,
>   I cannot see which way I can forgive it
>   With any modesty
>
> DE FLORES: Push! You forget yourself!
>   A woman dipp'd in blood, and talk of modesty!

Her attraction and submission to the man she hates, and her fascination with his ugliness, are part of the play's psychology of moral disintegration:

> BEATRICE: Already! How rare is that man's speed!
>   How heartily he serves me! His face loathes one,
>   But look upon his care, who would not love him?
>   The east is not more beauteous than his service.

The multiple perspectives, in which Beatrice, De Flores and the audience each understand Beatrice's comments differ-ently, contribute to feelings of moral chaos and to the dramatic irony. *A Game of Chess* (1624), Middleton's final play, comments on James's attempt to appease Spain, especially the proposed Spanish marriage of Prince Charles, and the supposed seduction of England by the Jesuits.

The authorship of many Elizabethan and Jacobean plays remains a problem. Hack work was common, plays were often written by two or more authors, writers were paid to add an act or two to older dramas, and scripts were sold to printers by actors, prompters and others without the author's consent. *The Revenger's Tragedy*, one of the great plays of the century, was published in 1607 without any author's name. The only contemporary reference to it is an entry by the printer in the Stationers' Register: 'Two plays, the one called *The Revenger's Tragedy*, the other, *A Trick to Catch the Old One*'. Although both are authorless in the Register, the latter play is known to be Middleton's. Usually plays by the same author were registered together. In 1656 the unreliable Edward Archer attributed *The Revenger's Tragedy* to Cyril Tourneur, author of *The Atheist's Tragedy*, and was followed without further evidence by others.

The Revenger's Tragedy epitomises much of the period's literature. The horrifying events take place at an Italian court so lecherous, adulterous, corrupt and murderous as to border on parody. Satire has moved into drama with the mocking spokesman now a revenger and, like Marston's malcontent, a bizarre character. There is intrigue, cunning, ironic exaggeration of speech and ironic, unexpected reversals at the play's conclusion. The verse is compressed, densely textured, highly imagistic, intense, witty and filled with conceits. There is a Middletonian feeling for humorous deflation. The serious, tongue-in-cheek and satiric are so intertwined that it is often difficult to know what is the main strand:

> Meet; farewell.
> I am next now, I rise just in that place
> Where thou'rt cut off — upon thy neck kind brother;
> The falling of one head lifts up another.

Is the play tragedy, comedy, morality, burlesque, melodrama or some Jacobean mixture such as tragic-satire or tragic-burlesque? What are we to make of a play in which, having raped a woman known for her virtue, who afterwards commits suicide, the villain when asked 'What moved you to'it?' replies, 'Why flesh and blood my lord: /What should move men unto a woman else?'

The plot presents a similar grotesque comedy. Vindice is hired by the very people on whom he intends revenge. No sooner does his brother, Hippolito, recommend him to Lussurioso than the latter asks Vindice to help him seduce or rape a woman. The woman is Castiza, the sister of Vindice and Hippolito. Lussurioso, not knowing who Vindice really is, laughs heartily at the irony of making Hippolito indirectly responsible for the defilement of his sister. Although this is typical of the villainous corruption of the Court in the play, it is also an example of how many actions by the characters ironically backfire. Every plan produces the opposite result. The Duke hires Vindice to bring him a woman. Instead he is brought the poisoned skull of Vindice's dead beloved. The Duke forces his kisses on the dressed-up skeleton and dies of poison. In the last scene of the play, when Vindice and Hippolito have managed to destroy all their enemies, they brag of having killed the Duke and are themselves arrested and executed. Villains and revengers are alike caught by themselves. Although the play could be given a conventional moralistic interpretation — evil doers will destroy themselves, leave justice to God — the comic justice, the grotesque events, the bizarre characters, the witty dialogue, the tongue-in-cheek tone, the cynicism, the rapid pace of events, the stylised, often comically absurd couplets and the way the characters are held at a distance, are closer to parody than an illustration of divine providence. The final rounding off of the plot with the death of both villains and revengers is aesthetically satisfying, but emotionally more an amusing joke than anything serious. Whatever Middleton or Tourneur or whoever wrote *The Revenger's Tragedy* intended, it is a great play.

Little is known about Cyril Tourneur (1580?–1626). Presumably the same 'Cyril Turner' published *The Transformed Metamorphosis* (1600), an obscure poem concerning the deformity of the world, contemporary politics and religion, influenced by Spenserian allegory and John Marston's satires. *Laugh and Lie Down: Or, the World's Folly* (1605), a satirical prose pamphlet by 'C. T.', is also attributed to Tourneur. *A Funerall Poem upon the Death of the Most Worthy and True Soldier, Sir Francis Vere* (1609) and a play, *The Atheist's Tragedy* (1611), were printed under his name. Two verse funeral elegies, *The Character of Robert, Earl of Salisbury* (1612) and *A Grief on the Death of Prince Henry* (1613), the latter printed with poems by John Webster and Thomas Heywood, have been shown to be Tourneur's. There

are records of a lost play, *The Nobleman* (1612), an agreement to write an act for another play which has also dis-
appeared, and possible attributions of two short poems. A
few documents and letters mention him. *The Atheist's
Tragedy: or the honest Man's Revenge* (1611), a didactic,
moralistic play, contrasts a rationalist's progress and downfall
with the sufferings, patience and eventual rewards of an
honest man. In this rather flat and undramatic work the
verse, although unrhymed, often enjambed and varied in
stresses, is rigidly strung into pentameter lines:

> Thus by the work of Heaven the men that thought
> To follow our dead bodies without tears
> Are dead themselves, and now we follow theirs.

The Isle of Gulls (1606), performed by the Children of
Blackfriars, was one of many plays of the early Jacobean
period which led to the imprisonment of the actors.
Although the plot is borrowed from Sidney's *Arcadia*, the
disguising of a man as a woman was understood as a satire on
the homosexuality of the Court. The author John Day
(*c*. 1574—*c*. 1640) was a hack writer who was the co-author
with Dekker and others of many, often lost, plays. His best
work is the charming *The Parliament of Bees* (published
1641) in which he uses 'the same method in my Characters
(or if you will Colloquies) as Perseus did in his satyres:
bringing in the Bees themselves, speaking themselves'. The
characters in verse and dialogue include 'the thrifty Bee, that
hoards up waxe', 'Two Rivall Bees', the 'Passionate Bee', a
poet bee and 'The Quacksalver', 'Who, to steale practise and
to vent / His drugs, would buy a Patient'.

The dramas of John Webster (*c*. 1580—*c*. 1634) — not to
be confused with John Webster (1610—82), the mid-century
educational reformer — remain controversial. Webster, who
early in the century collaborated on plays with Dekker,
Middleton, Drayton and Heywood, and who contributed to
the 1615 edition of Overbury's *Characters*, has been variously
described as a Stoic, a Christian moralist and as someone
whose plays reflect the aggressive individualism and moral
chaos of his time. He had pretensions to literary fame.
Rejecting the classical Senecan models of the closet dramatists,
he studied such contemporaries as Chapman, Jonson,

Marston and Fletcher with the aim of using their methods to create a serious drama which would be appreciated by the Court élite and the coterie that attended the private theatres. He deliberately wrote a harsh blank verse in a variety of metres, reworked in his plays passages from many authors whom he copied in his commonplace book, drew freely on well-known proverbs and sayings, used the generalised types found in the prose characters, heightened Fletcher's rapid changes in the personality of characters, used Marston's malcontent who is both observer and principal actor in the events, experimented with a variety of concepts of drama from the ironic to the didactic, while mixing in Senecan horror, villainy and generalised philosophical sentences. Although extremely theatrical, the result is a rather improbable mixture of Jacobean dramatic conventions. Bits of Stoic philosophy, terrifying injustices, long asides to the audience explaining motives and psychology, suggestions that corruption is the way of the State, and thematic motifs concerning jealousy, honour, honesty, family destiny and lust sit alongside repeated references to heaven, hell, devils and justice, and conventional moral tags concerning the immorality of revenge and the need for integrity.

The White Devil (1612) portrays an Italy of almost total duplicity and evil, where the innocent are weak; there are a vengeful cardinal, a brother pimping for his sister, adultery, treachery, murder, lust and a poisoned picture. The action is rapid and abrupt, the speeches packed with imagery and metaphor, and the characters are seen from the outside, as if they were actors playing roles. At times the play approaches greatness, but is confusing as the punishment of evil appears less convincing than the bravery with which Flamineo and Vittoria defy their enemies and fate:

LODOVICO :   O thou hast been a most prodigious comet,
    But I'll cut off your train: kill the Moor first.
VITTORIA :   You shall not kill her first. Behold my breast,
    I will be waited on in death; my servant
    Shall never go before me.
GASPARO :   Are you so brave?
VITTORIA :   Yes, I shall welcome death
    As princes do some great ambassadors;
    I'll meet thy weapon half way.

The main impression is 'O happy they that never saw the court'.

The Duchess of Malfi (1613) includes a poisoned book, masked murderers, a mistaken murder, madmen, a moral concerning revenge, and such great lines as 'I am Duchess of Malfi still', 'Look you, the stars shine still' and 'We are merely the stars' tennis-balls, struck and banded / Which way please them'. Malcontent Bosola, remorseful of his role in the Duchess's death, learns that rather than advancing by doing evil for the powerful he is unrewarded and has brought danger on himself; although his conversion follows he remains 'in a mist' by becoming a revenger. While Webster creates a convincing portrait of 'this gloomy world' of corruption, base motives and mistaken notions of honour, the rapidity of the play's action and character development, in which time appears to have been telescoped into intense scenes, makes *The Duchess of Malfi* seem like contrived melodrama; it teeters between the absurdly improbable and highly effective theatre:

CARDINAL: Is't possible?
  Can this be certain?
FERDINAND: Rhubarb, O for rhubarb
  To purge this choler! Here's the cursed day
  To prompt my memory, and here't shall stick
  Till of her bleeding heart I make a sponge
  To wipe it out.
CARDINAL: Why do you make yourself
  So wild a tempest?
FERDINAND: Would I could be one,
  That I might toss her palace 'bout her ears,
  Root up her goodly forests, blast her meads,
  And lay her general territory as waste,
  As she hath done her honour's.
CARDINAL: Shall our blood?
  The royal blood of Aragon and Castile,
  Be thus attainted?
FERDINAND: Apply desperate physic,
  We must not now use balsamum, but fire,
  The smarting cupping-glass, for that's the mean
  To purge infected blood, such blood as hers.
  There is a kind of pity in mine eye,
  I'll give it to my handkercher; and now 'tis here,
  I'll bequeath this to her bastard.

The tragicomedy *The Devil's Law Case* (1617?), sometimes referred to as an illustration of a didactic intention shaping the two major tragedies, similarly raises problems because the conclusion is both not credible and incompetent.

Webster's interest in women, his feeling that society is threatened by mankind's natural corruption and pride, his implication that the villainies of Renaissance Italy have their parallels in Jacobean England, result in powerful drama, even if the evils, with murder piled on top of murder, and the obsessive characters seem arbitrarily worked up to produce thrills. Webster brings together the retributive justice of the revenge play, the malcontent satiric drama and Chapman's high tragedy of state, to create a Jacobean *Grand Guignol* (like the French puppet-show combining melodrama, horror and farce) with Christian, even didactic, tendencies.

II Spenserian and other poets

The publication of a whole of the *Faerie Queene* with the *Mutabilitie Cantos* in 1609, followed by Spenser's *Works* in 1611, might be considered the start of the seventeenth-century Spenserians, a group of writers who favoured the pastoral and narrative poetry written in Elizabethan stanzas, idealised an old Merry England and used a certain archaism of diction. They usually wrote political, religious and moral allegories. Often Spenserianism really meant the influence of Joshua Sylvester (1563–1618), translator of *Devine Weekes and Workes* (1605) by the French Huguenot Guillaume de Salluste, Seigneur du Bartas (1544–90). A narrative based on the long traditions of commentary on the early books of the Old Testament, the *Devine Weekes* tells of the Creation and early history of the world. The encyclopedic range of information, the colloquialisms, ornateness, polysyllabic words and rhymes, striking and generalised descriptions, occasional Latinate idioms, diction and syntax influenced writers as different as Carew, Milton and Dryden, the last of whom confessed his early infatuation with such passages as:

> To Crystallize the Baltic ocean,
> To glaze the lakes, and bridle up the floods,
> And periwig with wool the bald-pate woods.

William Basse (1583?–1653?), author of *Three Pastoral Elegies* (1602), *Pastorals* (1616?) and a well-known epitaph on Shakespeare ('A little nearer Spenser, to make room/ For Shakespeare in your threefold-fourfold tomb'), wrote pleasant rustic verse with topical allusions in what he understood as the manner of *Shepherds' Calendar*, as likewise did the overproductive, popular Richard Brathwaite (1588–1673). William Browne (1590?–1645?), author of *Britannia's Pastorals* (1613, 1616), *Shepheards Pipe* (1613) and *The Inner Temple Masque* (1615), the latter based on the story of Circe and Ulysses, used the Spenserian pastoral manner for political allegories and was read carefully by Milton. George Wither (1588–1667) remained a popular author throughout most of the century. After leaving Oxford without a degree, he became part of a circle in London that included Browne, Drayton and Donne's friend, the minor writer Christopher Brooke. Wither began by writing for the Court, but his humourless satiric *Abuses Stript and Whipt* (1613), written in clear, closed couplets, and his Spenserian *Shepheard's Hunting* (1615) were not fashionable. As he turned towards a more popular readership, he became over-prolific and while his books sold well they became increasingly filled with dull moralising. His *Emblems* (1635) are of less interest than those of Francis Quarles. When serving on the Parliamentary side during the Civil War, he was captured by the Royalists in 1643 but saved by John Denham who claimed that as long as Wither lived Denham would 'not be the worst poet in England'.

The brothers Giles (1585–1623) and Phineas (1582–1650) Fletcher were the sons of the ambassador-poet Giles Fletcher senior (1548–1611) and first cousins of the playwright John Fletcher. At Cambridge they were part of a literary coterie devoted to the pastoral, Spenser and Italian poetry of the past century. Strong Protestants, with a taste of Renaissance high culture, allegory, narrative, and rich, sensuous, voluptuous imagery, they are a link between Spenser, du Bartas (1544–90) and Milton. In 'To the Reader' Giles Fletcher introduces *Christ's Victorie, and Triumph* (1610) by defending religious poetry, using as examples the 'sacred songs' of 'those heroicall Saints', Moses, David, Solomon and various Church Fathers. The four books allude to the main events of Christian history from the Creation to the Last Judgement, including the fall of Adam and Eve, the fall of Satan, and the war between the angels. Book One begins by propounding man's redemption by Christ ('The birth of him that no beginning knewe, / Yet gives beginning to all that are borne'), within the context of a debate between Justice and Mercy. The three subsequent books treat Christ's temptation by Satan, the Crucifixion and His resurrection and ascension. Using an eight-line stanza, divine paradoxes:

> How God, and Man did both embrace each other,
> Met in one person, heav'n, and earth did kiss,
> And how a Virgin did become a Mother,
> And bare that Sonne, who the worlds Father is,
> And Maker of his mother, and how Bliss
>   Descended from the bosome of the High,
>   To cloath himselfe in naked miserie,
> Sayling at length to heav'n, in earth triumphantly.

and in Book Two adapting Spenser's Bower of Bliss to the temptation in the wilderness, *Christ's Victorie* is an impressive poem which mixes the conscious artificiality of the late Renaissance with the spacious imagination of the Baroque.

Phineas Fletcher's works include the *Piscatorie Eclogues* (1606–14, published 1633) in which, following Sannazaro (1458–1530), the pastoral is adapted to fishermen, *Sicelides* (1615), a 'pescatory play', and *Venus and Anchises*, an erotic narrative first published in 1628 by Thomas Walkely as his own work, using the title *Brittain's Ida*. Phineas's long poems have the large, leisurely stanzas of the Spenserian tradition, although the language is less archaic. Similar to the writing of his brother, Phineas's religious poems look forward to the mystical, turbulent, paradoxical, conceited verse of Crashaw, Henry More and Benlowes during the mid-century. *The Locusts, or The Apollyonists* (1627) is a brief epic using Satan's continuing battle against God as the framework for a narrative concerning the Gunpowder Plot. *The Purple Island* (1633) uses the then popular analogy between man and an island — it formed the basis of Richard Bernard's (1568–1642) allegorical fiction, *Isle of Man* (1626), which later influenced Bunyan's *The Holy War* — as a basis for a complex allegorical epic. The parts of the body are described as the topography of an island in which there are three 'Metropolies' (Belly, Breast and Head). From Canto Six onwards the theme shifts to biblical history, personifications of the vices and virtues, and a battle between the forces of good and evil which concludes in Canto Twelve with the defeat of the Dragon and an impressive celebration of the marriage of the elect and divine love, in which pastoral becomes a vehicle for the mystical:

> Runne now you shepherd-swains; ah run you thither,
> Where this fair Bridegroom leads the blessed way:
> And haste you lovely maids, haste you together
> With this sweet Bride; while yet the sunne-shine day
>   Guides your blinde steps, while yet loud summons call,
>   That every wood & hill resounds withall,
> Come *Hymen, Hymen,* come, drest in thy golden pall.

While Spenserianism was mostly associated with the Pembroke circle and a new generation at the universities, and would in the next decades blend with the Cavalier lyric, metaphysical poetry had moved up from the Inns to those at Court. In many of the 'metaphysicals' the influence of Jonson and Fairfax is noticeable in the increasing use of heroic couplets, epistles and other formal kinds of verse. Sir Henry Wotton (1568–1639), Donne's friend from the Inns of Court, wrote short prose biographies and metaphysical verse. The Horatian 'Character of a Happy Life', the comic erotic landscape of 'On a Bench as I sate a Fishing', and the clearly articulated comparisons and logical progression of 'You Meaner Beauties of the Night' reveal skill, culture, taste and wit. He is also known for *The Elements of Architecture* (1624) and from Walton's *Life* which was first published in *Reliquiae Wottonianace* ('The Remains of Wotton', 1651).

A friend of Jonson, and probably of Donne, Richard Corbett (1582–1635), Bishop of Oxford and Norwich, was popular for his good-humoured verse on topical subjects. His elegies, epistles and epigrams often take a poke at the Puritans. At a time when James I had commanded the reading of the *Book of Sports* (1618) as a reply to Puritan attacks on the maypole and other traditional Sunday amusements as heathen idolatry, Corbett's 'The Faeryes Farewell' contributed to the identification of the Royalists and High Church with Merry Old England:

> Lament, lament, old Abbies,
>   The *Faries* lost Command:
> They did but change Priests *Babies*,
>   But some have changed your Land;
> And all your Children sprung from thence
>   Are now growne *Puritanes*:
> Who live as *Changelings* ever since
>   For love of your Demaines . . . .
> By which wee note the *Faries*
>   Were of the old Profession;
> Theyre Songs were *Ave Maryes*,
>   Theyre Daunces were *Procession*.

He experimented with the Horatian satire and epistle. If the closed satiric couplets look forward to Cleveland, they remain rooted in the more leisurely fun of the epic-romances:

> But for her breath, Spectatours come not nigh,
> That layes about; God blesse the Company.
> The man, in a beares skin baited to death,
> Would chose the doggs much rather than her breath.

Contemporaries humorously suggested that Jonson should be made Dean of Westminster after Donne and Corbett were made Deans of St Paul's and Christ Church.

George Herbert's eldest brother, Edward (1582–1648), later Lord Herbert of Cherbury, was probably the first poet directly to imitate Donne, whom he knew through his mother, Magdalen Herbert. Although his verse is simpler in diction, less dramatic and relies more upon narrative, it has the argumentative, closely knit, tight structure and philo- sophical concepts of Donne's poetry; he is, however, closer to the Italian Neo-Platonists in his views of love. He wrote poems on 'Platonic Love' and 'The Idea'. 'Ode upon a Question Moved, Whether Love Should Continue for Ever' is less physical than Donne's 'The Ecstasy'. Although Herbert uses long sentences, his diction is simple, sometimes mono- syllabic, and his phrases short and uncadenced. No doubt this was purposeful, as the verse seems contrived to prevent an easy response. The fourteen lines of 'Loves End', for example, are a continuous sentence in which the syntax is difficult to follow. The beginning may need to be read several times:

> Thus ends my Love, but this doth grieve me most,
>   That so it ends, but that ends too, this yet,
> Besides the Wishes, hopes and time I lost,
>   Troubles my mind awhile, that I am set
> Free, worse than deny'd.

De Veritate ('Of Truth', Paris, 1624) is said to be the start of English Deism. Where such Anglican theologians as Hooker and Chillingworth claim natural reason is an aid to faith, Herbert goes further in constructing a universal religion based upon five supposed common notions which are innate as God-given ideas or images within the mind: there is a God, he should be worshipped, virtue and piety are part of worship, repentance is necessary, and there are rewards and punishments in an after-life. Herbert claims that this is the natural universal religion and that all other articles and dogmas were thought up by priests for their own interest. Influenced by Platonism, he is sceptical of all claims of revelation; the soul is immortal and every mind contains the ideas required to understand religious truth.

Herbert's autobiography, written during the 1640s, is mostly concerned with his adventures abroad and his days at Court. Filled with anecdotes and digressions on philosophy, education and medicine, and covering a wide range of worldly experience, the autobiography differs from Presbyterian and other Puritan 'lives' in being unconcerned with conversion, grace and sin. Herbert sees himself as a chivalric knight, a Renaissance humanist, a man of the world, an ideal courtier, a hero of romance. The philosophical and chivalric passages are mingled, however, with realistic details which contrast with the idealised world he imagines. In his attempt at self-definition, in his need to create a persona, in his realism and egotism, Herbert reflects a society in transition. His life consists of achievements in the public world.

III Prose: Andrewes and Burton

Whereas fiction is now the most popular prose literature, in the early seventeenth century almost half the books published consisted of religious writings. Sermons and devotional guides were among the most significant forms of the century's literature, often expressing in their styles and themes the major trends in contemporary sensibility. While many Puritans objected to the witty, learned sermons of the Court preachers, and used oratory more for doctrine and moral exhortation, the popular Thomas Adams (c. 1580—c. 1660) could more than hold his own with the high churchmen. His sermons and meditations are vivid, rich in metaphor, satiric, humorous, topical, and his references range from Ovid to Montaigne and Chapman. He often develops his sermons around an allegorical figure. Less choppy than Andrewes, Adams mixes the long balanced sentences of the sixteenth century with the new Senecan style.

T. S. Eliot said 'the intellectual achievement and the prose style of Hooker and Andrewes came to complete the structure of the English Church as the philosophy of the thirteenth century crowns the Catholic Church'. Lancelot Andrewes (1555—1626) was one of the scholarship boys of the period who were educated at a newly founded grammar school and later distinguished themselves at university and in public life. At Merchant Taylors' School he early mastered Hebrew, Latin and Greek; at Pembroke Hall, Cambridge, he was famous for his knowledge of fifteen oriental languages. Ordained as Anglican priest (1581), he became Dean of Westminster (1601), Bishop of Chichester (1605) and Bishop of Winchester (1618). Friend of Hooker, Bacon and Herbert, a privy councillor, a famous preacher, Andrewes participated in the Hampton Court Conference of 1604 when the Puritans and bishops agreed to a new translation of the Bible, the Authorised Version which appeared in 1611. He was responsible for the scholars who translated the Old Testament from Genesis to II Kings. His sermons were first published in 1629, three years after his death, followed by translations of his *Devotions* or *Preces Privatae* (1648) written in Greek.

Andrewes's scholarship and interest in languages coincided with his desire for an English Church which was both

Reformed and Catholic. It was necessary to purge Roman additions to the primitive church; it was also necessary to avoid the excesses of the Protestant radicals. His concern with tradition, order, discipline, scholarship and moderation is shown in his sermons and devotions. His prayers are composed almost entirely of sentences and phrases taken from the Fathers and the Book of Common Prayer. In his sermons he avoids fine points of dogma and concentrates on the text and the occasion being celebrated. The sermons are orderly, with a clearly articulated structure, and the movement from division to division and point to point announced. The sermons usually begin with a statement of the text to be discussed and how it will be treated. The method is biblical exegesis, using Augustinian principles by which each phrase, word, even the syllables and letters of the words can be a source of commentary. The biblical word is seen as sacramental of truths to be recalled. The method is highly analytical, rational, calm and reflects centuries of Christian exegetical traditions in which words are symbols to be explored and prodded into their full significance through close analysis, using philology, typology (the prefiguration of persons and events in the New Testament by persons and events in the Old Testament; in the seventeenth century contemporary persons and events were also seen as biblical types) and even puns and other forms of word play which help to unravel the text to reveal the essentials of belief. His learned, witty, curt, Senecan style was admired by the King and Court; the Puritans, with their emphasis on doctrine, scorned it.

If Andrewes's manner is compressed, knotty, unemotional, it can be dramatic. The concern with words and types results in poetic repetition. The Sermon preached before the King on Easter 1620, with its symbolism of Christ the Gardener, is a fascinating example of pedantry creating rich metaphors:

1. A *Gardiner He* is then. The first, the fairest garden that ever was (Paradise) *He* was the Gardiner, it was of *His* planting. So, a *Gardiner*. 2. And ever since it is *He* that (as God) makes all our gardens greene, sends us yearely the Spring, and all the hearbs and flowers we then gather; and neither *Paul* with his planting, nor *Apollo* with his watering, could doe any good without him: So a Gardiner in that sense.

3. But not in that alone; But *He* it is that gardens our soules too, and makes them, as the Prophet saith, *Like a well watered garden*, weedes out of them whatsoever is noisome or unsavoury, sowes and plants them with true rootes and seedes of righteousnesse, waters them with the dew of *His* grace, and makes them bring forth fruit to eternal life.

But it is none of all these, but besides all these, nay over and above all these, this day (if ever) most properly *He* was a *Gardiner*. Was one, and so after a more peculiar manner, might take this likenesse on *Him*. *Christ* rising was indeed a *Gardiner*, and that a strange one, who made such an hearbe grow out of the ground this day, as the like was never seene before, a dead body, to shoote foorth alive out of the grave.

After Jonson experimented with Theophrastus' character types in his plays, ethical and moral characters were written by, among others, Joseph Hall, John Stephens (1615), Nicholas Breton (1615, 1616) and Richard Brathwaite (1626, 1631). A character is a description of the nature and qualities of some person or sort of person. It is usually brief, neat and witty. The character soon found a place in seventeenth-century sermons, autobiographies and satiric poems. The most popular characters of the century were attributed to Sir Thomas Overbury (1581–1613) and 'his friends'. Shortly after Overbury's death, his dull poem 'A Wife' was published. It was republished in 1614 with twenty-one *Characters*. New, enlarged editions of the *Characters*, with many of the university wits contributing pieces, brought the final total to eighty-eight. Webster is believed to have contributed to the first edition and added thirty-two characters in 1615; Dekker added six prison sketches in 1616; and Donne is credited with a piece in the 1622 printing. The first eleven characters, believed to be Overbury's, are obscure and intellectual in the manner of Marston's satires. The short, witty, epigrammatical characters written by 'his friends' offer a wide range of Jonsonian English social types. They are less concerned with ethics than with the foibles of human nature.

The best writer of characters was John Earle (1600?–65), whose popular *Microcosmographie. Or, A Peece of the World Characteriz'd* (1628, enlarged 1629, 1633) was published anonymously. Urbane, perceptive, witty, Earle's characters are written in an epigrammatic, antithetical, Senecan style.

They blend human comedy with seriousness and ethical concern, without losing sympathy for the contrast between what people pretend and what they are. Earle mixes the good and bad together in one person, unlike the Overbury sketches, to which his are often purposeful replies. He is also a master of form. The characters open wittily and without obvious transitions proceed smoothly to their epigrammatic conclusions. 'A discontented Man' 'Is one that is falne out with the world, and will be revenged on himselfe . . . . Hee is the sparke that kindles the Commonwealth, and the bellowes himselfe to blow it: and if he turne any thing, it is commonly one of these, either Friar, traitor, or mad-man.'

The ironic, satiric mode of Jacobean drama and the 'metaphysical' poets' witty use of obscure learning blended with the essay and character in *The Anatomy of Melancholy* (1621). There is no explanation for Robert Burton (1577–1640), a vicar of St Thomas's, Oxford, writing *The Anatomy*, beyond his claim that it was to keep busy to avoid his own melancholy. Burton's mask of Democritus, the laughing, cynical Greek philosopher, and his many comparisons of himself to Lucan, a Greek satirist, are clues to his tone. Written in an age in which the malcontent was both anti-hero and satiric mask, *The Anatomy* is an encyclopedia of human disorders; its claims to offer a cure for melancholy can be dismissed as ironic. It is a catalogue of human folly, portraying a mad world of appetites, hypocrisy, vanity and ideas. Burton pretends to a rigid scientific–philosophical organisation of his material; but the book is digressive, an accumulation of facts, opinions, misinformation, absurdities and sensational stories. Burton parodies his age in claiming to be a Senecan concerned more with matter than with words; *The Anatomy* is very un-Senecan with its long, rambling, digressive sentences, bewildering changes in subject, and delight in slang, coinages and unusual vocabulary. Rather than being about things, *The Anatomy* is a display of Burton's ironic, aggressive personality as it mocks mankind's dissatisfaction with the world. Rapidly shifting from donnish humour, Rabelaisian comedy, sardonic scorn, direct sarcasm, self-parody and mock-seriousness to the proverbial, picturesque, sensational, pedantic, spontaneous and vainglorious, Burton's satiric mask is Swiftian in its bewildering complexity.

The Anatomy is filled with parodies of the intellectual ideas of its day: 'I will yet, to satisfy and please myself, make an Utopia of my own, a new Atlantis, a poetical Commonwealth of mine own, in which I will freely domineer, build cities, make laws, statutes, as I list myself.' The Utopia is an impossible ideal, a comical parody of England. The ideals are undermined by the reality of human behaviour:

> If it were possible, I would have such Priests as should imitate Christ, charitable Lawyers should love their neighbours as themselves, temperate and modest Physicians, Politicians contemn the world, Philosophers should know themselves, Noblemen live honestly, Tradesmen leave lying and cozening, Magistrates corruption, &c.; but this is impossible, I must get such as I may.

Burton's solution to social problems is as ironically fantastic as the madness of the world:

> A bankrupt shall be publickly shamed, and he that cannot pay his debts, if by riot or negligence he have been impoverished, shall be for a twelvemonth imprisoned; if in that space his creditors be not satisfied, he shall be hanged.

5
The background:
1625–60

I Charles I

A struggle between the Court and the Commons began immediately after the accession of Charles I to the throne in 1625, when Parliament insisted redress of grievances must precede the granting of revenues, tried to impeach Buckingham, whom Charles retained as his principal adviser, and declared tonnage and poundage illegal. It was dissolved in 1626 without even voting the customs dues usually given to each king for life at the beginning of the reign. Charles, supported by the courts, started to collect customs dues, imprisoned those who refused to pay, and began forced loans, a medieval right of kings. The assassination of Buckingham in 1628 removed one cause of opposition to the Court, but William Laud, the leader of the Arminians, was made Bishop of London. The Arminians, who were to become the main support of the King, and a major cause of his downfall, represented a counter-movement within the Church to the militancy of the Calvinists. As the Arminians (their name derived from the Dutch theologian Arminius who defended free will against predestination) restored ceremony and beauty to church worship, they easily became targets for those who claimed that the Court was pro-Catholic. Arminians were promoted by Charles to high positions of Church and State, and increasingly seemed a new élite whose interests blocked the attempts by the opposition merchants, lawyers and squirearchy to wrest power from the throne. The Commons wanted the right to determine the religion of England, and by controlling Church government gain a significant source of authority; in attempting to silence the high-church party, the Commons declared that anyone recommending religious innovations which supported Arminians was an enemy of the Kingdom.

After the Commons passed resolutions against Arminianism and imposition of taxes, Charles dissolved Parliament in 1629 and imprisoned some of its leaders. There were no further Parliaments until 1640, while Charles tried to rule through his prerogatives and the high-church party. Although tonnage and poundage paid most of his debts, old laws were dug up and extended to provide additional revenue; this hurt the landowners who were normally a principal support of English monarchy. In various cases the courts ruled in favour of the King's right to make law when Parliament was not in session, and this led to increased resistance.

The leadership of the Church contributed to the atmosphere of repression and arbitrary government; in attempting to rid the Church of Puritanism, Laud, who was made Chancellor of Oxford in 1630 and Archbishop of Canterbury in 1633, imposed rigid press censorship, forbad the ordination of lecturers (the ministers paid by Puritans to preach instead of the local clergy), and revived an old policy of visitations, in which local ministers were examined for their conformity to national policy. The reissuing in 1633 by the King of the 1618 Declaration of Sports, the non-enforcement of laws against Catholics, the growth of a pro-Catholic party around the Queen at Court, the peace with France and Spain, the establishing of diplomatic relations with Rome in 1635, the publication of Catholic books and the conversion of several courtiers to Catholicism, seemed to indicate that the King and Arminians planned to impose Roman Catholicism on the English. Laud had replaced Buckingham as the King's chief political adviser and was in 1636 joined on the Privy Council by William Juxon, the Bishop of London, who became Lord Treasurer. Throughout the 1630s thousands of Puritans migrated from England to Holland or the North American colonies.

The decision to impose the Book of Common Prayer and new Arminian church canons on Scotland created a rebellion which Charles unsuccessfully attempted to subdue. What was known as the 'First Bishops' War' ended with the Treaty of Berwick in 1639. Needing to obtain money to raise a larger army, Charles was forced to call a Parliament, but in the

Short Parliament of 1640 the Commons would not grant subsidies for the army or vote any money until its grievances were satisfied. Although Parliament was soon dissolved and its leaders arrested, the convocation of the Church met and passed seventeen new canons. The first article declared the divine right of kings; another canon involved the inflammatory issue of the position of the communion table, which was to be placed at the east end of the church and raised from the congregation. There was to be bowing towards the altar when entering and leaving the church. Meanwhile the 'Second Bishops' War' of 1640 ended with the Scots invading the north of England. It was agreed that until the dispute was settled, they would occupy the north and be paid by the King.

II Civil War and execution of Charles I

Charles was once again forced to call Parliament. This was to be the famous Long Parliament of 1640 which sat until dismissed by Cromwell. Parliament impeached Laud and the King's adviser Strafford, and declared the new canons illegal, while the Root and Branch Petition called for a thorough change in the government and the Church. As those close to the Court started fleeing abroad, the London mobs surrounded Whitehall and threatened the Queen. Helpless, the King consented to a bill of attainder which led to Strafford's execution in 1641 without trial. Parliament passed the Triennial Act, requiring that it be called every three years after its dissolution, abolished the Star Chamber and other prerogative courts, and declared that the laws and taxes of the previous decade were illegal. When the House of Lords would not agree to radical reform of the Church, the Commons acted on its own and began to treat the assent of the House of Lords as unnecessary. When the House of Commons began discussing impeachment of the Queen, the King tried in 1642 to have five of its leading members arrested for treason. They fled and were given refuge in London. Unable to control Parliament or London, the King withdrew to Oxford which was to be his headquarters until 1646.

Parliament abolished the episcopacy in 1643 and called

together the Westminster Assembly to decide on religious policy. The Assembly, however, could not agree as it was divided between Presbyterians who wanted a national church governed by elders, Independents who wanted freedom for each congregation to decide its own policies, and the Erastians who wanted an Anglican Church subordinated directly to Parliament. Bishops, deans and chaplains of the Anglican Church, however, were abolished and church lands confiscated; one-half of the Anglican clergy were ejected and many were jailed; the liturgy and the Book of Common Prayer were forbidden, even in family worship. Whereas other Protestants could meet, Anglicans were prohibited the use of their churches and were deprived of such rites as baptism, burial and marriage. With the breakdown of central authority, radical Protestant sects which appealed to the artisans and labourers began to appear openly and soon flourished. What started as a struggle between the King and part of the ruling class over control of the State and Church soon became a more complicated conflict involving religion.

While the nobility and merchants divided their support about equally between the two sides, and many stayed neutral, the overwhelming majority of the 'gentlemen' supported Parliament. Although during the first year of the war the Royalists won battles throughout the country, they were unco-ordinated, with each commander going his own way. Fearing defeat, Parliament, over opposition by many of its members, formed a Solemn League and Covenant; in return for Parliament's imposing a Presbyterian form of Church government on England, the Scots would fight against the King. At the battle of Marston Moor, the first Parliamentary victory, Oliver Cromwell came to national attention by defeating Prince Rupert. After raising the New Model Army largely from sectarians, Cromwell and Lord Fairfax decisively beat the Royalists at the Battle of Naseby; by the end of June 1645 the first Civil War was ending.

Whereas Anglicans and Presbyterians had specific notions of what the Church should be, the sects, with their millenarian expectations, wanted a continuous reformation. The Independents, who evolved from the turn-of-the-century Brownists, claimed that each congregation had a right to govern itself and choose its own ministers from those God had called and given the gift of preaching; they separated from the established Church and claimed the right to individual interpretation of scripture and trust in their inner light. While the Independents were not social revolutionaries, their survival in England depended upon preventing the imposition of church conformity, and with the formation of the New Model Army, the fate of the Independents became intertwined with the soldiers. The Army and its Independent leaders soon found themselves at odds with Parliament about the fruits of their victory. As friction developed between the Presbyterian leadership in Parliament and the sectarians, radical democratic political ideas began to circulate within the New Model Army, calling for representation of those small landowners, small farmers and artisans who having won the war still had no right to elect members of Parliament, and who were joining the rapidly proliferating religious sects.

After the King surrendered in 1646 to the Scots, who passed him on to Parliament in 1647, there were signs of Royalists, Presbyterians and London compromising their differences and forming an alliance against the sects and Army. When the Army would not disband without being paid its arrears, Parliament threatened to declare the Army enemies of the State. The soldiers elected representatives, known as agitators, who along with the officers formed an Army council which passed radical resolutions against Parliament and its Presbyterian leaders. When a group of soldiers seized the King, Cromwell and the Independent officers regained control of the Army by themselves taking a radical anti-Parliamentary position. They started negotiating with the King, marched on London, and removed some Presbyterian leaders from Parliament. But once Parliament was purged, the Independents feared the democratic ideas of the Levellers; if all small landowners had the right to vote, they could vote themselves the property of the landed and rich. The Army officers wanted to keep the vote restricted to the landed, the wealthy merchants and others of their own class; when the Levellers demanded a more democratic form of government, with regular elections and a bill of rights, they were ruthlessly repressed by Cromwell, who executed disobedient soldiers and replaced the general council of the Army with a council of officers. Meanwhile the King had fled to the Isle of Wight, where he played for time, negotiating with the Army and Presbyterians; it soon became apparent that the King would compromise with the Scots by establishing a Presbyterian form of Church government for three years. A second Civil War started and was quickly won when Cromwell destroyed the Scottish army at the Battle of Preston.

Aware that Parliament and King would eventually agree to Presbyterianism, Cromwell seized the King in 1648 and occupied London, while Colonel Pride purged Parliament of one hundred and forty Presbyterians and moderates, leaving fifty members to rule England in association with the Army officers. The attempt to end the complexities of the situation by putting Charles on trial divided those whom Cromwell and the Army considered to be on their side, and only half of the commissioners the Commons appointed as judges and jurors attended the trial. All of Europe, whether Protestant or Catholic, was shocked by the execution. With the King beheaded, the moderates and Presbyterians suppressed, Parliament reduced to some fifty members, England was now governed by a clique with an Army. After the trial and execution of Charles I, the Rump Parliament abolished the monarchy and the House of Lords, and voted that the 'people of England' were the 'original' of all power and the 'Commons the supreme authority'. Having proclaimed a Commonwealth, the Rump set up a 'Council of State' consisting of forty-one members. The Council of State included Fairfax and others who had been against the execution of the King. When Ireland rebelled in 1649 against Parliament and Scotland planned to crown Charles II, Parliament ordered Cromwell and Fairfax to march north. Fairfax, however, retired to his country estate after refusing to conduct an offensive war with a country with which England had signed the Solemn League and Covenant. After Charles was crowned at Scone in 1651, Cromwell defeated the Scots at the Battle of Worcester.

III Cromwell and the Protectorates

Unsatisfied Army demands for religious toleration, payment of back wages, indemnity for any offences committed during the war, and legal reform, led to conflict with the Rump Parliament. Cromwell and the Army leadership demanded that new elections be held but the Rump clung to power. After Cromwell expelled the Rump in 1653 he asked the Congregationalist Churches to nominate members of Parliament; the Independents, however, were not cohesive and were already splitting into new 'Enthusiastic' religious groups who claimed to be divinely inspired and who as the elect had little respect for the existing Churches and would follow their inner light. The resulting 'Barebones' Parliament of 1653 was filled with enthusiastic 'saints' and Fifth Monarchy Men who controlled its committees and who claimed special status for themselves as the leaders of a world-wide revolution which would initiate the Kingdom of God. The Independents wanted, in place of a national church, a national ministry, financed by tithes, of recognised preachers who held fifteen fundamental Christian beliefs. As this suggested a new conformity, the Independent plan for a ministry was rejected; Cromwell then dissolved Parliament. The end of the Barebones Parliament destroyed all hopes of millenarian reform.

After the Instrument of Government framed in 1653 made Cromwell Lord Protector, assisted by a Council, the new Parliament immediately began a struggle over supreme power with Cromwell similar to past struggles between the Commons and the King. Cromwell demanded that its members pledge not to tamper with the Instrument of Government. When Parliament tried to reduce the size of the Army, Cromwell dissolved it and began to suppress the extremism and fanaticism which had played such an influential role in the turmoil of the past decade. Government and university appointments were given to moderates and Royalists. The utilitarianism which had sometimes been identified with English Puritanism and which was characteristic of the Royal Society after the Restoration was Cromwell's method of dampening the potentially revolutionary fires of religious enthusiasm. Although Cromwell was an admirer of Gustavus Adolphus, the King of Sweden, who led the Protestants against the Habsburg powers, he built up the Navy, from money gained by fining and confiscating the estates of Royalists, to support English traders against their principal

Protestant rivals. The Navigation Act of 1651 caused a war
with the Dutch. The 'Old Colonial System' was introduced
and colonies forced to trade only with England.

In 1655 England and Wales were divided into eleven zones
ruled by Major-Generals whom Cromwell nominated. The
Major-Generals, who often acted like war-lords, collected
taxes and were supposed to be responsible for moral
reformation of the people. The Protectorate spent annually
many times more than the total revenues Parliament had
given the Stuarts. The new taxes were similar to the controversial ship money. Excise taxes replaced monopolies. These
methods, which had been resisted under James I and Charles
I, were necessary for a modern state, but could only be put
into effect by a strong government with an army behind it.
There were various attempts to reform the nation morally.
Church festivals, including Christmas and Easter, were
forbidden and replaced with fast days. On Sunday and other
fast days, all sports, pastimes, work and travel were forbidden;
the Army, to enforce prohibitions, would enter homes
searching the kitchens and ovens to prevent food from being
prepared. Although the laws were not always enforced,
adultery was made a crime punishable by death, and there
were heavy fines against swearing.

The second Protectorate Parliament (1656) was largely
anti-Protectorate. After the Army prevented more than one
hundred members from being admitted and another fifty
members refused to attend in the circumstances, those who
met objected to military rule and, led by a pro-Cromwellian
faction, drew up a petition asking the Protector to become
King. While Cromwell was tempted the Army officers were
against it and a compromise was reached that he could name
his successor. Parliament then framed a new constitution
with a House of Lords and Privy Council both nominated by
Cromwell. Of the new lords seven were members of Cromwell's family and seventeen were senior Army officers. The
formal installation of Cromwell as Protector was elaborate
and resembled a coronation; Cromwell and his wife were
addressed as 'His' and 'Her Highness'. The distinctions
between Independent, Anglican, Cromwellian and Royalist
were rapidly blurring. When Cromwell heard of a plot to
proclaim a republic and recall the Presbyterian Long Parlia-

ment, he dissolved Parliament; new plans to make Cromwell king were ended by his death in 1658.

Richard Cromwell remained Protector for eight months. Leading generals intrigued against him and the Army would not obey him. The members elected to the third Protectorate Parliament (1659) had a majority of Presbyterians, Royalists and republicans who feared an Army *coup d'état*. The Army responded by further involvement in politics and demands that Parliament be dissolved; but the Army was itself split between ambitious senior officers who intended to use Richard Cromwell as a figurehead and junior officers who wanted a republic. The junior officers forced Richard to resign and called for the restoration of the Rump of the Long Parliament which had been dissolved in 1653. They hoped the Rump would establish a government with a single house and with no one individual as the head of the State. When the Rump met it tried to take power from the Army by dismissing the old Cromwellians, which resulted in the Army fragmenting into various mutually hostile groups, each of which was now opposed to the restored Rump. A faction of the Army took control of Whitehall and expelled the Rump. London radicals rebelled and restored the Rump to Parliament, which immediately began to purge the Army.

Meanwhile, General Monck in Scotland built up his army, marched south and demanded that the Rump admit the excluded members of the Long Parliament. When Parliament ordered him to destroy the city gates of London and arrest leaders of a tax revolt, Monck at last showed his hand. He forced Parliament to hold new elections and began negotiating for the return of Charles. Monck correctly thought that any freely elected Parliament would restore monarchy to England.

IV The arts under Charles I

It is sometimes thought that the Court of Charles I was a centre of immorality and hedonism. This is incorrect. The King and Queen were a close, faithful couple; they were, however, addicted to the arts, entertainment and luxury on a scale which shocked the puritanical. The immorality of the Court consisted more of huge sums spent on masques in which the Queen and her female attendants performed than in any debauchery. The Puritan William Prynne's (1600?–69) *Histriomastix* ('The Scourge of Learning', 1632) cost him his ears because in attacking players as immoral he wrote that dancing 'yea even in Queenes themselves . . . hath been always scandalous' and that women acting on stage is 'whorishly impudent'. There was, of course, the libertine poetry of Suckling and other courtiers, but libertine verse had been popular since at least the 1590s. More significant is how often the poetry of the period praises chaste mistresses — Lovelace's Lucasta, Habington's Castara — while Herrick uses *carpe diem* arguments to persuade women to marriage. Caroline Court drama often centred upon debates in which Platonic love is contrasted to love being fulfilled in marriage. Libertine spokesmen appear but are usually treated as villains or satirically. In keeping with the European Renaissance ideal of an aristocrat and Cavalier the courtiers dressed extravagantly by Puritan standards, gambled, drank, wrote love poetry and no doubt carried on love affairs, but the Court was not particularly immoral. The elegant taste of the Court, however, enraged the Puritan fanatics who objected not only to the costly entertainments but also to the classical pagan mythology with which Waller, Davenant and Carew flattered the monarchy.

Queen Henrietta Maria both influenced literary fashion and changed attitudes towards publication. The Queen brought with her from France a taste for the long prose romance fashionable on the Continent — D'Urfé's (1568–1625) *Astrée* was her favourite book — the mannered refinement of the *précieux* poets (the *précieux* movement in seventeenth-century France included much display of sentiment about love and honour), the cult of Platonic love, the pastoral, and the expectation that gentlemen and ladies would participate in stage performances. Charles first saw Henrietta Maria among the ladies dancing in a masque with the Queen of France; eventually, over Puritan protests, he allowed her continental tastes to dominate at his own Court. In 1626 Henrietta acted in a pastoral of her own composition with twelve of her ladies whom she had rehearsed. Walter Montagu (1603?–1677) wrote *Shepherd's Paradise* (1632), a pastoral drama which took eight hours to perform, in which

Henrietta acted; a fashion started and soon other courtiers, including Suckling, Lovelace and Carew, wrote plays and masques for Court and private performances. Platonic love was often a theme of the plays. The King and Queen took a direct interest in such entertainments, not only as actors and in paying the costs for elaborate scenery, but also in suggesting stories for plays, revising manuscripts, and overriding the objections of their censors as to what could be printed. Whereas Elizabeth and James had encouraged writers, but avoided direct involvement with the stage, the participation of Charles and Henrietta in the arts was influential. Previously manuscripts by courtiers circulated among friends; under Charles I courtiers began publishing lavish private editions. Henrietta attended public performances of plays, her favourite writers began to title themselves 'Her Majesty's Servant', and the plays of courtiers began being performed on the professional stage and sold at bookstores. Killigrew and Davenant advanced at Court and were eventually knighted, despite their continuing professional involvement with the theatre.

When Prince Charles visited Spain in 1623 to court the Infanta he saw the Venetian paintings of the high Renaissance and the royal portraits painted by Rubens, Titian and the young Velasquez. After his return he began one of the earliest English collections and attempted to bring English culture into the European tradition. His magnificent collection, which was confiscated and sold by Parliament during the Commonwealth, included many paintings by Titian, Raphael, Correggio, Rembrandt, Mantegna and Holbein. Charles I commissioned Rubens to decorate the ceilings of Inigo Jones's Banqueting House at Whitehall. The ceilings express the monarch's belief in the divine right of kings. Although Rubens was too much in demand throughout Europe to be persuaded to settle in England, Anthony Van Dyck (1599–1641), who visited London in 1620, took up permanent residence in 1632. Van Dyck brought a previously unknown sophisticated eloquence to English portraiture. Instead of the stiffness common to Jacobean art, Van Dyck's subjects often appear to have a refined, easy, languid manner. Van Dyck's portraits are rather patterns of beauty, breeding and good taste than studies from nature. A native-born painter of talent, William Dobson (1611–46) was more robust than elegant. Sir Peter Lely (1618—80) came to prominence during the late 1640s. Lovelace praised him and Lely's drawing of Lucasta was included in Lovelace's *Lucasta* (1649).

Charles I's love of the arts is shown by the enlargement of the King's Musick, his personal Court musicians, from an average of thirty under Elizabeth and forty under James to sixty-five. This does not include the musicians employed by the Queen and other members of the royal family. During the Caroline period madrigal singing went out of fashion and was replaced with songs and dances. Just as the Caroline lyric tends toward social situations and extroverted attitudes, so the musical settings, which follow the rhythms and argument of the poetic text, move somewhat in the direction of an operatic performance, with simple harmonies supporting the voice and underlining words. The poems of many of the best writers of the period, including Herrick, Carew, Suckling, Waller, Davenant and Cartwright, were set to music by the brothers Henry (1596—1662) and William Lawes (1602—45).

Caroline taste in home decoration and furniture followed the classical influence notable at Court. Whereas the Jacobean house was a more ornate, heavy, highly decorated version of the Elizabethan, under Charles houses had natural woods, columns, cornices, broken pediments, lighter furniture and, because of changes in window design, were brighter. As the old great hall grew smaller, there were more small rooms and smaller pieces of furniture. From the second decade of the century grand staircases became significant features of the houses of the wealthy and there was more use of framed oil paintings for decoration. The wood for furniture was oak, with cedar an alternative. Chairs were still not common and upholstery was rare. People usually sat on stools. As the English still had not mastered silvering, mirrors were uncommon. The old heavy chests were gradually being replaced by lighter chests with drawers.

After Denham's *Cooper's Hill* (1642) and Kynaston's *Leoline and Sydanis* (1642), little was published during the next three troubled years of the Civil War until Waller's *Poems* (1645), Milton's *Poems* (1645), Crashaw's *Steps to the Temple* (1646), Shirley's *Poems* (1646) and Vaughan's *Poems*

(1646). After 1646 nearly everyone, except for Marvell, was publishing — Cleveland, Hall, Stanley, Fane, Herrick, Lovelace. Although Parliament passed laws against acting and other public entertainments, a few plays were printed and there were some private performances; public drama was, however, effectively repressed for a decade until 1656, when Sir William Davenant leased Rutland House and began providing 'Operas', 'entertainments . . . by Declamations and Musick: after the Manner of the Ancients'.

V Arts and science during the Interregnum

The middle of the century saw the first significant use of journalism as political propaganda. The earliest English-language newspapers were started in Amsterdam in 1620, followed by journals published in England from 1622 to 1630. Journals were once more allowed from 1634 onwards, but until the abolition of the Court of the Star Chamber in 1641 they were permitted to publish only foreign news. By law any printed attack on the government could be treated as libel during the seventeenth century. At the start of the Civil War Parliamentary papers were founded, followed soon by Royalist journals. Cromwell, with Milton as censor, controlled the press from 1654 until towards the end of the Protectorate.

Despite the contribution of Gilbert and Harvey and the propaganda of Bacon, a scientific community developed slowly in England and only began to become evident late in the reign of Charles I. *The Discovery of a New World* (1638) and *A Discourse Concerning a New Planet* (1640) by John Wilkins (1614–72) popularised European research for the intelligent Englishman. In general the English interest remained utilitarian; Wilkins's *Mathematicall Magick* (1648) showed how the new principles of mechanics could be used to drain mines and coal pits.

During the Interregnum, groups modelled on those in Italy and France were formed to carry on scientific experiments and discuss their implications. The membership of such circles was as often Anglican and Royalist as Puritan and Parliamentarian. Many of the best scientific minds of the Interregnum were Anglican Royalists — Seth Ward (1617–

89), Savilian Professor of Astronomy at Oxford, the architect Christopher Wren, Thomas Wallis who performed research on the brain, Robert Boyle, and William Harvey. Many of those involved with science during the Interregnum served Cromwell, but after the Restoration supported the King and the national church.

The experimental, tentative, analytical methods of science offered an alternative approach to the rhetoric and ideals which inflamed the nation. The Baconian emphasis on experimentation and collecting of masses of facts before drawing conclusions, a method different from the more elegant deductive and theoretical approaches favoured on the Continent, was particularly suitable to avoid controversy. Whereas such European scientists as Galileo and Kepler (1571–1630) sought to discover the mathematical laws of nature, and Descartes (1596–1650) attempted to formulate a philosophy of science, the English proceeded to carry out endless experiments on small scientific problems, collecting information, while avoiding hypothesis and synthesis. Rather than the New Science challenging religion, the two realms were viewed as distinct until the end of the century when Isaac Newton harmonised science and religion by treating God as a Great Artisan who created a universe which operates by mechanical and mathematical laws. The approach which dominated the Interregnum and Restoration was, however, sceptical, in the sense of not drawing dogmatic conclusions, neutral in tone and utilitarian. The same people were later to form the Royal Society and since many of the Interregnum scientists after the Restoration became divines they carried over such attitudes into the Latitudinarian movement.

Sir Thomas Browne, Samuel Hartlib, John Drury and many others, including some of Cromwell's circle, were involved with science during the Interregnum. The principal groups were Gresham College, London, an 'invisible college' formed by Robert Boyle and his friends, and the Oxford Philosophical Society, centred upon Wilkins at Wadham College. During the 1650s some professional scientists, including Robert Boyle, Christopher Wren and Robert Hooke, joined Wilkins's amateur Oxford group. The actual discoveries of such circles were small — although John Wallis (1616–1703) invented differential calculus — but their experiments and concept of science were to bear fruit during the Restoration

While Cromwell and the Royalists alike saw science as potentially useful to society and as non-controversial, many sectarians viewed all formal study as 'heathenish and unnecessary'. The Barebones Parliament in 1653 discussed suppressing all universities and schools, as learning and reason were considered hindrances to spiritual illumination. Some Presbyterians were against the new science as they felt it would lead to religious innovation. Many of the supposed educational reformers of the period, such as the sectarian John Webster, who argued that the universities should exclusively teach science, might be more correctly viewed as social radicals who really wanted to prevent the educational system training gentlemen and an élite clergy. Their calls for reform were attempts at undermining one of the sources of English class structure. Despite complaints by Milton and others, the universities had in fact changed, and taught the Copernican system, analytical algebra, equations, magnetism, and recent ideas in anatomy and chemistry.

Although the Presbyterian-dominated Parliament in 1644 ordered the destruction of church organs along with 'images' and monuments, and the Chapel Royal was disbanded, music, as well as the other arts, began to flourish in the 1650s when the Protectorate increasingly began to acquire the trappings of a monarchy. Cromwell started concerts at Whitehall, enjoyed music at dinner, and employed a large number of former Court musicians, including organists and boy singers. Many of his musicians were from the old Chapel Royal. He had twelve trumpeters for ceremonial occasions. At the wedding of his daughter Frances, the musicians included forty-eight violins and fifty trumpets, and dancing continued until five o'clock in the morning. For the wedding of his daughter Mary in the same year, 1657, Marvell provided two pastoral dialogues to be sung and Cromwell performed the role of Jove. Cromwell's musicians were probably behind the 1657 decision to form a government committee for the advancement of music. The surprising expansion of the publication of poetry in the 1650s was paralleled by music publishing; the decade can be regarded as the start of professional music publishing in England. Besides masques and other musical entertainments performed in private houses and the Inns of Court, James Shirley's masque *Cupid and Death* (1653), using music by Matthew Locke and Christopher Gibbons, was performed for state occasions.

If secular music was encouraged during the Protectorate, the old tradition of church music came to an end. Although destruction of organs has usually been exaggerated, choir books were destroyed or lost, choirs forbidden, and after the Restoration there was little left upon which to build. The Presbyterians and other sects limited church music to the Psalms sung in unison by the congregation; the Psalms were lined out, with the minister first reading the verse to the congregation, which sang in response, line by line. The sixteenth-century Sternhold and Hopkins's metrical version of the Psalms had been improved upon by later writers; but the Psalms were still sung syllabically, very slowly, in, it would seem, a peculiar nasal tone which the Puritans adopted. Although the Puritans objected to church polyphony as 'Popish', versions of the Psalms in four-part harmony were published for use in homes.

6
Caroline literature

I New directions

After earlier experiments by Southwell, Donne and Jonson in transforming the secular into the devotional lyric, the second third of the century saw the emergence of a tradition of original religious poetry, often written by Anglican clergy, in contrast to versified biblical paraphrase. Influenced by the metaphysical lyric and Donne's religious verse, George Herbert showed how church symbols, hymns, Christian paradoxes and theological doctrines could form the basis of poetry treating of spiritual anguish, faith, hope and love. Herbert also brought to the century's religious verse the introspective, implied personal narrative of the Petrarchan sonnet sequence. Crashaw gave a more continental, Baroque expression to Anglo-Catholic and Catholic devotional practices and developed the ode to a new complexity in English, while Quarles popularised emblematic religious verse.

Under Charles I lyric poetry took on a sophistication, elegance and social grace appropriate to the Cavalier manners and attitudes now expected of a courtier. The styles of Donne and Jonson were refined and simplified by such writers as Carew and Suckling, to create witty, confident libertine love poetry, which if lacking in profundity was more cadenced and less obscure. In many of the minor poets the metaphysical conceit became an ornament of *précieux* gallantry and compliment. As the metaphysical and Jonsonian fused, and writers learned to adapt classical themes and models, a new style, which laid the foundations for Restoration Neo-Classicism, began to appear in the verse of Waller and Denham.

While Caroline dramatists claimed to be Sons of Ben, their

plays also reveal the continuing influence of Marston's city comedies and Fletcherian romance, along with a new concern, expressed in often elaborate plots, with upper-class manners, gallantry and the libertine and Neo-Platonic fashions of the Court. Alongside the longer cadences of Jonson's later verse and the poems of Carew, aphoristic, short-sentenced Senecan prose was being ousted by longer, looser, asymmetrical sentences which in their seemingly arbitrary shape reflected the movement of the author's thoughts. Often the writers seem to be soliloquising. Browne's playful eccentricities mask a scepticism towards attaining religious and other truths. As the Church of England increasingly split into Presbyterian, moderate and Anglo-Catholic factions, Chillingworth, influenced by the new mood of scepticism, argued the need for toleration.

II Poet priests: Herbert, Crashaw and King

The mother of George Herbert (1593–1633), Magdalen Herbert, was famous for her intellectual and artistic interests and was a patron of John Donne. Because of his learning and family connections, Herbert expected a distinguished public career similar to that of his elder brother Edward, Lord of Cherbury, who was English ambassador in Paris. He did not take deacon orders until 1626, was not ordained a priest until 1630, and probably hoped to combine a career in the Church with public office. The tension in Herbert's poetry between worldly desires and surrender of the will to God expresses lingering ambitions. *The Temple* (1633), published by Nicholas Ferrar after Herbert's death, consists of a long poem, *The Church-porch*, the many short lyrics which comprise *The Church*, and the narrative *The Church Militant*. Superficially the relation is obvious; it is necessary to be instructed how to behave before entering the Church and its communion; afterwards the communicant joins the body of believers. The moral advice in *The Church-porch* is, however, not exactly catechismal, while *The Church Militant*, which was written earlier, is a variation on the theme of Augustine's *City of God* in which the history of the world is seen as a mingling of the sheep and goats in the fallen earthly city until the end of created time when 'judgement shall appeare'.

The Church has a similar complexity. Although the poems refer to the sacraments, the physical church and the liturgical year, their main focus is on the individual experience of a member of the Church, especially the weakness and the joy felt in the journey through this life to the heavenly communion possible only after death ('Love III'). Entrance to *The Church* is through the 'Superliminare' with its invitation to 'the churches mysticall repast'. The following poem is visually shaped like a pagan altar, a typographical form which was sometimes used in fanciful Elizabethan love poetry; the altar, however, is the speaker's stony heart which needs Christ's sacrifice to be sanctified. The metaphoric relationship of the external church to the internal temple of the believer's heart is the basis of many poems, where Herbert's perspective shifts rapidly between Christ, the physical church, the body of Christians and the self. Clusters of poems follow on the Easter Season, catechismal topics, church architecture and services, and other themes, until the concluding group on death, judgement and the heavenly banquet. The poems, linked by allusions, themes and images, suggest an autobiography. The speaker is a sharply defined individual, sometimes bantering, often witty, who undergoes a fluctuating experience of repentance and faith. An Anglican who believes in ceremony, ritual, ordered devotion, the sacraments, holy days ('Whitsunday', 'Mattens', 'Church monuments', 'The Windows'), the use of art to 'dress' religion ('Antiphon', 'Even-song', 'Church-musick') and the mystery of the Eucharistic communion, he also accepts the Calvinist doctrine of predestination according to which fallen man is helpless without individual sanctification.

The poems in *The Church* are similar to the spiritual autobiographies of the age in having been written for self-analysis and to offer others examples of the spiritual turmoils and conflicts then considered a necessary part of a truly religious life. Many people, including Henry Vaughan, interpreted *The Temple* as such a record and claimed to be converted by it. Herbert expresses the doubts and anxieties which accompany spiritual progress through repentance, faith and perseverance, to grace. Even the social graces of 'Love III' subtly express divine power and the doctrine of election:

> Truth Lord, but I have marr'd them: let my shame
>   Go where it doth deserve.
> And know you not, sayes Love, who bore the blame?
>   My deare, then I will serve.
> You must sit down, sayes Love, and taste my meat:
>   So I did sit and eat.

As in Calvin's teaching, man can only be brought to faith by a gift of God; as man is helpless without personal grace, there can be no saving actions, only a record of the psychology of the faithful in growing towards spiritual assurance. Faith, despair and prayer are intertwined since fallen man can do nothing to save himself. As humility and repentance are divine graces, Herbert continually asks God to destroy his sinful ego.

Herbert surprises the reader by the variety of stanzaic forms and the unexpected directions in which his poems move. Each poem is an ingenious, daring experiment in the religious lyric. Some are parodies, in the sense of imitations, of secular lyrics. Others, such as 'The Sacrifice', based on the medieval complaints of Christ, dramatise theological paradoxes and church hymns. 'Easter Wings' is a pattern poem; the stanzaic form is shaped into a visual representation of its theme. The sonnet 'Prayer I' consists of a verbless chain of Christian symbols, paradoxes and typology. The calculated, seeming frenzy of disorder in rhyme scheme and line length in 'The Collar' is used to portray the speaker's rebellion against God, which then collapses in the reassertion of divine authority and grace:

> But as I rav'd and grew more fierce and wilde
>   At every word,
> Me thoughts I heard one calling, *Child*:
>   And I reply'd, *My Lord.*

Besides excellent control over syntax, song forms and oblique conceits, Herbert is also a master of sounds, especially varied internal patterns of rhyme. In 'Heaven' he parodies the secular echo poem for religious purposes:

> Then tell me, what is that supreme delight?
> > *Echo. Light.*
> Light to the minde; what shall the will enjoy?
> > *Echo. Joy.*
> But are there cares and businesse with the pleasure?
> > *Echo. Leisure.*
> Light, joy, and leisure; but shall they persever?
> > *Echo. Ever.*

Although Herbert's poetry has the drama, introspection, intellectual vigour, colloquial language, unexpected metaphors and sometimes obscure learning associated with Donne, it is different from the strong-lined metaphysical manner of the preceding decades. His poetry has a design on the reader; it is meant to 'Ryme thee to good, and make a bait of pleasure'. The style, at least on the surface, is clear, transparent, lucid. Herbert uses the conventional language of polite conversation, of commerce, of religious self-examination and other easily recognisable voices. The poems are varied in order and level of complexity so that there is sufficient intellectual difficulty to sustain interest despite the many pieces that are easy, didactic or playfully ingenious.

Fellow of Peterhouse, then a centre of High Anglicanism, and a participant at Little Gidding in Nicholas Ferrar's religious community with its Arminianism and cultivation of a devotional life, Richard Crashaw (1612?—49) was reported to Parliament as 'superstitious'. He fled Cambridge in 1643, weeks before Cromwell and his Army occupied the university, ejected the Laudians and demolished 'Superstitious Pictures . . . Crucyfixes' and other aids to devotion. He spent the remaining years of his life abroad and converted to Roman Catholicism in 1645.

Crashaw's poetry began with Ovidian wit applied to the divine paradoxes of Christian dogma. The method appeals to the intellect, aims at surprise and appreciation of ingenuity; the wit is a verbal, stylised contraction of a larger concept into a clever epigram. There is little difference between his early secular and translated sacred epigrams. A libertine could have appreciated the wit of 'Sampson to *his* Dalilah': 'Could not once blinding me, cruell, suffice?/ When first I look't on thee, I lost mine eyes'. Such epigrams as 'On the Miracle of

Loaves' are based on traditional Christian imagery, symbolism and typology: 'Now Lord, or never, they'l beleeve on thee, / Thou to their Teeth hast prov'd thy Deity'. 'Wishes To his (supposed) Mistresse' is, despite emphasis on chastity, an exercise in Caroline humour. 'On Hope', written with his friend Cowley in the form of alternating stanzas, is also an exercise in wit, although it proclaims Crashaw's exuberant Christian faith: 'Faire *Hope*! Our earlier Heaven! by thee / Young *Time* is taster to Eternity.'

Crashaw's poetry is an expression of what, in 'To the Name above Every Name', he calls 'the witt of love'. The devotional intention is clearly expressed in the anonymous preface to the *Steps to the Temple* (1646): 'So maist thou take a Poem hence, and tune thy soule by it, into a heavenly pitch; and thus refined and borne up upon the wings of meditation, in these Poems thou maist talke freely of God, and of that other state.' Although influenced by Herbert's *Temple*, Crashaw's great poetic meditations are neither introspective nor concerned with problems of conscience, guilt and man's fallen state. They do not express the spiritual anxieties of self-analysis. While his verse appears ecstatic and rhapsodical, it is controlled, the result of skilled craftsmanship, and, despite imagery of softness and colour, appeals to the intellect:

> We saw thee in thy baulmy nest,
> Bright dawn of our aeternall Day!
> We saw thine eyes break from their EAST
> And chase the trembling shades away.
> We saw thee: and we blest the sight.
> We saw thee, by thine own sweet light.

The notorious 'Two walking baths', 'Portable, and compendious oceans' and stanza IV of 'The Weeper' ('Upwards thou dost weep. / Heaven's bosome drinks the gentle stream') result from accurately and ingeniously expressing theological ideas without regard to how they appear literally.

Crashaw was influenced by the extremely popular devotional methods of St Francis de Sales (1567–1622), the Bishop of Geneva, who wrote an *Introduction to the Devout Life*. The emphasis on self-surrender to divine love and grace is Salesian as is Crashaw's method in his devotional poetry, where he immediately divorces himself from his environment, proposes his subject and then proceeds to an act of under-standing or to the meditation proper in which the mind darts like a bee — the image is a favourite of both de Sales and Crashaw — from flower to flower. The meditation is followed by a resolution and a small collection of spiritual flowers to serve as a remembrance. Whereas Herbert's poems both express a personal drama and serve as a model for spiritual progress, Crashaw's verse draws the reader out of the self into an elevation of spirit. There is little interest in Hell, pre-destination or death (except in the mystical sense of the going beyond the self); instead the poems create a world of divine love freely given, of God's friendship towards man, and of those, such as St Theresa, the Virgin Mary and Mary Magdalene, who have surrendered themselves to love. Crashaw's 'enthusiasm', the evolution of his lyrics towards narrative, the concern with elegancies of vowel sound and diction, the variety of line lengths and stresses, and the use of occasional unrhymed lines are part of a Baroque sensibility which was developing in England during the late 1630s and 40s. Many of his poems are odes in irregular stanzas with constantly changing metres. *Musicks Duell*, freely translated from the Latin poem of Strada, Jesuit author (1572–1649) of Neo-Latin poetry, is a showpiece of effects. The late hymns in *Sacred Poems* (1652) are virtuosi performances having a Miltonic complexity of form. Amazingly some of the poems were written for liturgical use.

Francis Quarles (1592–1644) was a popular writer who adapted the continental Baroque sensibility to English Protestantism. His development as a poet paralleled the changing literary methods of his time. His early work included verse narrative in couplets on such biblical subjects as Jonah, Esther, Job, the Lamentations of Jeremiah and the Song of Solomon. After *The Historie of Samson* (1631) and *Divine Fancies* (1632), four hundred short epigrams, 'meditations' and observations in verse, Quarles became for a time an interesting poet with *Emblemes* (1635), *Hieroglyphikes* (1638) and *Hosanna* (1647).

The printing of moralising poems with accompanying illustrations began in the sixteenth century. The European Jesuits of the seventeenth century made the Emblem Book into an art by bringing elaborate imaginative analogies to bear upon the religious texts or themes which the pictures symbolised. Quarles, who adapted the methods and sometimes used the plates of *Pia Desideria* ('Pious Desires', 1624) and *Typus Mundi* ('A Figure of the World', 1627), two European Jesuit books, tells his readers: 'An Emblem is but a silent Parable . . . In holy Scripture, He is sometimes called a Sower; sometimes, a Fisher; sometimes, a Physitian: And why not presented so, as well to the eye, as to the eare?' *Emblemes* portrays the progress of the soul through guilt-ridden anxieties towards the acknowledgement of divine love: 'The gift is thine; we strive, thou crown'st our strife; / Thou giv'st us faith: and faith a crown of life.' Each pictorial emblem is accompanied by an appropriate biblical quotation, a poem expanding or dramatising the theme, quotations from a Church Father and a concluding epigrammatic quatrain. The verse is easy to understand, inventive in stanzaic form, and makes use of paradox, antithesis and other rhetorical devices to dramatise the allegory of the episode. Often the structure of a poem or sequence is based on meditative practices and progresses from statements of anxiety through analysis of the problem to concluding prayer or resolution. Rather expansive and facile, lacking Herbert's intensity and concentration of effect, Quarles provided for the Protestant a new but easily understood religious art which expressed the troubled heart and its 'glorious misery to be borne a *Man*'. Quarles represents a side of the Church of England which could be Puritan, Royalist and conformist, until the divisions within the nation made such compromise impossible.

In *Partheneia Sacra* (1633), probably by the Jesuit Henry Hawkins (1571?–1646), images are systematically ordered as aids to devotion. Using the central emblem of the garden to represent the Virgin Mary, the book is divided into twenty-four sections, each of which is subdivided into an ordered nine-part devotion. Each section has its own symbol (Lily, Rose, Palm, Bee) and the devotion moves from emblematic symbol through various distinct stages of meditation. *Partheneia Sacra* is a beautiful book, filled with learning, and its logical but richly symbolic conceited style influenced Protestant poets. Its descriptions of the natural world, and imagery of light, jewels and colour, are delightful.

Henry King (1592–1669), a contemporary of George

Herbert at Westminster School and a friend of Donne, was made Bishop of Chichester in 1642, a year before Parliament abolished episcopacy. His style ranges from closely compressed, highly imagistic strong lines with extra stresses and clustered consonants to clear, bare statements phrased as epigrammatical wit. The poems argue, have long phrases of varied lengths and unpredictable pauses, and display ingenious wit. Although 'Tell mee no more how faire shee is' has often been admired for its clarity of articulation and cadence, King's early lyrics are not as poised as those of Carew and Suckling; they are still close to the Elizabethan Petrarchan tradition of amorous praise, devotion and rejection. His training in classical rhetoric shows in the clear, logical, concise articulation of 'An Epitaph on Richard Earle of Dorset' and in 'To my Dead Friend Ben Johnson'. He revealed a surprising talent for political satire from the 1630s onward in 'On the Earl of Essex' and 'Epigram: Hammond'.

King was uncommonly aware of death, especially through the loss of friends and family. He seldom shows Donne's anguish and fear; instead there is a quiet but alert resignation and an expectation of reunion in an eternal after-life. 'An Exequy', written in 1624 on the death of his wife, expresses a profundity of feeling through endearments, wit, metaphor and a logical, controlled argument:

> . . . For Thee (Lov'd Clay!)
> I Languish out, not Live the Day,
> Using no other Exercise
> But what I practise with mine Eyes.
> By which wett glasses I found out
> How lazily Time creepes about
> To one that mournes: This, only This
> My Exercise and bus'nes is:
> So I compute the weary howres
> With Sighes dissolved into Showres.
>   Nor wonder if my time goe thus
> Backward and most praeposterous;
> Thou hast Benighted mee.

The first half of the poem concludes with reference to the Last Judgement and the Resurrection, which is followed by the startling 'Meane time, thou hast Hir Earth: Much good / May my harme doe thee'.

III From Cavalier to early Neo-Classical poetry: Carew, Suckling, Waller and Denham

Although Church and Court circles overlapped, the courtiers were developing secular verse in such new directions as the Cavalier song and the Neo-Classical panegyric. Appointed Gentleman of the Privy Chamber of Charles I and regarded as one of the wittiest courtiers, the influential Thomas Carew (1594–1640?) was the most popular poet of the 1630s. Influenced by Donne's direct address, he is less dramatic, intense, passionate or profound; while his poems have Jonson's clarity of articulation in structure and development of theme, his phrases are longer, smoother and more elevated in diction. Using iambic pentameters and strict forms, he achieves a classicism and dignity revealing acquaintance with Catullus and the Greek Anthology. Many of his poems are variations on the later Petrarchan lyrics of Ronsard and Desportes, French poet (1546–1606), disciple of Ronsard. Samuel Daniel had earlier used the Italian poet Giambattista Marino's (1569–1625) witty poetic conceits, but Carew naturalised Baroque wit, giving it elegance and poise. Essentially a craftsman using various poetic manners and a range of dictions, with no particular philosophy beyond the libertinism fashionable at Court, Carew had a man-of-the-world sophistication. Although his poems about Celia include Petrarchan commonplaces, the implied narrative is invigorated by an aggressive realism. Carew's hedonism is tempered by social awareness; the poems are set within situations which involve the interplay of personalities. The style is the man, elegant, assured, playful, tough.

From such attitudes Carew creates striking phrases: 'Then crowne my joyes, or cure my paine; / Give me more love, or more disdaine'; 'A fayrer hand then thine, shall cure / That heart, which thy false oathes did wound'; 'Let fooles thy mystique formes adore, / I'le know thee in thy mortall state'. 'A Rapture', similar to Torquato Tasso's *Aminta*, begins with a denunciation of honour as inhibiting the natural sexual freedom of women; the persuasion to love moves on to a finely detailed fantasy of sensuous bliss and then surprisingly concludes in the contemporary social world of rivalry and public opinion. The poem includes a mixture of Donnean wit and Spenserian pastoral diction, used here for erotic description.

A social poet who wrote for the Court, Carew was a conservative who accepted Stuart claims to divine right. 'In answer of an Elegiacall Letter upon the death of the King of Sweden' commends King Charles's non-intervention in the Thirty Years War and contrasts the peaceful literature of England with European battles 'for freedom and revenge'. Carew's masque, *Coelum Britannicum* ('The British Sky', 1633), performed in Whitehall, had music by William or Henry Lawes, while the scenery and stage design were by Inigo Jones. The marvellous, malicious, witty speeches of Momus, with their parodies, puns and political allusions, are among the period's best verbal play.

Supposedly the greatest gallant of the time, a notorious gambler who used marked cards and invented cribbage, Sir John Suckling (1609—41?) was for later ages, along with Lovelace, the pattern of a Cavalier. Whereas Carew was influenced by Jonson's classicism, Suckling simplified the dramatic gestures and cynicism of Donne's early poetry, making the love song lighter, flippant, gay and at times self-mocking. Lacking Donne's introspection and profound analysis of the transformations of the lover's ego, Suckling contributed to Caroline anti-Petrarchism by a simple, clear, unsentimental view of love as appetite stimulated by imagination. Other poets adored, pleaded with, threatened or hated their mistresses; Suckling expressed a cheerful, worldly libertinism. Where Carew spoke in tones of elegant superiority, Suckling's short lines, simple stanzas and ordinary diction suggest casual indifference:

> Out upon it, I have lov'd
> Three whole days together;
> And am like to love three more,
> If it hold fair weather.

His poems are often playfully impertinent, as if he were laughing at himself. In 'The Metamorphosis', Love 'H'as metamorphos'd me into an Ass!' As Mrs A. L. 'dost all Hyperboles excell', the poet wishes 'some bad in thee, / For sure I am thou art too good for me'. He pleads with A. M.,

'Yeeld not, my Love; but be as coy, / As if thou knew'st not how to toy', because 'Men most enjoy, when least they doe'. Mocking the conventional poetry of absence and departure, he tells Lady E. C., 'I must confess, when I did part from you, / I could not force an artificial dew'. Suckling's 'Against Fruition' — 'Women enjoy'd (what s'ere before th'ave been)/ Are like Romances read, or sights once seen' — exactly caught the prose of polite cynicism favoured by the courtiers. Poetry was a game where wits attempted to top each other. Suckling's 'The deformed Mistress' ('Her Nose I'de have a foot long') is one of many seventeenth-century parodies of the traditional enumeration of a mistress's charms. He was inventive; 'A Ballade. Upon a Wedding', a comic epithalamion describing a noble wedding told in Kentish dialect by a rustic, and 'A Sessions of the Poets', created new sub-genres which were widely imitated. 'Of thee (kind boy)' is famous for its striking libertine attitudes ('Tis not the meat, but 'tis the appetite / Makes eating a delight'), while 'Oh! for some honest Lovers ghost' sensibly concludes: 'Give me the Woman here'. The Petrarchan languishing lover is mocked in 'Why so pale and wan fond Lover?':

> If of her selfe shee will not Love,
> Nothing can make her,
> The Devill take her.

While Carew brought elevation, social poise and longer, melodic cadences to Cavalier verse, Edmund Waller (1606—87) was the start of Neo-Classicism in English poetry. In the Dryden—Sir William Soames translation (1683) of Boileau's *L'Art poétique*, Waller is treated as the equivalent of Malherbe (1555—1628) who earlier in the century had reformed French verse in the direction of the classical. Waller is credited with teaching others how to place words forcefully, the refining of poetic diction, and the joining of 'easie words with pleasing Numbers' to form 'Soft Harmony'. He contributed to the evolving Neo-Classicism by transforming Ovidian wit and word play into balanced, graceful, closed couplets. By regularly observing the medial caesura, seldom varying his stress, and developing his rhetoric around 'turns' on repeated words (which are usually part of a compressed conceit), he changed the paradoxical wit of the metaphysicals into the smooth-flowing, antithetical Augustan couplet. If refinement seems to have replaced vitality, such characteristics as limitation, precision, controlled ornamentation and public address made Waller's verse a model for later poets.

In the 1630s Waller wrote good, if not outstanding, Petrarchan verses to Lady Dorothy Sidney, whom he called Sacharissa; perhaps the most interesting is the 'Story of Phoebus and Daphne Applied', which metaphorically tells of his unsuccessful pursuit. Such fine lyrics as 'Go, Lovely Rose', 'To Phyllis', 'To a Lady in Retirement', 'On a Girdle' ('Give me but what this ribband bound,/ Take all the rest the sun goes round') and the poems addressed to Flavia, Amoret and Chloris, may appear facile in comparison to the best of Carew's, but are gallant, poised and intelligently hedonistic. Waller's manner is polite, urbane, civilised, elegant, without the ethical and moral concerns of the earlier seventeenth-century poets. His language is both elevated and current. The lyrics are addressed to women, rather than intended for a circle of other male poets, and like many Restoration songs accordingly avoid difficulties of syntax and allusion. The lyrics are compliments, not expressions of deep thoughts and feelings.

The poems also reflect the increasing imitation of classical models throughout the century. Waller's style is based on conventional epithets and phrases, periphrasis (roundabout way of speaking), French and Latin verbs, polysyllabic nouns, an honorific vocabulary and attributive adjectives. From his study of Virgil (c. 70–19 BC), Ovid and other classical writers, Waller imitated such techniques of Latin and Greek syntax and poetic style as the zeugma, the piling-up of phrases and series of nouns, honorific similes, and the placing of the verb at the end of a line. His similes and metaphors are explicit, often treated as tentative analogies. While some of the lyrics are stanzaic, he usually writes in closed couplets in which the four major stresses are balanced in twos in each half of a line; the most important words coincide with the stresses of the metre.

The Stuart masque complimented its participants and the monarchy through its rich mythological and allegorical symbolism; Waller brought similar methods of analogy and figurative language into the public poem. Whether praising Charles I, Cromwell or Charles II, he contributed to the development of signifying through the use of mythological, classical and biblical analogies to contemporary persons, places and events. His allusions, similes and correspondences create comparisons and ideals. 'Upon His Majesty's Repairing of St. Paul's' suggests that Charles I's 'Art of Regiment' brings order to the Church and English life; in art and, it is implied, religion and politics, 'He, like *Amphion*, makes those quarries leap / Into fair figures from a confus'd heap'. In 'On St. James's Park' Charles II's improvements are implicitly understood as a restoration of graces and harmony to society; he is 'Born the divided world to reconcile'. He will 'Reform these nations, and improve them more, / Than this fair Park, from what it was before'. In the political poems of Denham, Marvell and Dryden such analogies and emblematic scenes will provide the larger assumptions which support the particular claims.

The paradoxically close relationships of Waller's panegyric manner to Restoration heroic satire can be seen by the way his *Instructions to a Painter* (1666) and 'On St. James's Park' were parodied by Andrew Marvell's 'Last Instructions to a Painter' and Rochester's 'A Ramble in St. James's Park'. In Restoration satire the elevated, figurative language and analogies of such poems as 'A Panegyric to My Lord Protector' and 'To the King, upon His Majesty's Happy Return' were retained, but for mocking purposes. Waller's own experiment with the mock-heroic in 'The Battle of the Summer Islands' (1638) is an early clumsy attempt at playfulness which compares unfavourably to the graceful seriousness of Marvell's 'Bermudas'.

Sir John Denham (1615–69) brought to the developing Neo-Classicism strengths, especially the pointed use of antithesis within the couplet, not found in Waller's style. Although his play *The Sophy* (1642), written in an energetic Shakespearean blank verse, is filled with scenes of horror and death, there is often in the speeches a reflective quality which is more pronounced in *Cooper's Hill*. Published in a pirated edition of 1642, Denham's best-known poem was substantially revised and enlarged for the 1655 version. His use of the description of a particularly landscape as a means of reflect-

ing upon history, politics, philosophy and art, and his famous
antithetical couplets, were an influence on later poetry. His
couplets are balanced, yet energetic:

> Oh, could I flow like thee, and make thy stream
> My great example, as it is my theme!
> Though deep, yet clear, though gentle, yet not dull,
> Strong without rage, without ore-flowing full.

The conciseness, the sharp antithesis, the balance of opposites,
the range of subjects from the majestic to the picturesque,
the contrast between the real and ideal, the linked association
of ideas, the memorable phrases, the subdued elegance and
the clear, witty precise metaphors made *Cooper's Hill* a
classic of its time. By packing much into a small space,
Denham brought the energy of the Jacobean strong line to
Neo-Classicism. Much is expressed through implied analogy,
as in the Thames couplets where the harmonious power of
'thy stream' is contrasted to inactivity and disorder. Windsor
Hill, associated with monarchy, is contrasted to London:
'Where, with like hast, through several ways, they run / Some
to undo, and some to be undone'.

In comparison to earlier poetry treating landscape, *Cooper's
Hill* is more public in its concerns. Whereas the 1642 text is
openly Royalist, the 1655 revisions tend towards a generalised
conservatism. The analogy of a hunted stag to the trial and
execution of Strafford ('Like a declining statesman') is
expanded in the 1655 version to imply general similarities
to the fate of Charles I, who was often associated with
emblematic stags, deer and fawns. Denham's use of emblematic scenes for social and political themes develops Waller's
technique of analogies and might be seen as marking a
transition between Caroline complimentary, panegyric verse
and the more profound, puzzling pastorals and lyrics of the
Interregnum. Part of Denham's style probably resulted from
his study and translation of Virgil. In his Preface (1677) to
The Destruction of Troy (1656), he said: 'if Virgil must
needs speak English, it were fit he should speak not only as
a man of this Nation, but as a man of this age'.

Denham was a friend of Sir Richard Fanshawe (1608–
66), the famous translator of the Portuguese poet Camões's

epic *Lusiads* (1655) into contemporary dress. In verses prefacing Fanshawe's version of Guarini's *Pastor Fido* (1647), Denham suggests that this is the first example of interpretative paraphrase in contrast to Jonson's literal methods of translation. Denham and Fanshawe set an example later followed by Cowley and Dryden.

The second quarter of the century was particularly rich in good minor poets who brought their own touch to contemporary styles. Aurelian Townshend (1583?–1650?), who in 1632 briefly followed Jonson as Inigo Jones's librettist for two masques, *Tempe Restored* and *Albions Triumph*, wrote graceful, intelligent lyrics, precise yet almost Elizabethan in diction, often Donnean in logic. Townshend's stanzaic forms and rhyme schemes are varied, and sometimes surprising. The beautiful 'Dialogue betwixt Time and a Pilgrime' has the graceful seriousness of the best metaphysical poetry:

> If thou art Time, these Flow'rs have Lives,
>   And then I fear,
> Under some Lilly she I love
>   May now be growing there.

Sidney Godolphin (1610–43) wrote short lyrics and began the influential translation of the Fourth Book of Virgil's epic, the *Aeneid*, completed by Waller. Although he catches the graceful cadences of Carew and Suckling, and uses some Elizabethan Petrarchan rhetoric, Godolphin's verse is more intellectual; logical ideas develop in long sentences which run throughout the stanza and sometimes into the next stanza. The style is taut, lucid. The clarity is Jonsonian; but the compression, feeling and thought are closer to the metaphysical strong line, where rhythm follows the movement of a thinking mind. 'Or love me less, or love me more' is an interesting variation of Carew's 'Mediocrity in Love'. 'Chorus' is a surprising mixture of late Elizabethan Senecanism and what appears to be the sensationalist psychology of Godolphin's friend Thomas Hobbes. 'Vain man, born to no happiness' is dissatisfied because he either desires what he lacks or is satiated by what he has.

William Habington (1605–54) prefaces his *Castara* (1634, 1635, 1640) with the declaration: 'In all those flames in which I burnt, I never felt a wanton heate; nor was my invention ever sinister from the straite way of chastity.' He 'never set so high a rate upon' poetry and believed it 'hath too much ayre'. Originally written as part of his courtship of Lucy Herbert, the sequence of poems proceeds through the usual Petrarchan themes of 'Inquiring why I loved her', 'Upon a dimple', 'departure', 'absence', 'An Apparition'; but unlike the usual sonneteer, Habington praises chastity and celebrates the rewards of innocent love with Castara's transformation into a wife. The love poems are often Elizabethan with their syntactical phrases conforming to the line, their stereotyped imagery and monotonous rhythms; but Habington's use of the couplet and compressed conceits is Caroline. He had no interest in the Neo-Platonism and libertinism of the Court; the third part of *Castara* (1640) begins with a prose character of 'A Holy Man', followed by religious verse meditations, of which 'Nox nocti indicat Scientiam' ('Let night proclaim Knowledge') is best.

Thomas Randolph's (1605—35) *Poems* (1638, 1640) are social, addressed to friends, or funeral elegies and epithalamia, or humorous exercises on conventional themes. They include 'A Pastoral Courtship' ('No herb nor balm can cure my sorrow — / Unless we meet again to-morrow'), the humorous 'Upon a Hermaphrodite' and the playfully erotic 'A Complaint against Cupid, that he never made him in Love' ('Who, like good proselytes, more in heart than show / Shall to thy orgies all so zealous go'). In contrast to the intense metaphysical poem, the Caroline poet seldom takes love seriously. In 'A Platonic Elegy':

> Were't possible that my ambitious sin
> Durst commit rapes upon a cherubin,
> I might have lustful thoughts to her, of all
> Earth's heavenly choir the most angelical.

Many of Randolph's plays — *Aristippus, The Drinking Academy, Hey for Honesty* and *The Jealous Lovers* — are based on the plots of Greek or Roman comedies, but the characters are Jonsonian humours. *The Entertainment* (1630) satirises the Puritan view of the theatre, 'Colleges of transgression, where the seven deadly sins are studied'. *Amyntas* (1630) is in the pastoral tradition of Guarini and John Fletcher.

Allegorical interpretation of heroic and Ovidian romances was common throughout the first half of the century. Besides Bacon's discussion of parabolical and allusive fiction in *The Advancement of Learning*, Edward Fairfax's translation of Tasso's *Jerusalem Delivered*, Leonard Digges's Ovidian *The Rape of Proserpine* (1617) and Shackerley Marmion's *Cupid and Psyche* (1637) were published with allegorical explanations:

> By the City is meant the World; by the King and Queen, God and Nature; by the two elder Sisters, the Flesh and the Will; by the last, the Soul, which is the most beautiful, and the youngest, since she is infused after the body is fashioned. Venus, by which is understood Lust, is feigned to envy her, and stir up Cupid, which is Desire, to destroy her; but because Desire has equal relation both to Good and Evil, he is here brought in to love the Soul, and to be joined with her, whom also he persuades not to see his face, that is, not to learn his delights and vanities.

Marmion (1603–39), who like his friend Jonson had a scholarly interest in myth, also wrote such humours comedies as *Holland's Leaguer* (1631) and *The Antiquary* (1635). The allegorical Ovidian romance is a distinct sub-genre from such humorous erotic romances as *Leoline and Sydanis*, by Sir Francis Kynaston (1587–1642), a minor 'metaphysical' poet.

The two main allegorists of the period were George Sandys (1578–1644) and Henry Reynolds. Sandys's *Ovids Metamorphosis* (1626), written in closed couplets and influenced by Sylvester's poetic diction, was republished in 1632 with an allegorical commentary. In *Mythomystes* ('An Initiate of Myths', 1632) Reynolds dismisses tropes, rhyme and metre as the flowers and accidentals of poetry. Influenced by Pico della Mirandola, he claims that true poetry is philosophical, mystical and divine knowledge expressed through allegory, myth and other veils. Reynolds unfavourably compares modern with ancient writers, seeing in the legends and myths of the past moral and mystical significance. His references to the Jewish *Cabbala* (Jewish mystic interpretations of the Scriptures which evolved during the ninth to thirteenth centuries), number symbolism, early Church Fathers, Augustine, and Italian Renaissance philosophers are representative of the varied sources of the 'Art of Mysticall Writing'.

IV Dramatists: Ford, Massinger, Shirley and Davenant

While most of the Caroline dramatists claimed to be
Jonsonians, John Ford (1586—1640?) continued to explore
such Jacobean tragic themes as incest, adultery and the
ambiguities of revenge. Often his plots are contrived to create
ambivalent sympathies. The incestuous love of Giovanni and
Annabella in *'Tis Pity She's a Whore* (1633) appears more
honest than the marriage into which Annabella is forced; but
if the friar, Bonaventura, cannot satisfactorily answer
Giovanni's arguments in favour of the free enjoyment of love,
the events in the plot, and the facility of Giovanni's speech,
demonstrate the spuriousness of such Renaissance golden age
libertinism. In *Love's Sacrifice* (1633) Bianca visits Fernando
at night, resists the temptation of adultery but is murdered
by her husband after he finds her with her lover. Fernando
praises her purity:

> *glorious Bianca,*
> Reigne in the triumph of thy martyrdome,
> Earth was unworthy of thee.

Interpretation of Ford's plays is difficult because his verse
is cool, distant, controlled, while the scenes are often
melodramatic and sensational. There is no consistent guidance
in the tone of speeches; in the debate on incest and God's
punishment in *'Tis Pity*, both the friar and Giovanni are
given speeches which sound tinged with the author's irony.
An excellent dramatist with an unusual theatrical sense of
movement, gesture and grouping, Ford seems more concerned
with art as patterned contrivance than with the moral
implications of his plots. Perhaps it is best to see him in the
context of the Caroline Court with its debates on Platonic
and libertine love, delight in poised, mannered conduct, and
languid aristocratic superiority. The stoicism, intense feelings
and individual assertion of his plays are modified by stylised
speeches and the aesthetics of dying well. More interested in
individual psychological and personal relationships than
morality, Ford views honour as a way of life. He treats the
conflicts arising from chastity, love, marriage, jealousy,
adultery, revenge and fate as lyric themes. His plays reflect
the tensions of a Court society where marriages were

political, but where sensibility was concerned with love, chastity, personal relations, and aristocratic behaviour. The psychology of the depressive, obstructed lover is clear in *The Lover's Melancholy* (1628) and *The Broken Heart* (1633), both influenced by Burton's *The Anatomy of Melancholy*.

Philip Massinger's (1583—1640) mixture of Jonsonian satiric humours and Jacobean city comedy, and his plain, unmetaphoric verse, were influential on the Caroline dramatists. The son of a former Oxford fellow who was an agent for the Pembrokes, Massinger was one of the new generation of impoverished gentlemen who turned to the stage as a career. Whereas formerly a specially prepared manuscript was given to patrons, Massinger published his plays with dedications. The plays reflect loyalty to the older, landed aristocracy in contrast to the newly rich of the city and the ambitions and designs of the court. *A New Way to Pay Old Debts* (1625) shows the influence of Jonson in the characters of Sir Giles Overreach and his clerk Marrall, modelled on Volpone and Mosca. In contrast to Overreach there is Wellborn, one of the new-style, likeable, spendthrift heroes who will be found in Caroline and Restoration comedy. The austere *Roman Actor* (1626), influenced by Jonson's classicism in *Sejanus*, is notable for its three inserted playlets within the play.

Massinger's plots have a neatness of exposition, a clarity of story movement, unlike the digressiveness and carelessness of his predecessors. There are seldom any abrupt shifts of scene, loose ends left hanging at the conclusion of a play, or unresolved themes. The plays begin with scenes in which characters explain the situation which forms the basis of the subsequent action; often some information or secret is withheld from the audience but comes to light in a discovery or reversal of fortune. Tragic characters die in the fourth act, the villains are punished in the fifth act and the play ends with a moral. *The City Madam* (1632) concludes:

> Make you good
> Your promis'd reformation, and instruct
> Our City dames, whom wealth makes proud, to move
> In their own spheres, and willingly to confesse
> In their habits, manners, and their highest port,
> A distance 'twixt the City, and the Court.

The neat interweaving and resolution of two different subjects and plots is characteristic of Massinger, as are the long verse sentences, with many clauses, which anticipate a style that became common later in the century and was made famous or notorious by Milton. In the context of the theatre such long sentences, however, seem somewhat rhetorical and undramatic.

In the comedies and tragicomedies of James Shirley (1596—1666) Jonsonian humours and social satire blend with Fletcherian romance, wit and love battles and, in the sub-plots, a touch of Marston's city comedies, to provide elements that later went into Restoration comedy — battles of repartee, rakish heroes, love intrigue, witty ladies, and satire on the country. Shirley has a Jonsonian sense of pretences and eccentricity of character. He was prolific, often turning out three or four plays a year. By the time of *The Wedding* (1626) he had learned how to build Fletcherian tragicomedy, full of surprises, in which tragedy concludes with a clever happy ending. Not very serious, it is good theatre. In such plays as *The Witty Fair One* (1628), *Hyde Park* (1632) and *The Lady of Pleasure* (1635), Fletcherian romance blends with Jonsonian satire to produce witty comedies of manners. Shirley's masques include *The Triumph of Peace* (1634), produced with Inigo Jones, which the Inns of Court presented to Charles after Prynne's notorious attack on the theatre and the Queen, *Histriomastix*. Less forceful and individual than Carew's, Shirley's poems have the social poise and intimacy of the Jonsonian lineage, with a neatness, gracefulness of articulation and fullness of cadence that are attractive. Seemingly effortless and very socially aware, the lyrics and epistles are among the fruit of Caroline culture.

A former servant of Jonson, whose influence can be seen on his exposition of theme and dramatic organisation, Richard Brome (*c*. 1590—1653?) used Jonsonian satire and humours characters to provide a light, comical portrait of society. His plays are often based on such contemporary social conflicts as the attempt of fathers to recover their fortunes through the marriage of their children. They are skilful dramas, with the elaborate plots popular in the Caroline era, and contain a range of moods from bawdry to stylised romance. Brome seems especially sensitive to the new

Court manners which he contrasts unfavourably to the responsibilities of the older aristocracy. *The Court Beggar* (1640) satirises those who flocked to the Court seeking to obtain monopolies; it includes Sir John Suckling and Sir William Davenant among its various targets. *A Joviall Crew* (1641), acted on the eve of the Civil War, humorously expresses a desire to escape to a romantic English past of a generous, stable aristocracy.

Sir William Davenant (1606–68) entered literary circles as an employee of Fulke Greville and became, under the sponsorship of Endymion Porter, one of the writers for the Court. His London comedy *The Wits* (1634) was 'corrected by the King'. The Queen, who liked his tragicomedy *Love and Honour* (1634), which was influenced by French romances, became his patron and commissioned him to write a masque, *The Temple of Love* (1635), in which she played the part of Indamora. The Court fashion for Platonic love was brought to the professional stage with Davenant's *The Platonic Lovers* (1635), a pastoral romance set in Sicily. After Jonson's death, Davenant became Poet Laureate and wrote *Madagascar* (1638), a heroic poem meant to encourage Prince Rupert, the son of Elizabeth of Bohemia, to conquer Madagascar and turn it into an English colony. He co-operated with Jones on *Salmacida Spolia* (1640), the last of the masques before the war ended such Court entertainments; the King appeared in it as 'Philogenes' or 'Lover of His People'.

Towards the end of the Protectorate, Davenant began presenting 'operas' as a means of circumventing the laws against public performances of plays. 'A heroique story in *Stilo Recitativo*', (recitative style – declamation usual in the narrative and dialogue parts of operas and oratorios), *The Siege of Rhodes* (1656), with the first English actress to perform in public, music by Henry Lawes and scenery by Jones's protégé John Webb, has been called the beginning of English opera. Other productions followed, including *The Cruelty of the Spaniards in Peru* and *The History of Sir Francis Drake*, both of which were probably regarded as propaganda for Cromwell's war against Spain. Dryden said that Davenant showed how Waller's reform of verse could be used in the rhymed speeches of the heroic plays. In demonstrating how large narrative material could be condensed into a play, the operas prepared the grounds for the epitomising of the epic-romance in Restoration heroic drama. A more lasting influence was on the art of the theatre. Using perspective and changeable scenes, Davenant brought the stagecraft and illusionism of the masque and Court entertainments to the professional stage. From his operas the new art of the theatre passed to the Restoration. After the Restoration his Duke's Theatre specialised in perspective scenery.

Davenant's best work is his poetry, especially 'The Larke now leaves his wattrey Nest', 'The Philosophers Disquisition directed to the Dying Christian', his dialogue songs, 'Endimion Porter, and Olivia' and 'The Philosopher and the Lover', and the songs 'The Souldier going to the Field' and 'O Thou that sleep'st like *Pigg* in Straw' from *News from Plymouth* (1635). There is a natural progression to his imagery which, if sometimes surprising, is complementary to the thoughts expressed. Although he can be humorous and playful, his tone is weightier and more serious than that of many Caroline poets; he has an intellectual and colloquial vigour even when writing on trivial subjects. His 'Jeffereidos' and 'The long Vacation in London' are early and pleasant examples of mock-heroic and burlesque poetry. *Gondibert* is an attempt to create a modern epic using Hobbesian psychology and celebrating the new science. Davenant's preface (1651) was published a year before the poem with an essay by Hobbes on the theory of the projected epic. Both the epic and Hobbes's 'Answer' show the exiled English Court being influenced by the rationalism and Neo-Classicism which was becoming dominant in France. A concern with literary 'rules' and genres was part of the new rationalism which brought an end to *précieux* verse in France and metaphysical poetry in England. Earlier Italian-influenced Petrarchism, pastoralism and 'conceited' wit were being overtaken by a new sensibility more in keeping with the clarity and generalising processes of scientific thought.

The influence of Jonsonian comedy and masques on Caroline drama and the parallel evolution of tragicomedy towards the heroic play of the Restoration can be seen in such minor Sons of Ben as Henry Glapthorne (1610–43?), whose *The Hollander* (1635) is influenced by *The Alchemist*.

The specifically Caroline mode is represented by his pastoral drama *Argalus and Parthenia* (1638) and the tragicomedy *The Lady's Privilege* (1637), where ethical entanglements lead to discussions of love, honour and friendship. In the tragicomedies of the poet William Cartwright (1611—43) there are noble Neo-Platonic lovers, witty debates, and scenes that later were imitated by Dryden. Jasper Mayne's (1604—72) *The City Match* (1636), a comedy of manners presented at a royal visit to Oxford, satirises the Puritans and Court Platonism, and includes an attack on Prynne. Besides Mayne and Cartwright, Jonsonian clerical dramatists include Peter Hausted (1605?—45) and William Strode (1602—44), whose *Floating Island* (1636), a moral masque, was presented before the King with elaborate scenery and machinery, including movable wings and an island seeming to float above the stage. Thomas Nabbes's (1605—41) masque *Microcosmus* ('A Small World', 1637) is a dramatic allegory in which Bellanima, the soul, is in conflict with Physander, the body. *Hannibal and Scypio* (1635) carries to an extreme the methods of Jonson's Roman tragedies; the effect is similar to a pageant. His comedy *Tottenham Court* (1633) ridicules the libertines and attacks the sexual double standard.

Thomas May (1595—1650), another Jonsonian, wrote plays and in 1627 translated the *Pharsalia* of the Latin poet Lucan (AD 39—65), followed by his own *Continuation of Lucan's Historical Poem* (1630). A Royalist, he turned into a propagandist for Parliament (supposedly because after Jonson's death William Davenant was made Poet Laureate), and wrote a *History of the Parliament of England* (1647). He was buried at Westminster Abbey, from which his body was removed by order of Charles II. William Cavendish (1583—1676), Duke of Newcastle, was talented at writing comical scenes, but needed the help of such professional dramatists as Shirley, and later Dryden, to 'tie' his plays together. His *Country Captain* (1640) illustrates how Jonsonian comedy as modified by Shirley was moving in the direction of what was to be Restoration comedy. A portrait of high society, it includes a Sir Francis Courtwell, a Lady Huntlove, French gallants, libertines, country gentlemen and adultery.

V Prose and Sir Thomas Browne

The prose fiction of the first half of the century is mostly of historical interest. The better-known works include Robert Anton's *Moriomachia* ('Battles of the Fates', 1613), a Cervantes-influenced parody of chivalric and pastoral romances of the previous century; Alexander Hart's *Alexto and Angelica* (1640), a high-flown bookish romance of idealised love and valour; Francis Godwin's imaginary voyage, *The Man in the Moon* (1638); and John Reynolds's curious *The Triumphs of Gods Revenge Against . . . Murther* (1621, 1635), which consists of thirty violent, erotic stories demonstrating what happens to the wicked. Another curious work is Sir Kenelm Digby's autobiographical *Loose Fantasies*, written in 1628, in which his courtship of and marriage to Venetia Stanley is treated as a romance. Written in a euphuistic style (so-called after the style of John Lyly's prose romance *Euphues* (1579, 1580), an artificial or affected way of writing, often elegant and witty), with Greek pseudonyms, and including discussions of free will and determinism, some erotic description, and the language of Platonic idealism, *Loose Fantasies*, which was not intended for publication, shows a contradiction between the idealised pastoral-romance types Digby wanted to portray and his psychological concern with his attraction to a woman who was known previously to have had many lovers.

The best Caroline prose is often highly personal and reflects an emerging scepticism about religious and philosophical truths. Although such scepticism was caused by the religious and scientific controversies of the age, it was part of a larger intellectual movement as represented by Montaigne and the philosopher, mathematician and Christian apologist Pascal (1623–62) in France. At a time when, influenced by Augustine's *Confessions*, Puritans were keeping diaries (to record their spiritual progress from sinfulness through a sense of guilt and awakening despair to examination of conscience, conversion and assurance of election), Sir Thomas Browne's (1605–82) *Religio Medici* ('A Doctor's Religion', 1642) is a revelation of the self by a cosmopolitan scientist. A practising doctor who had studied at the best continental medical schools, Browne also read deeply in the early Church Fathers, Renaissance Neo-Platonism (a synthesis of the doctrines of Plato with those of medieval Christianity, from which came doctrines of love and notions of the relation of spirit and matter reflected in many seventeenth-century poems), Hermeticism (falsely believed to be an ancient Egyptian philosophy learned from the God Thoth; the Hermetical books related to a system of occult philosophies in which correspondences between earthly and heavenly things are studied), number symbolism and the various occult sciences which were popular during the late Renaissance. Where others found conflicting authorities, he moved easily between various opposing claims to truth. Browne's casual, tentative, digressive manner is a means of poeticising possible heresies while remaining a loyal member of the Church of England. He could do this because he was sceptical of reason discovering truth on its own.

Science and philosophy should support religion, as they are the contemplation of God's Creation. Where they seem to challenge it, Browne was willing to submit to the Church. He felt 'there is no Church whose every part so squares unto my conscience, whose articles, constitutions, and customes seeme so consonant unto reason' as the Church of England, but he accepted: 'As there were many Reformers, so likewise many reformations; every Countrey proceeding in a particular way and Method, according as their nationall interest together with their constitution and clime inclined them.' He is similar to Pascal in that his faith is a counter-assertion to the scepticism produced by reason. Lacking Pascal's discipline, and enamoured with curious speculation, Browne, who was only thirty at the time of writing *Religio Medici*, creates a persona of an eccentric, whimsical elder:

> Me thinkes there be not impossibilities enough in Religion for an active faith; . . . I love to lose my selfe in a mystery, to pursue my Reason to an *o altitudo*. 'Tis my solitary recreation to pose my apprehension with those involved aenigma's and riddles of the Trinity, with Incarnation, and Resurrection. I can answer all the objections of Satan, and my rebellious reason, with that odde resolution I learned of *Tertullian, Certum est quia impossible est.* I desire to exercise my faith in the difficultest points, for to credit ordinary and visible objects is not faith, but perswasion.

Pseudodoxia Epidemica ('Common False Opinions', 1646) is an encyclopedic refutation of vulgar errors which are founded in superstition and the authority of the past. Bacon had wished someone would write such a book. Browne is typical of the mid-century in attacking the received wisdom of the past while remaining in love with metaphysics and the occult. *Hydriotaphia, or Urne Buriall* (1658) and *The Garden of Cyrus* (1658) are related meditations on death and life. The former contrasts pagan ritual and the desire for immortality with Christian faith which offers the only answer to the vanity of the world. Its fifth chapter contains magnificent prose in the elevated, polysyllabic, biblical and Latin-influenced, longer sentences of Browne's later writing, in contrast to the more relaxed style of *Religio Medici*. *The Garden of Cyrus* is a study of the number five, 'Artificially, Naturally, Mystically Considered'. Browne's concern is with the analogies between the book of nature and history, the Bible and the spiritual; symbolic correspondences reveal an order which Browne keeps suggesting without assertion. As usual he is tentative, digressive, explorative and untormented. The thought circles, the style is richly textured, playful and paradoxical. The manner is consciously pedantic, quaint and purposefully creates a witty, tolerant, likeable, eccentric personality. Browne's delightful mixture of science, scepticism, religion, wonder and nostalgia for the occult made him famous throughout Europe.

William Chillingworth (1602–44), a godson of Laud, was part of Lord Falkland's Great Tew circle. During an era when many High Anglicans were leaning towards Rome, Chillingworth was converted by a Jesuit priest; a year later in 1631 he returned to Protestantism but did not take the Articles until 1638. During the intervening years he tried dispassionately and sceptically to examine the religious controversies of the age. The results, published as *The Religion of Protestants A Safe Way to Salvation* (1637), laid the foundation for a middle way of rationalism and toleration within the Church of England. In lucid, vigorous, unadorned prose, Chillingworth argued that the Bible contains all that is necessary for salvation, that each person has a private right to interpret scripture, and that although different persons may reach different degrees of truth, God will judge each person by his effort. Sceptical of all authority and prejudice, willing to suspend judgement on matters of controversy, Chillingworth was later highly praised by Tillotson and Locke.

Early travel literature includes *Haklytus Posthumus or Purchas His Pilgrimes* (1625) by Samuel Purchas (1577?– 1626) and the unusual, energetic *Coryats Crudities Hastily Gobled up in Five Moneths Travells* (1611) by Thomas Coryate (1577?–1617). Coryate was satirised in the whimsical *An Epicidum or Mournfull death-Song for Coriats supposed drowning* and *The Eighth Wonder of the World* by John Taylor (1580–1653), the popular Water Poet, who earned his income by taking gentlemen to the theatres along the river. Taylor's doggerel verse and prose pamphlets were numerous. He raised subscriptions to write pamphlets describing his trips around England and abroad; when the subscribers did not pay, he satirised them in verse. James Howell's (1594–1666) *Instructions for Forreine Travell* (1642, enlarged 1650) was perhaps the earliest guide book in English for those intending to tour France, Spain and Italy. Howell commented upon the politics of his age in *Dodona's Grove or the Vocal Forest* (1640, 1650), a political allegory in which trees represent individuals and forests stand for countries. His popular *Epistolae Ho-Elianae* ('Messages') went through four editions between 1645 and 1655, and reveals his broad interests, ranging from manners, current affairs, religion and foreign languages, to wine. Influenced by Seneca, the epistles are pithy essays.

Owen Felltham's (1604?–68) *Resolves: Divine, Morall, Politicall* (1623), a form of essay practised earlier by Joseph Hall, Tuvill and others, was expanded from one hundred to two hundred by the eighth edition of 1661, which also included *A Brief Character of the Low-Countries* (1652) and forty-one poems under the title *Lusoria*. He used brief Senecan sentences and well-turned antithetical phrases: 'No armor can *defend* a fearful heart. It will kill itself, within.' Although Felltham's poems show the influence of Donne in such fine lyrics as 'The Vow-breach', 'The Sympathy' and 'The Amazement', smoother, longer, Caroline cadences are noticeable in 'To Mr Dover on his Cotswold Games' and 'When, Dearest, I but think of thee' (which was for many years considered one of Suckling's better poems).

7
Civil War and Interregnum literature

I Disillusionment, mysticism and rationalism

THE 1640s and 50s were an unusually rich and varied era of English poetry. At first the Cavalier lyrics of Herrick and Lovelace reflected public events through political allusions, but as the war brought political chaos, the destruction of the Church and the ruin of many families, both Royalists and moderates retired to the countryside and sought solace in writing satires, translations and religious verse. Their lyrics and pastorals are often charming but private, guarded and obscure; it is sometimes difficult to be certain whether the subject of a poem is love, King, Church or God. The epistle, ode and other recently revived classical genres took on political and religious significances as Royalists obliquely referred to the Interregnum as a 'winter' requiring stoical, Horatian endurance. Other new directions in poetry included an exploration of the bizarre and playful as a literary manner. While Benlowes and others delighted in fanciful, humorous conceits and obscure, pedantic allusions, Cleveland transformed Ovidian word play and metaphysical wit into a technique of satire. The middle years, rather than the early decades of the century, are the richest period of wit writing, although sometimes the results are trivial and bizarre.

The banning of Anglican church services, the increasing knowledge of books of Christian and other mysticisms, along with the wild expectations created by the belief that the revolutionary political situation was connected with the Apocalypse, probably influenced the evolution of the meditative religious lyric into the mystical and contemplative. Augustine's *Confessions* were a seminal influence and the

Augustinian contemplative mystical tradition, especially as represented by Bonaventura, cast a spell on the poets of the mid-century who saw the natural world as symbols that lead the mind towards illumination and communion with God. Many poets wrote in an 'enthusiastic' manner, mixing metaphysical wit and mysticism with a new striving for the sublime. While the blending and attenuation of earlier styles resulted in poetry reaching new, Baroque heights of complexity, the sermons of Jeremy Taylor are the final blossoming of witty, metaphysical, Senecan, Latinate prose.

If public events, especially the exile of the Court, contributed to the eventual displacement of the love lyric, Neo-Classicism continued its steady development towards the dominant position it would hold after the Restoration. Although the reaction against enthusiastic, inspired, extremely subjective writing partly resulted from the turmoil caused by the Civil War, its main source was the new rational view of nature and behaviour which developed alongside the increased understanding of modern science. The clear, logical prose of Thomas Hobbes and the demand by Wilkins and others associated with science that preaching be reformed are part of a new sensibility also reflected in Cowley's poetry and perhaps even in the generalised, abstract vocabulary of such mystical poets as Benlowes and Henry More. The now surprising association between rationalism and Neo-Classicism can also be seen in France where Cartesian writers and critics formulated from the practice of the ancients rigid Neo-Classical rules to ensure clarity and regularity in contrast to fanciful *précieux* poetry and romances. If the religious literature of the Interregnum was the last expression of the Christian sacramental vision of the world, writing from the mid-1650s onwards became a reflection of a concern with order, clarity and rationality. The Interregnum also saw innumerable pamphlets and books that offered radical, new, often modern theories of government, morals and society.

II From Cavalier to mystical poetry: Herrick and Lovelace to Marvell and Vaughan

As was the practice of the time, Jonson's friend the clergyman Robert Herrick (1591–1674) included both secular poems, *Hesperides*, and 'pious pieces', *Noble Numbers*, in the same book (1648). Published during a time when Charles I was the prisoner of Parliament, *Hesperides* associates classical and Hebraic ceremonies with English festivals and Anglican ritual. Concerned with love, beauty and the brevity of youth, the poetry relates the past to the present in a celebration of a universal order now threatened by the Puritans. Herrick's careful craftsmanship, imitations of Roman verse, epigrams, epistles, odes, Horatian poses, delight in artifice, playfulness and good-humoured tolerance are affirmations of a culture which should include classical and Christian, Court and country.

The poems in *Hesperides* are arranged in a significant pattern. After 'The argument of his Book' ('I sing of *May-poles . . . Youth . . . Love . . .* cleanly-*Wantonnesse . . . Times trans-shifting . . . Fairie-King . . . Heaven*, and hope to have it after all'), there follow seven more poems about 'his Booke'. Sprinkled throughout the book there are many poems treating of art and literature. Herrick praises Mildmay Fane, John Denham, John Hall, John Selden, William Alabaster and 'Saint Ben' Jonson to whom six poems are given. Other poems refer to classic writers. The final eight poems in *Hesperides* treat of Herrick as an author ('and maidens set / Upon my curles the *Mirtle Coronet*'). 'The pillar of Fame', visually shaped to resemble a pillar, speaks of the eternity and fame provided by art: 'Tho Kingdoms fal, / This pillar never shall'. A similar significant pattern is noticeable in *Noble Numbers*, which begins with 'His Confession' ('those Lines, pen'd by my wanton Wit, / Treble the number of these good I've writ'), 'His Prayer for Absolution' ('For Those my unbaptized Rhimes') and concludes with poems on the Passion and entombment, including the visually cross-shaped 'His Anthem', in which Herrick refers to the devotional purposes of his verse.

'To the Virgins, to make much of Time' begins with 'Gather ye Rose-buds while ye may' and urges 'be not coy', but its message is 'while ye may, goe marry'. Although not all of the pastoral love lyrics express 'cleanly-*Wantonnesse*', their apparent hedonism is usually a modification of civilised artifice. Herrick praises 'Delight in Disorder', but the erotic is the effect of a 'wilde civility' which 'Doe more bewitch me, then when Art / Is too precise in every part'. When Corinna is told it is a 'shame', 'sin', and 'profanation' to delay 'going a Maying', the significance may not be Christian morality despite the reference to 'plighted Troth', but it would hardly matter as the natural world is a temple where 'all the Birds have Mattens seyd, / And sung their thankfull Hymnes'. Herrick does not follow early Donne in making a religion of love; religious analogies contribute towards the ideal pastoral world formed by art. In 'A Hymne to the Muses' Herrick asks for inspiration:

> Then I'le your Altars strew
> With Roses sweet and new;
> And ever live a true
> Acknowledger of you.

An Anglican Royalist, Herrick mocks duty to Cromwell ('Touch not the Tyrant; Let the Gods alone / To strike him dead, that but usurps a Throne') and uses in 'Farewell Frost' the Royalist analogy of winter to the Civil War. While the Interregnum was a great period for the pastoral lyric, Herrick's reputation as a pastoral poet is rather ironic. Believing in manners, decorum, artifice and classical ideals, in 'To *Dean-bourn*, a rude River in *Devon*', he speaks of 'A people currish; churlish as the seas; / And rude (almost) as rudest Salvages'; in 'Discontents in *Devon*', he complains of being 'sad, / In this dull *Devon-shire*', but admits that 'I ne'r invented such / Ennobled numbers for the Presse, / Then where I loath'd so much'.

Often called the handsomest man at Court, Richard Lovelace (1618–57) fought for the King against the Scots, was imprisoned in 1642 for presenting the Royalist Kentish petition to Parliament, fled to Holland and France, returned to England only to be imprisoned during 1648–9 and die impoverished in obscurity. *Lucasta: Epodes, Odes and Sonnets* (1649) was followed by *Lucasta: Posthume Poems* (1659). No other writer of the period so perfectly expresses the Cavalier code of honour, loyalty and love, or appears so personally disillusioned by the disintegration of traditional values with the Civil War and Parliament's victory. Often sombre in tone and sometimes obscure in syntax and allusion, Lovelace's poetry mixes Petrarchism, metaphysical wit and the classicism of Jonson with the longer cadences and strikingly articulated phrases of Carew.

Many of the best poems reflect the consequences of the Civil War. 'The Grasse-hopper' begins as another loose Caroline translation of Anacreon's poem, similar to Stanley's or Cowley's, but changes direction with 'Poore verdant foole! and now green Ice'. The call to drink and be merry is a sombre challenge to the times; the insect's past joys 'Bid us lay in 'gainst Winter, Raine, and poize / Their flouds, with an o'reflowing glasse'. Unexpectedly Lovelace shifts the address from the grasshopper to his friend Charles Cotton the elder, the father of the poet Charles Cotton, and transforms Jonsonian praise of friendship and conviviality to a defiant celebration of the King and the Christian festivals that had recently been outlawed by Parliament: 'he hath his Crowne againe!' Jonson's stoicism was transformed by the defeated Royalists into a withdrawal into the self and friendship: 'Thus richer then untempted Kings are we, / That asking nothing, nothing need'.

'To Althea, From Prison', in its fusion of Horatian imperviousness to fate with Royalist sentiments and the Caroline love lyric, is an example of the Cavalier spirit at its best:

> Stone Walls doe not a Prison make,
> Nor Iron bars a Cage;
> Mindes innocent and quiet take
> That for an Hermitage;
> If I have freedome in my Love,
> And in my soule am free;
> Angeles alone that sore above,
> Injoy such Liberty.

The epigrammatic conciseness, song rhythms, striking cadences, stanzaic paragraphing of thoughts, clear construction of argument and lightly deployed 'religion of love' imagery of 'To Lucasta, Going to the Warres' permits the witty juxtapositions of

> True; a new Mistresse now I chase,
> The first Foe in the Field;
> And with a stronger Faith imbrace
> A Sword, a Horse, a Shield

and their resolution:

> I could not love thee (Deare) so much,
> Lov'd I not Honour more.

'To Lucasta. From Prison' shows, however, Lovelace's sense of a world in disorder:

> I would love a *Parliament*
>   As a maine Prop from Heav'n sent;
> But ah! Who's he that would be wedded
>   To th' fairest body that's beheaded?

'The Ant', 'The Snayl', 'Another', 'The Falcon' and 'A Fly caught in a Cobweb' are unusual emblematic poems which obliquely, sometimes puzzlingly, refer to political events and the uncertainty of life, while offering a version of self-centredness which is far from classic in its disillusionment. 'The Snayl' is 'Wise Emblem of our Politick World . . . within thine own self curl'd'.

Forced to retire from public affairs a small group of Royalists, linked by kinship and friendship, provided many of the translators and poets of the Interregnum. Thomas Stanley's (1625–78) relatives included George Sandys, Richard Lovelace, the minor poet William Hammond (1614–?), and Sir Edward Sherburne (1616–1702), a Catholic who lived with Stanley during part of the Interregnum and whose *Poems and Translations* (1651) Stanley influenced. They were attracted to the witty, artificial conceits which made Marino, the Italian master of 'preciosity', one of the favourite poets of the mid-century. Stanley's friend, the essayist and educational reformer John Hall (1627–56), wrote 'A Satire' in run-on iambic couplets which in their fantasy, learning and unusual rhymes could be mistaken for Cleveland. He is at his best in such amused, fantastic lyrics as 'The Call', 'An Epicurean Ode' and 'The Antipathy'. The mid-seventeenth century may be the only time when a poet could write to his university tutor: 'And as we go, / We'll mix these atoms that crawl to and fro'; and include in the same book of *Poems* (1647): 'Yet do the lazy snails no less / The greatness of our Lord confess'. Hall translated *Dionysius Longinus of the Height of Eloquence* (1652), the first English version of what was to become an influence on later notions of the sublime. In keeping with his age Hall thinks of the sublime as a highly rhetorical style rather than as great thoughts in simple words, the interpretation which later became popular after the publication of Boileau's translation of Longinus into French as *Traité du sublime* (1674). Like many others who believed in order, Hall urged Cromwell, in *The True Cavalier Examined* (1656), to become King.

Stanley was a careful craftsman who took over the gestures, ideas and conceits of Donne, Carew, Suckling and various European poets and created intelligent variations on the poetry of his own and the preceding age. Working within the tradition of Donne's logical development of an argument as modified by Carew's more elevated and restricted range of voice, Stanley's amatory verse makes use of the metaphysical conceit while avoiding the harshness and unruliness of the late Jacobean strong line. Influenced by his classical learning, concerned for the harmony of sound and metre, experimental in the use of Latinate syntactical inversions and precisely limited witty analogies, Stanley illustrates later developments of the metaphysical style parallel to the Neo-Classicism of Waller and Denham. While he created a variety of stanzaic forms, of which 'The Exequies' is a remarkable instance, his couplets anticipate Restoration wit. He sometimes had difficulty in fitting his meaning into his stanzas and the syntax can be ambiguous or obscure. The Caroline abandonment of Jacobean direct, dramatic speech patterns and the concern to achieve a regular metre, created hurdles over which Stanley sometimes tripped. A Royalist, his *Psalterium Carolinum* ('A Caroline Psaltery', 1656), a verse adaptation of John Gauden's *Eikon Basilike* ('A Royal Image'), was set to music by John Wilson.

Mildmay Fane, Earl of Westmorland (1602—66) fought for Charles I, was imprisoned and returned to his estate where, like many Anglican Royalists, he celebrated 'A Happy Life' in the countryside and meditated upon 'nature's book'. In *Otia Sacra* ('Sacred Peace', 1648), which includes engraved emblems and patterned poems, 'My Country Audit' speaks of his 'Happy retreat, wherein / I may cast up my reck'nings, audit sin'. Based on Herbert's 'Redemption', the poem recalls the distinction between the old and the new covenant to show 'the Landlord's grace / Full of compassion to my drooping case'. Although he gestures towards mystical contemplation, Fane is more concerned with salvation through 'conquering th' rebellions of sense'. The life of retirement provides an opportunity for self-examination, meditation and increase of grace. Fane also wrote some plays and masques for private performances, including *De Pugna Animi* ('The Fight of the Soul', 1650), in which Mind eventually wins over the disorderly five Senses. A relative of Lord Fairfax, Fane in his poetry often anticipates the themes, phrases and conventions of Marvell's verse.

Although Andrew Marvell (1621–78) began writing Caroline pastoral love lyrics in the 1640s to 'Clora' and 'Clorinda', the poems for which he is famous probably belong to the period 1649–53 and within smaller forms have the Baroque complexity characteristic of Crashaw's and Milton's poetry. They blend metaphysical wit, Caroline grace, classical parallels and Spenserian pastoral with the new contemplative mode and show a strong awareness of poetic genre:

> D.   These once had been enticing things,
>   *Clorinda*, Pastures, Caves and Springs.
> C.   And what late change?
> D.   The other day
>   *Pan* met me.
> C.   What did great *Pan* say?
> D.   Words that transcend poor Shepherds skill,
>   But He ere since my Songs does fill:
>   And his Name swells my slender Oate.

'A Dialogue between the Resolved Soul and Created Pleasure' begins with an address to the soul, reminding it of its nature ('Now, if thou bee'st that thing Divine, / In this day's Combat let it shine'). In the dialogue which follows, the soul firmly resists the temptations of the five senses and then is encouraged by a chorus to 'persevere' in its subsequent combat against the worldly temptations of beauty, riches, glory and knowledge, before the chorus returns to sing the soul's triumph. The material for a long medieval or Renaissance allegorical debate is compressed into a richly varied, charming short poem which implies more than it says. A similar gracefulness blended with more serious tones can be heard in such apparently secular lyrics as 'Bermudas', 'The Picture of Little T. C.', the four Mower poems and 'The Nymph Complaining for the Death of Her Fawn': 'There is not such another in / The World, to offer for their Sin'.

'On a Drop of Dew', probably influenced by Hawkins's emblem book *Partheneia Sacra*, blends the emblematic with Herbert's inventive stanzaic patterns and biblical typology into a meditation on the relationship between the natural world, the divine image within the soul, and the Bible as history, revelation and prophecy. The poem economically alludes to stages of the Augustinian mode of contemplation ('remembering', 'shuns', 'recollecting', 'does upwards bend') and the concluding four lines refer to the biblical manna symbolic of Christ's birth and sacrifice. The restlessness of a world in process expressed by the continually varied line lengths and rhymes of the first half of the poem moves towards resolution in the increasingly regular next sixteen lines, until the two concluding couplets proclaim 'the Glories of th' Almighty Sun'.

'The Garden' similarly moves from meditation upon the book of nature to recollection ('Withdraws into its happiness') and the higher stages of contemplation:

> What wond'rous Life in this I lead!
> Ripe Apples drop about my head;
> The Luscious Clusters of the Vine
> Upon my Mouth do crush their Wine;
> The Nectaren, and curious Peach,
> Into my hands themselves do reach;
> Stumbling on Melons, as I pass,
> Insnar'd with Flow'rs, I fall on Grass.
>
> Mean while the Mind, from pleasure less,
> Withdraws into its happiness:
> The Mind, that Ocean where each kind
> Does streight its own resemblance find;
> Yet it creates, transcending these,
> Far other Worlds, and other Seas;
> Annihilating all that's made
> To a green Thought in a green Shade.

> Here at the Fountains sliding foot,
> Or at some Fruit-trees mossy root,
> Casting the Bodies Vest aside,
> My Soul into the boughs does glide:
> There like a Bird it sits, and sings,
> Then whets, and combs its silver Wings;
> And, till prepar'd for longer flight,
> Waves in its Plumes the various Light.

In many of Marvell's best poems, probably written when he was tutor to Fairfax's daughter, allusions, echoes, images, parodies and ironies imply possible radically different significances from what is being literally said. Often, as in the Spenserian pastoral, there is a suggestion of a religious or political meaning. In *Musicks Empire* Marvell puns: 'First was the World as one great Cymbal made'. Even the persuasive argument to make the most of time in 'To His Coy Mistress' has its religious ironies:

> But at my back I alwaies hear
> Times winged Charriot hurrying near:
> And yonder all before us lye
> Desarts of vast Eternity.
> Thy Beauty shall no more be found;
> Nor, in thy marble Vault, shall sound
> My ecchoing Song: then Worms shall try
> That long preserv'd Virginity:
> And your quaint Honour turn to dust;
> And into ashes all my Lust.

In 'Upon Appleton House' Marvell points to his technique, although teasingly and playfully. A survey of the history of the house and of the Fairfaxes, contrasting its use by the family to its previous misuse as a convent, the orderly farming of its lands with the contemporary Civil War, and Fairfax's retirement with the ambitions of others, the poem is filled with various ingenious perspectives:

> No Scene that turns with Engines strange
> Does oftner then these Meadows change.
> For when the Sun the Grass hath vext,
> The tawny Mowers enter next;
> Who seem like *Israelites* to be,
> Walking on foot through a green Sea.
> To them the Grassy Deeps divide,
> And crowd a Lane to either Side.

The playful description of the seasonal agricultural activities of the Fairfax estate reflects, as a parody, both the chaos of contemporary England and the biblical typology which Cromwell, the Parliamentarians and the New Model Army applied to themselves. In a time of absurd paradoxes, retirement to Appleton House is seen as analogous to Noah's ark:

> But I, retiring from the Flood,
> Take Sanctuary in the Wood,
> And, while it lasts, my self imbark
> In this yet green, yet growing Ark;
> Where the first Carpenter might best
> Fit Timber for his Keel have prest.
> And where all Creatures might have shares,
> Although in Armies, not in Paires.

One of the many themes is the use of retirement for study and contemplation.

The ironies and ambiguities of Marvell's 'An Horatian Ode upon Cromwell's Return from Ireland' (July 1650?) possibly reflect Fairfax's retirement as head of the Parliamentary Army after he disagreed with Cromwell's execution of Charles I and plan to invade Scotland. The unusual tone of the poem, objective yet capable of being seen as either satiric or laudatory, mixes Horace's flat, understated, ambiguous irony with the witty, extravagant, satirical praise of Lucan's *Pharsalia*. Also Horatian is the building of a poem from juxtapositions of opposites:

> 'Tis Madness to resist or blame
> The force of angry Heavens flame:
> And, if we would speak true,
> Much to the Man is due.

The ambivalences created by the many contrasts are further complicated by sentences which may be read in contrary ways: 'Nor yet grown stiffer with Command, / But still in the *Republick's* hand'.

The First Anniversary of the Government under His Highness the Lord Protector (1655), written after Marvell had become close to Milton and Cromwell's circle, is a panegyrical defence of the dissolution of the 'Barebones' Parliament, with its millenarian radical fantasies, and the establishment of the Protectorate. Characterised by reasoning in verse, compressed statement, and use of analogies in analytical thought, *The First Anniversary* is an example of the metaphysical style moving towards an Augustan clarity. The classical and biblical analogies and the sustained similes heighten the tone and elevate the events. The active, emphatic verse evokes in its sound and movement the energy and achievement of Cromwell as someone who has created a new order and as, it is suggested, a providential force.

Similar to many Royalist Anglicans, Henry Vaughan (1621–95) was transformed by the Civil War from a minor Caroline Son of Ben to a poet of retirement and mystical contemplation. *Poems, with the tenth Satyre of Juvenal* (1646) begins with praise of Jonson and Randolph, some songs to 'Amoret', and offers examples of the plain evolving into the Cavalier style. *Olor Iscanua* ('Swan of Usk', assembled but not published in 1647) includes verse translations of Ovid, the Roman philosopher Boethius (*c*.475–524), Casimirus (a Polish Jesuit whose mystical poems of retirement were an influence on the period), several prose translations and elegies on dead Royalist friends. Largely Jonsonian in style there are the usual friendship and retirement themes common to Royalist verse of the time.

A major poet suddenly appeared in *Silex Scintillans* ('sparkling flint', Part I, 1650; Part II, 1655). Although inspired by Herbert (the emblem of a stony heart on Vaughan's title page uses the same symbolism as Herbert's 'The Altar') to write 'private Ejaculations' (the subtitle of *The Temple*, suggesting the Protestant spiritual drama of desiring election), Vaughan's poems are different in their longing for transcendence, their sacramental vision of nature and their memories of an edenic 'home'. Influenced by the mysticism of the mid-century, including Neo-Platonism and hermeticism, but especially by St Augustine's *Confessions*, with its mixture of contemplation and self-analysis, Vaughan's poems also differ from Herbert's in their narrative allegories, looser structure and almost literal use of biblical phrases, images, types and symbols. Many of his symbols are common to the emblem books. While both Herbert and Vaughan were Calvinistic Anglicans, concerned to show the soul's anxieties in the experience of conversion and the desire for election, Herbert's verse assumes the Church as the body of true believers, while Vaughan's poems, written after Parliament had forbidden Anglican worship, are private and seek transcendence in the natural world and in silence. Although his sensibility is unlike Marvell's, there is a similar use of the pastoral for sacred allegory and contemplation of the natural world as a step in the soul's ascent towards the divine.

The difference between Herbert and Vaughan can be seen by comparing the former's 'Redemption' with the latter's 'Regeneration' (although Herbert's 'The Collar' is Vaughan's actual model). 'Redemption' is a tight sonnet using a legal metaphor and is an explicit allegory of the old and new law. 'Regeneration' is five times the length and is based on the Augustinian concept that once we were happy, but

> surly winds
> Blasted my infant buds, and sinne
> Like Clouds ecclips'd my mind.

Then follow a series of emblematic scenes in which, although the speaker recognises his lack of merit, he is shown examples of grace. Seeking rational explanations, he can find no cause:

> But while I listning sought
> My mind to ease
> By knowing where 'twas, or where not,
> It whisper'd; *Where I please*.

> Lord, then said I, *On me one breath,*
> *And let me dye before my death!*

> Cant. Cap. 5 ver. 17.

> *Arise O North, and come thou South-wind, and blow*
> *upon my garden, that the spices thereof may flow out.*

Many of Vaughan's poems recapitulate or are related to 'Regeneration'. 'The Retreate' is based on Augustine's uncertainty whether our original notions of happiness derive from childhood or are racial and collective:

> Happy those early dayes! when I
> Shin'd in my Angell-infancy.
> Before I understood this place
> Appointed for my second race,
> Or taught my soul to fancy ought
> But a white, Celestiall thought.

The soul yearns 'to travell back' to its original vision, which it can regain only after death:

> But (ah!) my soul with too much stay
> Is drunk, and staggers in the way.
> Some men a forward motion love,
> But I by backward steps would move,
> And when this dust falls to the urn
> In that state I came return.

In 'Rom. Cap. 8 ver. 19' the natural world waits and groans for the Revelation, but 'I am sadly loose and stray'; Vaughan petitions God, 'O let not me do less! shall they / Watch, while I sleep, or play?' In the linked sequence this is followed by 'The Relapse' ('I had slipt / Almost to hell') and 'The Resolve' ('A longer stay / Is but excus'd neglect'). 'The World':

> I Saw Eternity the other night
> Like a great *Ring* of pure and endless light,
>   All calm, as it was bright,
> And round beneath it, Time in hours, days, years
>   Driv'n by the spheres
> Like a vast shadow mov'd, In which the world
>   And all her train were hurl'd.

is followed by 'The Mutinie' ('weary of this same Clay, and straw') and 'The Constellation':

> Fair, order'd lights (whose motion without noise
>   Resembles those true Joys
> Whose spring is on that hil where you do grow
>   And we here tast sometimes below).

Filled with feelings of misery, sinfulness and unholy rebellion, the poems are also alive with the drama of grace; there is both the personal urgency and the historical expectation of renewal. Vaughan longs for and awaits the soul's return to its spiritual home. The recurring images of light, mists, veils, night, day, stars, water, darkness, Eden, time and eternity create a feeling of a mind on the verge of revelation; at times Vaughan's vision is similar to that of the early Christian mystics. While accepting Reformation theology of man's helplessness without grace, Vaughan has the mystics' desire to ascend directly to a world of purity, light, peace and oneness.

If Edward Benlowes's (1602–76) *Theophila* ('Dear to the Gods', 1652) were more readable, it might well serve as an introduction to the literature of Anglican mysticism and contemplation of nature during the Civil War and Interregnum. Written in thirteen cantos, each of one hundred stanzas, mostly of a curious mono-rhymed triplet of ten, eight and twelve syllables, packed with archaisms, odd words, coinages, bizarre rhymes, syntactical contortions and fantastic conceits, it treats in nine cantos of the ascent of the soul into mystical communion, followed by two cantos on the vanity of the world and two cantos on 'The Sweetness of Retirement'. *Theophila* appears to be directly inspired by Bonaventura's mysticism and, in the final two cantos, by G. Hills's influential translation of the Latin *Odes* (1646) of the Polish Jesuit Casimirus. The ecstatic enthusiasm of *Theophila* treats of the mind's road to God in a style which draws upon all kinds of 'wit' writing while Benlowes's abstract, conceptual diction illustrates how the poetry of the mid-century was moving towards Restoration generalisations:

> Praise best doth Inexpressibles express:
> Soul, 'th Architect of wonders bless;
> Whose all-creating Word embirth'd a nothingness.

By contrast, Patrick Cary's (1624–57) thirteen religious poems, each prefaced by a hand-drawn emblem, reflect slightly older meditative practices in their structure; they move from a proposed subject to an examination or analysis, to a final colloquy, resolution or prayer. In the Ignatian manner, Cary imagines the scene before his eyes. Using 'common, cleare, and pure' diction, with consciously commonplace phrases, but inventive in his stanzaic forms and varied line lengths and rhyme schemes, he continues the tradition of Herbert and Quarles. The thirteen poems form a sequence beginning with 'Worldly Designes, Feares, Hopes, farwell!' to the 'Dies Irae'. His twenty-three 'Triviall Ballades', composed to popular tunes, range from facile lover's complaints to satires on Cromwell's Protectorate.

III From bizarre wit towards a rational poetry: Cleveland to Cowley

While the Interregnum resulted in many authors turning to religious verse, John Cleveland's (1613–58) poetry illustrates tendencies to use metaphysical wit both for sheer playfulness and for a new kind of topical satire. Learned, playful, with a university don's self-mockery in the display of obscure knowledge and uncommon words, Cleveland continues the tradition of university wit also exemplified by Corbett and Burton; he is delightfully humorous when carrying to ingenious extremes well-known poetic topics and styles or absurdities of the time. A poetic convention was the comparison of a mistress waking in the morning to the rising sun and the hyperbolic compliment of the natural world paying homage to her; in 'Upon Phillis walking in a morning' the convention is parodied by grotesque descriptions of nature:

> The Plants whose luxurie was lopt,
> Or age with crutches underpropt;
> Whose wooden carkases were grown
> To be but coffins of their owne;
> Revive, and at her generall dole
> Each receives his antient soule.

An oath was required in 1640 to be taken by all clergy from archbishops to 'archdeacons,&c.', approving the doctrine and government of the Church; Cleveland wrote 'A Dialogue between two Zealots' in which '&c' comically recurs — it is absurdly unacceptable to the religious fanatics and an absurdity in itself. Such double-edged humour is Cleveland's satiric manner.

As the Civil War progressed, Cleveland's sense of the absurd developed into mockery of the realities of his own Royalist side in contrast to its ideals; he could not write panegyric without it becoming satiric. His satiric sense when turned against the Scots and Parliament soon made him the favourite Royalist writer of the age. Although his topical allusions are often tedious and obscure, in such poems as 'The Mixt Assembly' and 'On the Archbishop of Canterbury' Cleveland created a style which caught the disorder and chaos of the age: 'There is no Church, Religion is growne / From much of late, that shee's encreast to none'. Elizabethan and Jacobean satire was often rough rhythmically, obscure in expression, and had little shape, unity or moral coherence. Cleveland gave this disorder a purpose. He understood that an unrelated sequence of closed couplets and poor rhymes create comic discontinuity and can express a society in fragmentation. The early poems are relaxed and tolerant; the later poems are bitter and more obscure, as was befitting the change in political climate during the 1640s.

A physician, John Collop (1625—post-1676) wrote such comic poems as 'Against Phlebotomy to a Leech' and 'For Phlebotomy'. Always on the alert to attack ignorance and eccentricities in 'On the Astrologicall quack', 'Oglio of quacks', 'A Piss-pot Prophet' and 'The fugitive Chymick', he claimed to favour religious toleration, but attacked 'The Presbyter', 'Enthusiasticks' and Catholics, while praising Laud for strengthening church ceremonies and discipline. He wrote poems 'On Monocula, A one ey'd Lady', 'To Dionysia the plump Lady', 'On a Crooked Lady' and other tongue-in-cheek exercises. Collop's literary manner is as wilful and inconsistent as his opinions; like Cleveland he jumps from conceit to conceit. His religious lyrics, however, are surprisingly skilful in their invention, stanzaic variety, local effects ('I, I, ah I thee Lord betraid!'), typological puns ('Thy blood sweet *Jesu*'s a Red-sea') and paradoxical rhetoric ('I'le wash thee Lord, till I be clean'). If Collop's secular verse shows ways in which the metaphysical strong line had become comical displays of wit by the 1650s, his religious lyrics suggest that Herbert's revitalisation of the Jacobean lyric for religious self-analysis remained useful.

The writings of William Chamberlayne (1619—89), author of the 14,000 line *Pharonnida: A Heroick Poem* (1659) and *England's Jubilee* (1660) on the restoration of Charles II, are illustrative of the curious, long, involved sentences, elaborate grammatical constructions, purposefully haphazard syntax, odd rhymes, contorted phrases and forced elisions of syllables which became popular during the Interregnum.

Although *Pharonnida* is seemingly tossed together from previous romances without the author bothering to keep his characters and settings coherent from canto to canto, Chamberlayne's word coinages and long sentences are purposefully absurd, close in spirit to Cleveland's bizarre verbal wit. He subverts the couplet with his run-on sentences, opposition of syntax and line, descriptions within descriptions, and use of adverbs, prepositions and conjunctions in rhymes. The effect is confusion, a conscious anti-order.

The poetry of Abraham Cowley (1618—67) is transitional in the evolution of seventeenth-century taste from the short personal lyric characterised by ingenious conceits to longer public forms in which concise analogies are illustrative. This movement from a metaphysical towards a classical style already noticeable in the Caroline period was quickened by the reaction during the 1650s to the political chaos when the disillusioned of both sides of the Civil War became distrustful of all signs of excess and subjectivity and turned to experimental science as a neutral intellectual activity. Although the development of his poetry reflects the change from private metaphysical to public Neo-Classical verse, Cowley, unlike Waller, never mastered the new style. He had the humorous tone often expected of public verse and contributed to the domestication of the Pindaric ode (called after Pindar (518—438 BC) the Greek lyric poet) in England, but remained a writer of witty Interregnum conceits.

The Mistress (1647) shows his limitations; exercises in the Petrarchan tradition (of a series of linked love lyrics with an implied narrative) as it evolved over centuries, the poetry is more playful than serious. Although the eighty-three lyrics tell a vague story of yearning love and its eventual success, the narrative is an excuse to write witty, often self-mocking poems. They are charming exercises by a sceptic in an older genre. The opening 'Request' sets the tone:

> I'Have often wisht to love; what shall I do?
>   Me still the *cruel Boy* does *spare*;
>   And I a double task must bear,
> First to woo *him*, and then a *Mistress* too.
>   Come at last and strike for shame;
>   If thou art any thing besides a *name*.
>   I'le think Thee else no *God* to be;
> But *Poets* rather *Gods*, who first *created Thee*.

Poems (1656) contain *Miscellanies, Pindarique Odes* and *Davideis*. The *Miscellanies* include excellent translations, in irregularly stressed octosyllabic couplets, of the Greek lyric poet Anacreon (*c*. 570–*c*. 480 BC). Cowley's translations of the Greek poet compare favourably with Thomas Stanley's more literal versions; he neatly catches the modulations in tone, the carelessness, and the enjoyment of the present moment. A similar recasting can be seen in the *Pindarique Odes*, where Cowley modulates between various tones and line lengths to catch the soaring, changing 'furor poeticus' of his source. The imitations were printed with explanatory notes and the relevant passages of Greek for comparison. The notes to 'The Resurrection' show at what Cowley supposedly was aiming: 'This Ode is truly *Pindarical*, falling from one thing into another, after his *Enthusiastical manner*'. Each of the odes begins well, but Cowley sometimes has trouble, as in 'To Mr Hobs' (a friend and influence), in keeping up the high style and invention of topics after a few stanzas. The ode 'Of Wit' is an instance of the new rationalism influencing sensibility; Cowley uses the concise illustrative analogies which were replacing the extreme ingenuity of the early Baroque:

> In a true piece of *Wit* all things must be,
>   Yet all things there *agree*.
> As in the *Ark*, joyn'd without force or strife,
> All *Creatures* dwelt; all *Creatures* that had *Life*.
>   Or as the *Primitive Forms* of all
>   (If we compare great things with small)
> Which without *Discord* or *Confusion* lie,
> In that strange *Mirror* of the *Deitie*.

Davideis, an attempt to write a Christian epic, was left unfinished with only four of the twelve projected books completed. Often imitated by Milton it avoids the pagan machinery of previous epics, but Samuel Johnson's criticism of it as 'narrative spangled with conceits' summarises its faults.

The later poetry includes *Upon His Majesties Restoration and Return* (1660), 'Ode. Upon Dr Harvey', 'The Complaint', 'Hymn. To light' and 'To the Royal Society'. Written in iambics, but with long and short lines in a variety of stanzaic shapes, the odes provided Dryden and others with an alternative to the rigid structure of the heroic couplet and such genres as the panegyric and elegy. Although the sense of humour and tendency to digress for a witty analogy remained, Cowley's post-Restoration style is more poised and Horatian.

Cowley's prose includes *A Proposition for the Advancement of Experimental Philosophy* (1661) and *Several Discourses by way of Essays* (first published in *The Works of Mr Abraham Cowley*, 1668, edited by Thomas Sprat). Informal, playful, full of learning, concerned with himself in the manner of Montaigne, Cowley writes in a plain, clear style upon such topics as liberty, solitude, life in the country, gardens, greatness, avarice and procrastination. The essays are easy reading, occasionally anecdotal, often refer to Cowley's own experience, offer an Horatian ideal of retirement to the country, and are followed by excellent translations of Latin authors.

Katherine Philips (1632—64), 'the matchless Orinda', continued the Caroline cult of Platonic love into the 1650s and early years of the Restoration. 'Love' is 'the being and the harmony of things'. Retirement, life in the country and self-centred contentment among a circle of like-minded friends, common themes of the Cavalier 'winter', are treated without originality: 'Kings may be slaves by their own passions hurl'd, / But who commands himself commands the World'. Metaphysical argument and wit is simplified, fused with Jonsonian discrimination and disdain, and set to the alternating four and three stressed lines of Caroline song. Although Katherine Philips imitates Carew and Lovelace, her poetry reflects the new rationalism. There are echoes of Hobbesian psychology and of deism and natural religion in her more philosophical poems. In 'Against Pleasure' the libertine gestures of Suckling are in the process of transformation to the Hobbesian scepticism of Rochester:

> There's no such thing as Pleasure here,
>   'Tis all a perfect cheat,
> Which does but shine and disappear,
>   Whose charm is but deceit:
> The empty bribe of yielding souls,
> Which first betrays, and then controls.

1. Garden of Plenty. Design for triumphal arch in Cheapside for Royal Entry of James I into London, 1604. Drawn by chief architect Stephen Harrison; texts for the pageant written by Thomas Dekker and Ben Jonson.

2. Oberon's Palace. Inigo Jones's design for scene ii of Jonson's *The Masque of Oberon* (1611).

3. Preaching at St Paul's Cross. Unknown Jacobean artist (*c.* 1616).

4 b. A Dwarf Postillion from Hell. Costume design by Inigo Jones for an antimasque to Jonson's *Chloridia* (1631).

4 a. Gilt Jacobean wine-cup (1616—17).

5. Five Children of Charles I, painted by Antony Van Dyck, 1638.

6. Emblematic title page to Henry Vaughan's *Silex Scintillans,* 1650. Within the heart a face can be seen.

7. Portrait of Oliver Cromwell's daughter Bridget, attributed to Sir Peter Lely.

8. Nell Gwyn, actress and mistress of Charles II, painted by Sir Peter Lely.

9. Gilt Restoration Cup and Cover (1669).

10. From Act V of Settle's *The Empress of Morocco* (1673), the first play to be published with illustrations of its scenes.

11. *An Owl Mocked by Small Birds*, painted by Francis Barlow, 1673.

12 b. St Paul's Cathedral (1695–1710), also restored by Wren.

12 a. St Laurence Jewry (1671–77), one of the churches restored by Christopher Wren after the Great Fire.

13. Abingdon Town House (1680), built and probably designed by Christopher Kempster, a mason in Wren's circle of workmen.

14. Portrait of Sir Christopher Wren by Sir Godfrey Kneller.

15. Wood carvings by Grinling Gibbons and portrait of Old Sir John Brownlow in Belton House, Lincs.

16. Belton House by Henry Bug (1695). Belton House was built by the mason William Stanton, following Roger Pratt's (1620–84) design for Clarendon House (1667). Its classical symmetry is closer to Jones than Wren in spirit.

In creating a persona and accompanying set of attitudes Philips is inhibited by what was permitted to a woman. A wide range of social and sexual attitudes either are not available to her or seem inappropriate in the context of Platonic love between women.

IV The Cambridge Platonists

The Cambridge Platonists reacted against the extremes of Calvinism and radical Protestantism. Blending the study of Plato (c. 427—c. 347 BC) the Athenian philosopher and Plotinus (AD 205—270) the Greek Neo-Platonic philosopher (who believed everything in the universe was an 'emanation' which flowed from The One as light from a candle; he greatly influenced Christian mysticism) with such early Christian theologians as Origen, and with the new rationalism of their own century, they reconciled reason and faith, Christianity and philosophy. God, The One, is the source of Reason, and all Reason leads to God and goodness. While their writing is filled with philosophical and mystical jargon and images, they were a link between the Christian Neo-Platonism of such writers as Vaughan and early Milton and the natural theology of the later seventeenth century. Their moderation in terms of current sectarian conflicts, their toleration of different opinions, and their appeal to reason and liberty of thought, along with their wide-ranging friendships, made them equally favoured by Cromwell, who wanted a moderate influence at the universities during the Protectorate, and those during the Restoration who favoured a comprehensive Anglican Church. The Restoration Latitudinarians were often their students.

Benjamin Whichcote (1609—83), leader of the movement, published nothing but gave influential sermons at Cambridge during the 1640s. His pupil, John Smith (1616?—52), whose *Select Discourses* were published in 1660, could speak of the divinity of human reason, participation in the divine life and The One, in terms which were both Christian and influenced by Plotinus. In the *Discourse* (1652) of Nathanael Culverwel (1618—51?), fellow of Emmanuel, reason and faith are allied in a curious blend of Platonism, Calvinism and Latitudinarian toleration. Peter Sterry (1613—72), Independent, chaplain to Lord Brooke and Cromwell, although not one of the

Cambridge group, shows a similar eclecticism. Natural theology, mysticism and Calvinist distrust of free will are somehow blended.

Henry More (1614—87), the most prolific writer among the Cambridge Platonists, was well read in Plotinus, Ficino and hermetical literature. Influenced by the Spenser of the *Four Hymns* and the *Mutabilitie Cantos*, he often uses Spenserian diction and stanzaic forms for long expositions of the soul's progress towards illumination and assurance. The lack of poetic resonance looks forward to the generalised abstraction of Traherne's verse. Believing Plato and Plotinus taught the same philosophy as Christianity, in *Psychodia Platonica* (1642) More narrates in verse the life, immortality and 'Confutation of the Sleep of the Soul'. More's writing indicates the crisis of religious verse which resulted from the eccentricity and mysticism of the mid-century. Long mystical religious poems concerning the soul had become commonplace. After More's *Philosophical Poems* (1647), a High Anglican, Joseph Beaumont (1616—99), published *Psyche: or Love's Mysterie in XX Canto's: Displaying the Intercourse Betwixt Christ, and the Soule* (1648), an elaborate exercise in history, allegory and metaphysics, supposedly the longest poem in the language.

V Anglican prose: Taylor and Walton

The writing of Jeremy Taylor (1613—67) shows the 'metaphysical', 'Senecan' prose of Donne and Andrewes evolving towards long, sonorous, cadenced sentences, mixing Latinisms and Latinate syntax with colloquialisms. This style might be described as 'African' and was possibly influenced by Augustine. In *An Apology for Authorised and Set Forms of Liturgies* (1649), dedicated to Charles I, Taylor claimed that the extemporaneous prayer favoured by the Puritans encouraged carelessness in worship. Although he warned against splitting the Church into an ever-increasing number of sects, he was a liberal Anglican who emphasised free will, believed the Apostle's Creed a sufficient guide, and thought that much could be left to the individual conscience.

His famous *Holy Living* (1650) and *Holy Dying* (1651) were Anglican devotional manuals written in response to the

Presbyterian destruction of the established Church. A guide to and a collection of prayer and meditations, *Holy Living* offers rules of conduct for the soul during the difficulties of the age. Taylor opposes the rapturous, ecstatic spirituality of the period with a God of love, sweetness and tranquillity. *Holy Dying* warns that human life is short and temptations increase by illness. It is necessary to begin preparing for death while still healthy.

Taylor's *Sermons* (1651, 1653) and a book of prayers, *The Golden Grove* (1655) were followed by *A Collection of Offices or Forms of Prayer* (1658) written to be used in place of the proscribed Prayer Book; it is notable for including devotions based on the liturgical practices of the Greek, Ethiopian and other early churches and for its emphasis on the Resurrection. The sermons reflect the Anglican love of beauty; Taylor's concern with the book of nature as a microcosm of God's Creation is shown in the many images drawn from the natural world. *The Life of Our Blessed Lord and Saviour* is based on the older narrative meditations on the life and passion of Christ. Although he was criticised by some Restoration divines for his elaborate style, Taylor's tolerance, concern with ethics and charity are transitional between the high-church doctrines of Laud and the rationalism of the Latitudinarians.

Among the Anglican divines Thomas Fuller (1608–61) was a popular author with a quirky, garrulous personality. *The History of the Holy War* (1639), or Crusades, offers many examples of his epigrammatical wit: 'The best way to keep great princes together is to keep them asunder.' *The Holy State and the Profane State* (1642), a very popular book, uses characters, short biographies and essays to show good family, professional, social and public lives in contrast to the bad or profane state. Fuller had a knack of putting common sense into epigrams and being amusing; he uses homely expressions and racy idioms. Although an orthodox Christian, he is sceptical of most miracles. A saint 'made no more to caste out a devil than a barber to draw a tooth, and with less pain to the patient'. *The Church History of Britain* (1656), from the Druids to 1649, is surprisingly exuberant, anecdotal and shocked contemporaries with its puns and quibbling wit. Fuller was interested in people, customs, local proverbs and often trivial facts in his most famous work, *The History of the Worthies of England* (1662).

Biography and autobiography before the last decades of the century are seldom objective attempts to record the truth. History, biography, eulogy, mirrors for magistrates and saints' lives were still not distinct forms and were often confused, since biography was seen as morally instructive. As a result of the Civil War there were many ecclesiastical biographers. Izaak Walton (1593–1683) pretended to an artless simplicity, but neither *The Compleat Angler* (1653) nor the *Lives* of John Donne (1640), Sir Henry Wotton (1651), Richard Hooker (1665), George Herbert (1670) or Robert Sanderson (1678) are disinterested. Walton was not a natural writer, but he was a conscious craftsman who disciplined his style, revised carefully and distorted truth to create works of art favourable to High Anglicanism. Part of the Royalist literature of retirement, *The Compleat Angler* created nostalgia for an Elizabethan golden age of the poetry of Marlowe, Du Bartas and Ralegh, of rustic songs, of good food and easy comradeship. Published during the Protectorate, it includes Herbert's Anglican poems and, more remarkably, Christopher Harvey's poem, 'The Book of Common Prayer' (from *The Synagogue* [1640], Harvey's imitation of Herbert's *Temple*), which Walton altered to strengthen its Anglicanism. Walton playfully claims that the Angler (read 'Anglican') is a descendant of the four Apostles and of the biblical patriarchs. His fisherman is within the pastoral tradition which inculcates spiritual truths through simple guides. Walton's friend, Charles Cotton, wrote a Part II for the fifth edition (1676), which is included in most editions.

Although well documented, the *Lives* are often factually inaccurate and sometimes untruthful. Whereas Fuller records faults as well as virtues, and wants to be entertaining, Walton's calm, balanced, alliterative, epigrammatic prose aims at a contemporary saint's life. Donne's secular poetry is neglected and the facts of his life distorted to emphasise the preacher and the divine. The *Life* of Hooker was part of the High-Church reaction at the Restoration and was occasioned by passages in John Gauden's *Life of Hooker* (1662) favourable to the Low Church. Walton's *Life* of Herbert uses the poetry as autobiography to create an ideal parson; to do so he has to tailor his quotations, omitting the stresses and conflicts which would have detracted from an idealised character of a virtuous clergyman. Walton's *Lives*, however, are an advance on previous biography in their sense of a life having a shape. Although Walton digresses and sometimes rambles to bring in an entertaining anecdote, each life has a form and is rounded off with a beautiful death.

VI New philosophical and political ideas: Hobbes and others

Thomas Hobbes's (1588–1679) application of the logic and terms of mechanics to language, psychology, government, morals and religion seemed the most scientific philosophy of the age; even those who disagreed with him (and few, except the Restoration libertines and rakes would admit to be Hobbists) were influenced by his mechanistic psychology and treatment of the origins of government. Hobbes tried to reshape the study of man along the lines of the new physical sciences. *Leviathan, or the Matter, Forms and Power of a Commonwealth, Ecclesiasticall and Civill* (1651) begins:

> For seeing life is but a motion of Limbs, the begining whereof is in some principall part within; why may we not say, that all *Automata* (Engines that move themselves by springs and wheeles as doth a watch) have an artificiall life? For what is the *Heart*, but a *Spring*; and the *Nerves*, but so many *Strings*; and the *Joynts*, but so many *Wheeles*, giving motion to the whole Body.

Man is matter put into motion by the stimulus of what he hopes to enjoy or the fear of pains to be avoided. The dissatisfactions of life are normal, following from our limitless desires and fears. There can be no repose, no tranquillity. Life is continual motion; desire is frustrated both by the absence of gratification and by satisfaction, since the latter can only be temporary and is followed by further appetites including the desire to ensure future enjoyment of present pleasures.

Man has no natural, or innate, moral sense: 'The secret thoughts of a man run over all things, holy, prophane, clean, obscene, grave, and light, without shame, or blame.' In a hypothetical state of nature each man is at war with every

other man for possessions, security and self-glorification.
Since no man can be secure, and the fear of death predominates, men contract to form a government. But no social
contract is secure as men will continue enemies unless there is
an absolute power which can assure the safety of the state
and individuals. All laws, morals and religious observations
derive from this authority. Any attempt to challenge it
returns man to the state of nature where all have a right to
all and life is 'solitary, poore, nasty, brutish, and short'.
Hobbes makes what were traditionally spiritual matters the
concern of the secular state, which will decide what is just
and unjust conduct.

Hobbes also contributed to the change in literary style
during the middle of the century. A translator of Thucydides'
history of the *Peloponnesian Warre* (1629) and of Homer's
Iliad (1675) and *Odyssey*, he wrote an *Art of Rhetorique*
(1655) and an 'Answer to Davenant's preface to Gondibert'
(1650). He distrusts fanciful language in which words obscure
what he regards as a rational approach to cause and effect.
In his psychology of sensations, the imagination or fancy is
merely 'motions within us, reliques of those made in the
sense'. Hobbes separates judgement from wit. Judgement is
rational, wit is fanciful. Metaphor is loose reasoning. This
aesthetic contributed to the distrust of metaphor during the
Restoration, when it became an ornament, an illustration,
a comparison of two closely similar things or qualities.
Hobbes's own style is one of the best prose manners found
among those associated with the new science. Sprat's description of it as 'bold, resolved, settled', 'sparing of similitudes,
but ever extraordinarily decent in them' ignores the irony,
the scornful rhetoric when Hobbes is attacking and even the
strategy of arguing while pretending to write an impersonal,
mathematical prose. The appearance of controversy is
avoided as definition follows definition in what is supposed
to be a scientific approach to problems of government and
religion.

In *Patriarcha: A Defence of the Natural Power of Kings*
(written sometime between 1635 and 1642, published 1680),
Sir Robert Filmer (1588?–1653) shifted the argument
concerning political legitimacy away from the older sacra-
mentalism and the newer contractual theories to a seemingly

natural explanation of the origins of government. He dismissed contractual and democratic theories by asking when the people supposedly convened to form a government. History offers no example of a nation being formed through such a gathering of the populace. History, as shown in the Bible and in the seemingly universal organisation of society, demonstrates that authority is invested in the patriarch or father. By analogy the King is the father of his people; Adam's dominion over the earth and its creatures was passed on through his children and the sons of Noah to modern monarchs. Any attempt to limit such arbitrary power must lead to conflicting claims of obedience and to anarchy. Filmer's views were the opposite of Philip Hunton's (1604– 82) *A Treatise of Monarchie* (1643), in which it was claimed that as England is a 'balanced polity' neither King nor Parliament is supreme. When the two are in conflict the individual must follow his conscience.

James Harrington's (1611–77) *The Commonwealth of Oceana* (1656) is a Utopian romance which presents a transparent allegory of Roman history and of recent social and economic changes within England to show the relationship between property, power and government. Influenced by Harvey's work in physiology and Hobbes's mechanistic treatment of human nature and necessity, Harrington studied changes in the distribution of property in an attempt to create an objective, scientific theory of government. Regarding land as wealth and the basis of power, he showed that since the time of Henry VIII property ownership had passed from nobility to gentry, yeomen and merchants. To have a stable government it was necessary both to reflect this shift in power and to ensure a balance between classes. During the political controversies of the Interregnum, *Oceana* was an attempt to find an alternative form of government which would meet both Leveller demands for an extension of power beyond the nobility and the fears of the Army leadership, Presbyterians and Royalists that a republic would inevitably lead to a social revolution.

During the late 1640s the brilliantly written Leveller pamphlets and petitions spread revolutionary democratic ideas through the New Model Army. In *A Remonstrance of Many Thousand Citizens* (1646), the *March* (1647) *Petition* and *An Agreement of the People* (1647) and the *Agreements* of 1648 and 1649, they develop a theory of government based on the natural rights of the people. The Levellers wanted religious toleration, election by manhood suffrage, no king, no lords, the supremacy of the Commons, annual parliaments, written constitutional guarantees and economic reform. They were, however, willing to exclude servants and wage earners from the right to vote and agreed that the 'levelling' of estates be made illegal. The Leveller pamphlets were written by various hands, often in co-operation, and in response to specific political events of the 1640s. Although the pamphleteers refer to God-given rights, there is little theology; the arguments presented are secular, historical and rational. The style is forceful, logical, without pedantry and quibbling. Images arise naturally from the context and the diction is vigorous. The best-known Leveller propagandist was John Lilburne (1615?–57), imprisoned for treason when he challenged Parliament's authority; the best writer and theorist is the satiric Richard Overton:

> You shall scarce speak to *Crumwell* about any thing, but he will lay his hand on his breast, elevate his eyes, and call God to record, he will weep, howl and repent, even while he doth smite you under the first rib.

Gerrard Winstanley (1609–?), the leader of the Digger movement in 1649–50, was a freeman of London and a cloth merchant. The war ruined his business and he retired to the country where he lived off friends while writing mystical theology. Winstanley brought his religious vision to the radical politics that surfaced after the King's surrender. During April 1649 he led a group of poor men to St George's Hill, near Cobham, where they dug the waste land and planted; they claimed that all land and property originally belonged to the community. The Council of Army ordered the Digger colony destroyed. Although Winstanley's early pamphlets, such as *The New Law of Righteousness*, called for a primitive communism which would be achieved by example, his last work, *The Law of Freedom* (1652), is similar to Leveller proposals in asking Cromwell to create a government based on manhood suffrage, regular elections and religious toleration. Winstanley's diction, analogies and assumptions reflect his Protestant mysticism. God is the inner light within each man. The Reformation is part of a divine plan reflected in each soul. Varied in manner, clear, yet rich in biblical phrases and metaphors, *The New Law of Righteousness, Fire in the Bush*, the *Letter to Lord Fairfax* and *An Appeal to the House of Commons*, although political discourses, share similarities with the mystical poetry of Vaughan and Marvell. A visionary who wished to reverse the effects of man's fall, with the consequent division of property and labour, Winstanley understood that the Civil War had merely redistributed power among the ruling classes:

> In the midst of this garden likewise there is the tree of life, who is this blessing, or restoring power, called universal love, or pure knowledge; which when mankind by experience begins to eat thereof, or to delight himself herein, preferring this kingdom and law within, which is Christ, before the kingdom and law, that lies in objects without, which is the devil:
>
> Then man is drawn up into himself again, or new Jerusalem, which is the spirit of truth, comes down to earth, to fetch earth up to live in that life, that is a life above objects: even to live in the enjoyment of Christ, the righteous spirit within himself, and to tread the earthly life, that lies in objects without, under foot, This is the life that will bring in true community, and destroy murdering property. Now mankind enters into the garden of God's rest, and lives for ever. He enjoys his kingdom, and the word within himself. He knows sin and sorrow no more, for all tears now, which blind imagination brought upon him, are wiped away, and man is in peace.

I Life and prose writings

JOHN MILTON (1608–74) was the son of a scrivener, a combination of notary, clerk and usurer, who was also a well-known musician and composer. After St Paul's School, London, known for its teaching of the classical languages and use of contemporary literature in the study of rhetoric, Milton went to Christ's College, Cambridge (1625–32), where he was a contemporary of Richard Crashaw, Henry More, Jeremy Taylor, Thomas Randolph and John Cleveland. Because of the direction the national church was taking, under Laud, Milton decided not to become a clergyman. He studied privately from 1632 to 1638, preparing himself to be a poet. The sonnet 'How soon hath time' (1631) is one of Milton's many references to the passing of his youth: 'But my late spring no bud or blossom sheweth'. Feeling he has accomplished little, he retains faith in fulfilling a vocation; but, as usual with Milton, his proclamation of purpose is made conditional on divine will:

> Toward which time leads me, and the will of heaven;
>   All is, if I have grace to use it so,
>   As ever in my great task-master's eye.

Milton's continental tour through France and Italy (1638–9) included visits to the Dutch writer and philosopher Hugo Grotius (1583–1645), and to Galileo. His treatment as an equal by the intellectuals, scholars and patrons of the famous academies was aided by his close friendship at St Paul's School with Charles Diodati; the Diodatis were an exiled Italian family, influential in international intellectual circles both as theologians and as advocates of a Protestant alliance.

On Charles Diodati's death in 1639 Milton published *Epitaphium Damonis* ('Damon's Epitaph', 1640). After the outbreak of the Civil War Milton returned to England where he soon began writing for the Parliamentary side. During 1641–2 *Of Reformation, Of Prelatical Episcopacy, Animadversions upon the Remonstrants Defence, The Reason of Church Government,* and *An Apology for Smectymnuus* argued against the hierarchical system of Church government. Written during a time when Parliament claimed to be fighting for the King but against evil advisers, bishops and claims to arbitrary rule, Milton's tracts are not anti-monarchical; they argue that worldly bishops weaken the King by alienating him from the people. The tracts reveal a major difference between Milton and Presbyterians; whereas they wanted Church discipline, Milton wanted broad toleration except to Catholics. Liberty is necessary to test the truth and individual:

> Other things men do to the glory of God: but sects and errors it seems God suffers to be for the glory of good men, that the world may know and reverence their true fortitude and undaunted constancy in the truth. Let us not therefore make these things an incumbrance, or an excuse of our delay in reforming, which God sends us as an incitement to proceed with more honour and alacrity. For if there were no opposition where were the triall of an unfained goodnesse and magnanimity?

Why Milton married the daughter of a Royalist family on the eve of the Civil War (1642), why Mary Powell soon left him, and whether he would have in other circumstances written the divorce tracts are matters of speculation. Whereas most Protestant Churches had rejected the Catholic view of marriage as a sacrament and allowed divorce, the Anglican Church still took an ambiguous position. While matrimony was not a divine sacrament, there was no provision for divorce and remarriage. Early in the Civil War, Parliament discussed possible reforms concerning divorce. Milton's tracts were attempts to influence opinion, but were too radical for the time; they shocked the Presbyterians by making incompatibility a cause for divorce beyond the usual grounds of adultery and desertion. Milton believed that marriage is a union of minds, complemented by physical union; where a union of souls is lacking, the physical union is corrupt.

Although it would be naïve to see no relationship between Milton's writing and life, *The Doctrine and Discipline of Divorce* (1643), *The Judgement of Martin Bucer* (1644), *Tetrachordon* ('The Tetrachord', 1645) and *Colasterion* ('Instrument of Correction', 1645) should be viewed in perspective with the tracts for radical reform, *Of Education* (1644) and for freedom from licensing laws, *Areopagitica* (1644). The relationship of Milton's attack on episcopacy to his desire for a radical reformation of society, restoring it, he claimed, to a primitive Christianity, unadulterated by Catholic tradition, can be seen throughout his writing of this period.

Written against the Licensing Order of 1643, which renewed the old practice of requiring approval before publication, *Aeropagitica* does not advocate unlimited freedom of the press:

> And yet on the other hand unlesse warinesse be us'd, as good almost kill a Man as kill a good Book; who kills a Man kills a reasonable creature, Gods Image; but hee who destroyes a good Booke, kills reason it selfe, kills the Image of God, as it were in the eye. Many a man lives a burden to the Earth; but a good Booke is the pretious lifeblood of a master spirit, imbalm'd and treasur'd up on purpose to a life beyond life.

Censorship before publication prevents open discussion of issues, once a work is published, if subversive, immoral or libellous, it can be tried in a court of law. Such testing is part of the reformation of the Church and society in contrast, Milton argues, to the Popish suppression of discussion.

On the Licensing Order and divorce Milton openly broke with the Presbyterians who, he felt, were blocking further reformation. He saw truth as the object of a continuing quest through which, using reason and inspired by grace, man could regain his prelapsarian (unfallen) state:

> I cannot praise a fugitive and cloistered vertue, unexercis'd and unbreath'd, that never sallies out and sees her adversary, but slinks out of the race, where that immortall garland is to be run for, not without dust and heat. Assuredly we bring not innocence into the world, we bring impurity much rather: that which purifies us is triall, and triall is by what is contrary.

Milton's tracts were controversial and brought him unfavourably to the attention of Parliament; he retired from public disputes for a few years.

His anti-monarchical tracts and three Latin *Defenses* belong to the period of the King's trial, execution and the international outcry which followed. *The Tenure of Kings and Magistrates* (1649) claims that government power is based upon a covenant with the people; if power is abused the people have a natural right to change the government. The tract, which is filled with the period's mystical notions of the coming of Christ and the Millennium, attempts to persuade readers of their duty to punish tyrants and their right to change the kingdom into another form of government. In March 1649 Milton was appointed Secretary for Foreign Tongues to the Council of State of the purged Parliament. Shortly afterwards he published *Eikonoklastes* ('Image-breaker', 1649), a reply to John Gauden's famous *Eikon Basilike: the Portraiture of His Sacred Majesty in his Solitudes and Suffering*, supposedly written by Charles I before his death. Gauden created the image of the executed King as a pious Christ-like martyr who had died for his people's sins. Besides attempting to destroy the image of the Royal Martyr, Milton defends the purging of Parliament and accuses the Presbyterians of turning against their sectarian allies.

In 1651 Milton became censor of Marchamont Needham's *Mercurius Politicus*, a government newspaper. By 1652 he had become totally blind. The sarcastic, often scurrilous three Latin *Defenses* (1651, 1654, 1655) defend the execution of the King and the rule of the Commons against European protests that England had committed a sacrilege and that government had fallen into the hands of the rabble. The *Defenses* are of interest for their many autobiographical passages; they also show that Milton's concept of rule by 'the people' changed. In the *First Defense* he wanted government by the well-off and well-educated, in the *Second Defense* he claims that as the people are sinful and unable to agree, it is necessary for Cromwell to be Protector and defender of their liberty.

Milton again entered public controversy during the months when Richard Cromwell's Protectorate fell to pieces,

Parliament met and monarchy was being restored; as the government changed six times within two years, the eight tracts Milton wrote in 1659—60 make for confusing reading. Religious and civil liberty and the prevention of the restitution of monarchy are the common themes. The first and second editions of *Readie and Easie Way to Establish a Free Commonwealth* (March and April 1660) were last-minute attempts to persuade General Monck not to restore monarchy. Within months Charles II was recalled to power and a proclamation was issued suppressing the Latin *Defenses* and *Eikonoklastes*. Milton went into hiding. Originally proposed for the short list of regicides to be tried and executed, he was imprisoned but saved through the aid of Andrew Marvell, then a member of Parliament, Sir William Davenant, and others. *Paradise Lost* (1667), a book on grammar (1669), *The History of Britain* (1670), *Paradise Regain'd* and *Samson Agonistes* (both 1671) were published during the Restoration. The most complete and radical statement of Milton's religious beliefs, *De Doctrina Christiana*, was not translated and published until 1825.

Milton's prose usually consists of long sentences with many clauses, Latinate diction and syntax, and often follows the divisional structures of formal classical oratory. Although he also uses colloquial expressions, they sit oddly in their context. Latin was still the international language of Europe and Milton was educated to speak and write in Latin as if it were his native tongue. His style has similarities to the Latin constructions, long sentences and mixed diction of other prose writers of the time, but is more extreme.

II Poetry to 1650: 'Nativity Ode' to sonnets

The greatest English poet of the Baroque, Milton's achievement remains controversial because, unlike Donne, Jonson and Herbert who use artifice to create an impression of directness and intimacy, Milton's conscious artistry presents a barrier to easy involvement. Elaborate styles, experimentation with genres, elevation of manner, vast designs, complex forms, spatial constructions, dramatic interplay of contrasting elements and of such opposites as light and dark, and the display of wondrous and amazing effects, were common to Mannerist and Baroque art before they were subdued by Neo-Classicism and the Rococo (apparently a fanciful formation on the stem of *rocaille*, shell- or pebble-work, creating an effect of lightness and gaiety). The Baroque came late to England and in Milton the varied elements came together to produce a poetic equivalent to the sculpture, painting and architecture of Bernini (1598–1680), Borromini (1599–1667) and Caravaggio (1569–1609). In contrast to Milton's expansion of form and use of space, such writers as Donne, Herbert and Vaughan put their best energies into smaller forms, and into the stanza, the conceit, 'wit', and self-dramatisation. Milton appears out of place between Donne and Dryden because English literary history has usually concentrated on the schools of Donne and Jonson and the line of Waller – Denham – Dryden, while neglecting the development of a 'sublime' Baroque Neo-Classicism from Spenser through Sylvester and the Fletchers to Milton. Dryden would have recognised part of his Neo-Classical inheritance from such a lineage. The high style was particularly favoured in the mid-century when Crashaw and Henry More developed their own version.

The early *On the Morning of Christs Nativity* (1629), one of the greatest English odes – a form which had hardly yet been naturalised in England – reveals many characteristics which we think of as Miltonic. Although the English tradition of nativity poems derived from the medieval carol through Robert Southwell, Jonson, Herbert, Crashaw, Vaughan and Herrick, Milton uses the soaring, diving, hear-and-there movement of the Pindaric ode to shift the focus from the Christ child to the Incarnation of the Redeemer of fallen man and nature, and to set His birth within the vast perspective of human and eternal history. The focus of the poem moves vertically through heaven, earth and hell, and horizontally across the ages from the Creation to the end of time. These movements are not treated sequentially; the poet's imagination moves backward and forward in time, linking key moments of created time to the significance of the Christ child's birth. The poem is a celebration of the nativity in which doctrines concerning the mysteries of the faith are recalled along with ideas which centuries of Christian scholarship had evolved to harmonise pagan with Christian history and myth, into a comprehensive cosmological view:

> Such music (as 'tis said)
> Before was never made,
>   But when of old the sons of morning sung,
> While the creator great
> His constellations set,
>   And the well-balanced world on hinges hung,
> And cast the dark foundations deep,
> And bid the welt'ring waves their oozy channel keep.
>
> Ring out, ye crystal spheres,
> Once bless our human ears,
>   (If ye have power to touch our senses so)
> And let your silver chime
> Move in melodious time;
>   And let the base of heaven's deep organ blow,
> And with your ninefold harmony
> Make up full consort to the angelic symphony.

Biblical typology, allegorisation of myth, the personification of nature, opposition of light and dark, and contrasting time schemes are used to create a universal perspective in which the birth of Christ is a new Creation of the world and will lead to the Last Judgement and restoration of paradise. The poet's vision and art have similarities to the divine vision and art in encompassing all time, seeing relationships between past, present, future, and all Creation, whether angel, the spheres, man, or the natural world. By comparison the earlier English odes of Drayton, Jonson and Herrick seem tame and rudimentary.

The companion poems *L'Allegro* and *Il Penseroso* (1631) are exercises in the pastoral; similar to Herrick's 'The Hock-Cart', Milton's two poems are part of a sensibility which was evolving alongside the metaphysical lyric and which led to the generalised, idealising, moralising, reflective verse of the eighteenth century. Milton's paired poems, parallel in structure and incident, are philosophical considerations of mirth and melancholy. Each begins with an invocation banishing its supposedly opposite mood and then progresses through representative descriptions of day or night. *L'Allegro* presents pleasures ranging from the merry English countryside to a city day of extroverted festivities and concludes with a tranquil evening of entertainment and poetry. *Il Penseroso* praises the pleasures of contemplative, solitary, introspective life with its study of the mysteries of nature, art and philosophy. Although the activities of *L'Allegro* offer a good sociable life, the contemplative life brings the serene spiritual wisdom of old age:

> And may at last my weary age
> Find out the peaceful hermitage,
> The hairy gown and mossy cell,
> Where I may sit and rightly spell,
> Of every star that heaven doth shew,
> And every herb that sips the dew;
> Till old experience do attain
> To something like prophetic strain.

The conclusion of *Il Penseroso* is less conditional: 'These pleasures Melancholy give, and I with thee will choose to live'.

A Mask (1634, revised 1637), usually called *Comus*, was performed at Ludlow Castle in 1634, with music and direction by Henry Lawes, to celebrate the Earl of Bridgewater's election as Lord President of Wales. *Comus* uses the pastoral mode for an emblematic allegorisation of the testing of a young mind by the temptations of the senses; it celebrates virginity as a divine mystery. By virginity Milton does not necessarily mean physical chastity, although that is applicable to the children performing in the masque; he means a purity of mind which, according to his reading in early Church Fathers and Renaissance Platonists, will free the soul from the corruptions of the material world and contribute towards the restoration of mankind:

> Celestial Cupid her famed son advanced,
> Holds his dear Psyche sweet entranced
> After her wandering labours long,
> Till free consent the gods among
> Make her his eternal bride,
> And from her fair unspotted side
> Two blissful twins are to be born,
> Youth and Joy; so Jove hath sworn.

Those who resist temptation, if aided by grace, will participate in the heavenly marriage. In the *Apology for Smectymnuus* (1642) Milton explains that the 'high mysteries' of Revelation 14:14 ('These are they which were not defiled with women, for they are virgins') does not prevent marriage, which 'must not be called a defilement'. The doctrine of virginity assumes a continuum from the divine through spirit and matter; according to whether the individual is untempted or falls, the soul can either rise 'Higher than the sphery chime' or grow 'clotted by contagion' 'till she quite lose / The divine property of her first being'. Written mostly in blank verse, using the theme of temptation, *Comus* is concerned with the proper use of time and the plentitude of God's Creation. The Tempter Comus elegantly argues for the need to seize the day: 'If you let slip time, like a neglected rose / It withers on the stalk with languished head'. While he can imprison the lady's body, her mind is free to resist him. But free will in itself is insufficient; her salvation requires divine grace represented by the attendant spirit, Sabrina, and the mysterious plant, haemony.

Milton's *Comus*, with its allegory of the Christian's journey through life, the need to restore the divine image in man by resisting the temptations of the world, and allusions to mystical doctrine, is similar to the profound symbolism found in Jonson's masques. The relationship between the actors, actual life and the audience is also part of the significance. *Comus* celebrates a reunion of the Earl of Bridgewater's children with the family. By analogy they travel to the castle through the surrounding woods and Sabrina river, facing dangers, until the family, reunited, joins in a dance or revels. The Lady is the Earl's youngest daughter, Alice, the two brothers are his sons John and Thomas, Sabrina was probably an older sister, and the attendant spirit was played by Henry Lawes, their tutor. The evil Comus, because of notions of social and moral decorum, was probably played by a professional actor. The metaphor of the journey, in keeping with the allegorising mode of the masque, also stands symbolically for the children's spiritual future; by celebrating an ideal they participate in it. Although Milton's text depends less on dance, music and scenery, its combination of symbolism, moral allegory and topicality is similar to the court masques of Jonson and Jones.

Lycidas, written on the death of Edward King, was published in 1638 in *Justa Edouardo King*. The subtitle in which Milton 'foretells the ruin of our corrupted clergy then in their height' was added for the 1645 publication of his *Poems*. *Lycidas* is a monody, or song for solo voice, and a pastoral funeral elegy. Influenced by Italian experiments in stanzaic form, especially the *Canzone* with its lines of varied length, Milton's poem, with its verse paragraphs of unequal lengths, its varied rhymes and ten unrhymed lines, its digressions on fame and on the corruption of the clergy, and its epilogue in which the narrative suddenly distances with a shift from the first to the third person, is a major example of the Baroque. The dynamic form, with its interwoven contrasting rhythms, rhymes and themes, has similarities to Italian architecture of the age. As usual Milton richly elaborates a few basic ideas into complex, massive stanzas. Although the formal movement of *Lycidas* is complicated by digressions and shifts in focus, the poem progresses logically, if elliptically, from an introductory invocation through a primarily pagan view of life, then a Christian perspective, to the vision of Lycidas reborn in heaven, one of the blessed saints of the Church enjoying heavenly marriage. Asking what is the meaning of life, the narrator fails to find any adequate consolation for death except the Christian promise of heaven:

> Weep no more, woeful shepherds weep no more,
> For Lycidas your sorrow is not dead,
> Sunk though he be beneath the watery floor,
> So sinks the day-star in the ocean bed,
> And yet anon repairs his drooping head,
> And tricks his beams, and with new spangled ore,
> Flames in the forehead of the morning sky:
> So Lycidas sunk low, but mounted high,
> Through the dear might of him that walked the waves;
> Where other groves, and other streams along,
> With nectar pure his oozy locks he laves,
> And hears the unexpressive nuptial song,
> In the blest kingdoms meek of joy and love.
> There entertain him all the saints above,
> In solemn troops, and sweet societies
> That sing, and singing in their glory move,
> And wipe the tears for ever from his eyes.

The power of *Lycidas* does not derive from any originality

of thought or intensity of feeling; its greatness, including its emotional tensions, results from its art. The thought rushes forward as the short contracted lines expand into larger paragraphs; the imagery of water, river, seas, and tears unifies; the shifting metaphor of the narrator as shepherd, student, priest and poet, intensifies; the various modulations of tone range from elegaic, oratorical and lyric to prophetic and visionary. The many themes, the movement from funeral to wedding, from death to rebirth, the sympathetic response of the natural world, the wide range of classical material referring to similar situations, the climaxes ('of so much fame', 'stands ready to smite once, and smite no more') contribute to the rich artistry as do the economical, musical repetitions of phrases: 'Yet once more . . . For Lycidas is dead', 'Shall now no more be seen', 'Weep no more, woeful shepherds, weep no more, / For Lycidas your sorrow is not dead'. *Lycidas* is a performance. It is in the Spenserian tradition of high art; its conscious artifice, shown in its sometimes Spenserian archaic diction, demands as much recognition as its themes and subject.

A similar, if lesser, artistry and joy of experimentation with form went into the sonnets. Mostly written in response to the political controversies of the 1640s and 50s, the sonnets argue, attempt to persuade, satirise and celebrate: '*Fairfax*, whose name in arms through Europe rings' (1648); '*Vane*, young in years, but in sage counsel old' (1652). The sonnets addressed to Fairfax, Cromwell and Vane are connected with the conflict between the Parliamentary Presbyterians who wanted religious conformity and a controlled press and the sectarians who wanted liberty of conscience and a continuing reformation. The address to Cromwell, a fourteen-line sentence, concludes 'Help us to save free conscience from the paw/ Of hireling wolves whose gospel is their maw'. 'Avenge O Lord thy slaughtered saints' (1655) takes up the cause of international Protestantism at a time when Cromwell was attempting to form an alliance of Sweden, Holland and the Swiss to defend the Vaudois. In contrast to the subjectivity of Donne or the social intimacies of Jonson, Milton's public voice assumes that it speaks for England and Protestantism.

Possibly influenced by the 'heroic sonnets' of Tasso,

Milton welds the normal divisions of the sonnet into a unified whole; the sentences run over the lines and the thought does not respect stanzaic division. Similar to Jonson's avoidance of heavy pauses at the end of a line, Milton's full stops and colons often fall early in a line. As the remainder of the line springs the thought forward into subsequent lines, there is both unity and purposeful, energetic tension. Milton's verse in the sonnets is rich in local movement. In 'O Nightingale', an early exercise (1630?) he uses a twelve-line sentence to integrate the stanzas; but he creates tension between thought and stanza by a rhyme scheme which does not correspond to the movement of thought. In 'I did but prompt the age' (1646), written in response to the controversy over the divorce pamphlets, the final sentence is a quatrain, which integrates the last line of the first tercet with the concluding tercet. The satiric diction shows the distance Milton has moved from the amorous Elizabethan sonnet: 'owls and cuckoos, asses, apes and dogs'. 'A book was writ of late' (1647?) in defence of *The Doctrine and Discipline of Divorce* (1643) is an example of Milton's sense of humour, with its comic rhymes *'Tetrachordon'* / 'pored on' / 'word on' / 'Gordon':

> Cries the stall-reader, Bless us! what a word on
> A title page is this! and some in file
> Stand spelling false, while one might walk to Mile-
> End Green. Why is it harder sirs than Gordon.

III 'Paradise Lost'

While Milton accepted that a vernacular literature needed an epic before it could be accorded the same dignity as Latin and Greek, he originally planned *Paradise Lost* as a drama, *Adam Unparadiz'd*, similar to other European tragedies written on the fall of Adam and Eve. By 1658 Milton had started his epic poem. Composing and dictating ten to forty lines during the winter nights and in the morning editing them to half their number, Milton probably took four or five years; *Paradise Lost* was supposedly complete by 1665. It was first published divided into ten books (1667, 1668 and 1669). The second edition of 1674 was published as twelve books, the traditional number for an epic: Milton divided Books Seven and Ten and made a few minor alterations in the text.

In *Paradise Lost* Milton attempts to go beyond all previous epics by using a grander theme. Although Marino, Sylvester, Giles Fletcher and Cowley had written biblical epics, Milton's subject matter, the Creation of the world, the Fall of man and the divine scheme for his redemption, was capable of an encyclopedic inclusiveness ranging from events before the Creation to the end of the world. If the biblical accounts of the Creation and Adam's Fall are the beginning of human history in the Old Testament, for Christians they are part of a historical drama of which other acts are the coming of Christ, His sacrifice and the last days foretold in Revelation, followed by the passing away of this world and the restoration of man to paradise in a newly created heaven and earth. Viewed from an eternal or divine perspective, Adam's Fall. although it brings death and sin to his heirs, is fortunate as God through His foresight and mercy will bring about a greater good.

Because of the paradox of the fortunate fall Milton can 'assert eternal providence, / And justify the ways of God to men'. In Book XII the Archangel Michael says that after the Last Judgement:

> then the earth
> Shall all be paradise, far happier place
> Than this of Eden, and far happier days.

Adam exclaims:

> O goodness infinite, goodness immense!
> That all this good of evil shall produce,
> And evil turn to good; more wonderful
> Than that which by creation first brought forth
> Light out of darkness! Full of doubt I stand,
> Whether I should repent me now of sin
> By me done and occasioned, or rejoice
> Much more, that much more good thereof shall spring,
> To God more glory, more good will to men
> From God, and over wrath grace shall abound.

Having shown him the divine scheme for the future, which is

'the sum/ Of wisdom', Michael claims Adam will 'not be loath/ To leave this Paradise, but shalt possess/ A paradise within thee, happier far'. Although achieving its effects in a different manner, *Paradise Lost* has similarities to Augustinian contemplation. It restores man's original 'memory' of truth, the light of which has been clouded by the distractions of our fallen condition.

A major theme of the poem is the contrast between free will and the claims by Satan and his followers that the world and God are governed by necessity and chance. Free will was a controversial issue of the age; influenced by Calvin's teachings on predestination, the Presbyterian Parliament outlawed Arminian teaching of free will since, they claimed, it limited original sin and God's power to elect whom and how he chose. Similarly the new science seemed to argue for a deterministic causality; the scientific revolution itself brought about a revival of interest in stoic fate and the Lucretian notion that the universe was made from matter and governed by chance. Perhaps the most significant evidence of the controversy over free will was Bishop Bramhall's debate with Hobbes in which the latter argued that free will is a delusion. Hobbes claimed that since God is the cause of all motion, divine foreknowledge is the same as necessity. Milton's God says 'Man shall not quite be lost, but saved who will, / Yet not of will in him, but grace in me'. The position is Arminian in contrast to Calvinist; general grace renews the power of the will to contribute towards salvation, although some are saved through 'peculiar grace'.

The style, structure and themes of *Paradise Lost* are a development from Milton's previous poems. As in *Comus* a central theme is temptation, and the Tempter is made to speak more cleverly, rhetorically and sympathetically than those who uphold the truth. Satan offers very human arguments to justify his actions and more than one reader, despite Milton's irony and cautionary descriptions, has seen the devil as the hero. In contrast to the false hero with his cunning, maliciousness and energy, the true heroes of Milton's poems, the Lady in *Comus* and the Son of God in *Paradise Lost* and *Paradise Regain'd*, conquer through patience, fortitude and obedience. Christ is the second Adam who reverses the consequences of the Fall; He is the seed promised Eve who will bruise the head of the serpent and end the reign of death.

During a century when many English poets and dramatists were experimenting with the possible resources of the heroic and the epic, Milton incorporated and transformed epic material in *Paradise Lost* into a rich new kind of Christian heroic poem. The epic conventions include the opening statement of theme, invocation, catalogue of soldiers, battles by opposing armies, contrasting heroes, beginning in the middle of the story, and events which shape the future of a race; but the conventions have taken on a greater significance. The poem is comprehensive. It not only offers a history of the world as found in the Old and New Testament and as elaborated by biblical commentators, but also incorporates pagan mythology (which is seen as distorted histories of the fallen angels and other biblical truths), recent scientific ideas, and some non-European history, along with references to and imitations of classical literature, into a harmonious vision. The vision is similar, or at least as similar as narrative which depends on temporal sequence can be, to God's vision in which all eternity is simultaneously present. The movements backward and forward in time, the ascents and descents to and from heaven, earth and hell, the seeming tangential digressions, the extended similes which assimilate comparisons to other comparisons, the unusual syntax which suspends normal temporal expectations of relationships, all contribute to a God-like vision. Milton is a poet—priest, a *vates*, inspired by the Holy Spirit which was present at the Creation of the world:

> Instruct me, for thou know'st; thou from the first
> Wast present, and with mighty wings outspread
> Dove-like sat'st brooding on the vast abyss.

The spaciousness, architectural form, interplay of contrasting elements, vitality and drama of *Paradise Lost* carry further the ambitious experimentalism, expansion of form and completely organised spatial relations of the *Nativity Ode* and *Lycidas*. Besides the shifts in focus between heaven, earth, hell and intervening spaces and the movements backward and forward in time, there is also the poet who

'On evil days though fallen, and evil tongues; / In darkness; and with dangers compassed round, / And solitude', sings of a cosmos which is in its sweep and imagination worthy of science fiction.

Paradise Lost has a complexity which makes it one of the greatest achievements of our literature. A principal structural method is pattern through opposition, contrast and parody. The first half of the epic treats of the cause of the Fall and is dominated by Satan; the second half treats of the Fall itself and divine providence. Oppositional contrasts include heaven and hell, the Son of God and Satan, Paradise before and after the Fall, man before and after the Fall, eternal bliss and damnation, light and dark, the Fall of Satan and the Fall of man, ascent and descent, bliss and woe, and such specific contrasts as the heavenly trinity and the trinity of Satan—sin—death, the councils in heaven to save man and the councils in hell to destroy man, the stairs to heaven and the causeway to hell, Christ and Satan as volunteers, Christ's love and Adam's love, and the sexual bliss of Adam and Eve and Satan's frustration. Hell, like Paradise, even has its four rivers. Throughout the epic Satan parodies the Father, Son and Holy Spirit in his actions. Sin is born from Satan's head in parody of the Father's creation of the Son; and sin is Satan's perfect image, as Christ and man are God's images. Alongside the narrative the devils offer their own epic view of the events. Satan in Book I gathers his twelve disciples, and parodying the fortunate fall claims that he will bring good from the fall of the angels:

> From this descent
> Celestial virtues rising, will appear
> More glorious and more dread than from no fall.

The care with which Milton has constructed his epic can be seen from the symbolism of Christ ascending his triumphal chariot at the exact centre (counting the lines of the first edition) of the poem (Book VI, line 762): 'Ascended, at his right hand Victory'. (Previously Satan 'High in the midst exalted as a god / The apostate in his sun-bright chariot sat / Idol of majesty divine'.) Although the exact interpretation of the number symbolism is still controversial, many events, descriptions and speeches in the epic are significantly arranged. It is probable that even the length of the speeches and songs has a meaning and forms an invisible language, or symbolic sub-text, to the poem.

The controversy during the first half of our century over the style of *Paradise Lost* has died down and Milton's verse can now be historically placed with more objectivity. Milton's explanation of 'The Verse', prefacing the second edition, explains: 'The measure is English heroic verse without rhyme, as that of Homer in Greek, and of Virgil in Latin'. Following the example of 'both Italian and Spanish poets of prime note' and 'our best English tragedies' he claims to be 'the first in English' to write an 'heroic poem' without 'the troublesome and modern bondage of rhyming'. The musicality of the verse will consist of 'apt numbers, fit quantity of Syllables, and the sense variously drawn out from one verse into another'. Although Milton is influenced by the classics and the continental Baroque, his prosody has some similarities to the strong lines of Donne and Jonson. The line is of ten syllables, largely iambic, but with many variations. Adjoining vowels are run together into a single syllable. The stresses and pauses are varied. The lines are energetic and packed with many harsh consonants, double stresses, compressed syntax, and concentrated meaning achieved through puns, ambiguities, ironies, symbolism and double syntax (in which a sentence may carry more than one meaning according to how it is read). The sentences, however, are usually long, and form paragraphs in which the many phrases and clauses, allusions and similes pile up associations, qualifications and related ideas to the main statement. The dislocation of English syntax, often with inverted word order and constructions based on Latin grammar, elevates the style and can be regarded as part of the Neo-Classical tendencies of the seventeenth century. More specifically, long, loose, unbalanced sentences with multiple connectives and many parenthetical clauses are characteristic of the mid-century, as can be seen from the prose of Browne and Taylor. In rejecting both the balanced Ciceronian and the compressed, aphoristic Senecan styles, but seeking elevation and sonority, and possibly influenced by the hither-and-yon movement of Augustinian contemplation, writers developed a long, loose asymmetrical Latinate sentence which was varied by shifts into colloquial diction. Many of Milton's verses are, however, a variation of the Ciceronian sentence, although less symmetrical; long phrases and clauses are massed on both sides of the principal verb.

In places Milton's style is extremely tactile and the sound and movement of the line echo the sense. It can be tough, sensuous, tight, a model for dramatic blank verse. In other places, however, the style feels extremely artificial, inflexible and distant from the topic. Milton probably thought that in a long poem it was necessary to vary the texture, especially to avoid overloading didactic passages with dramatic qualities. Although the often-commented-upon Latin influence on the diction has been shown to be exaggerated, especially as other English poets had previously used the same words in their Latin sense, the cumulative effect of such usages is part of the elevated manner appropriate to the poem's divine vision. The symbolic repetition of such words as fruit—fruitless—fruition in various contexts, the complex similes which act as metaphors, the puns on Latin meanings, the way the same words are used with different significances before and after the Fall, the often unconsciously ironic use of self-justifying terms by Satan or Eve, and the biblical allusions, give *Paradise Lost* an extremely rich verbal texture.

While Milton's elevated style is in keeping with the subject of his poem, it is one of the developments away from the low diction of the early seventeenth century. Although Milton's style and manner may seem unique, its characteristics can be seen in the verse of his contemporaries. The Latinate diction, coinages, idioms, word order and syntax were both part of the mid-century's 'sublime' style, a manner noticeable in many of the Interregnum metaphysical poets, and were also part of the century's Neo-Classicism. Often, as in Waller and early Dryden, the verse progresses by a 'turn' which repeats a word while advancing a new, sometimes antithetical thought. Milton took such Latinisms further, creating an elevated, artificial style in which English was meant to be given a dignity comparable to that of the classical languages; the elevation of the vernacular to the classical was one aim of the Renaissance. While Milton uses many Latinate techniques which create elegance, he goes beyond the English Neo-

Classical poets in raising his verse towards the sublime. His vocabulary is rich-sounding with many adjectives and nouns:

> He trusted to have equalled the most high,
> If he opposed; and with ambitious aim
> Against the throne and monarchy of God
> Raised impious war in heaven and battle proud
> With vain attempt. Him the almighty power
> Hurled headlong flaming from the ethereal sky
> With hideous ruin and combustion down
> To bottomless perdition, there to dwell
> In adamantine chains and penal fire,
> Who durst defy the omnipotent to arms.

Whereas a Waller or Dryden uses a classical manner to achieve a well-bred dignity, Milton, like Spenser, creates a purposefully artificial manner suitable to his grand themes. Donne and Jonson argue and persuade, Waller and Dryden converse, but Milton evokes and describes a world of inspired imagination.

IV 'Paradise Regain'd' and 'Samson Agonistes'

Milton's choice of the devil's temptation of Christ in the wilderness as the main episode of *Paradise Regain'd* (1671) is surprising. Jesus's sacrifice, which brings atonement, is logically the central event in Christian history. Spenser, Marvell and Milton, however, treat the individual resistance to temptation as symbolical of, and as contributing to, the reversal of the temptation of Eve and Adam's Fall; Jesus provides Milton, as He did the sixteenth-century Christian humanists, with a model for behaviour. In *Paradise Regain'd* Jesus suffers as a human; He does not, nor does Satan, fully understand His nature or His significance in fulfilling the prophesy in Genesis that Eve's seed will bruise the head of the serpent. Offered temptations He becomes conscious of Himself as the Son of God who conquers through obedience.

In *Paradise Lost* Milton contrasts 'the better fortitude / Of patience and heroic martyrdom / Unsung' to the usual topics of the epic. Written in a bare style, with few epic similes (extended comparisons between the fabled and familiar, using an 'As . . . so . . . ' formula), but with many of the conventions of an oral tale, *Paradise Regain'd* is a heroic poem which incorporates and transcends classical features by Christianising them. The opening lines, with their Virgilian echoes, state the argument:

> I who erewhile the happy garden sung,
> By one man's disobedience lost, now sing
> Recovered Paradise to all mankind.

The invocation to the muse is to the Holy Spirit ('Thou spirit'). The temptations follow the order in Luke (IV; 1–13) but are elaborated from speculations formed in biblical commentary. As in some medieval and Renaissance narrative lives of Christ the focus shifts to include the baptism by John and to Mary's concern at Jesus's disappearance, an event which parallels His earlier disappearance when He impressed the rabbis in the temple. Such references to the early life of the hero create a significant background for his confrontation with his adversary. Satan is similar to Comus in offering attractions, arguments and, finally, force in trying to conquer a chaste mind by temptation. But neither hunger, the world nor promises of spiritual power have any effect on Jesus. Horatian, stoic fortitude is transcended by the inner light which justifies the rule of saints:

> Yet he who reigns within himself, and rules
> Passions, desires, and fears, is more a king; . . .
> But to guide nations in the way of truth
> By saving doctrine, and from error lead
> To know, and, knowing worship God aright,
> Is yet more kingly, this attracts the soul,
> Governs the inner man, the nobler part.

Although *Paradise Regain'd* and *Samson Agonistes* were published together (1671) the date when the latter work was written is controversial. Because of the use of rhyme and metrical experiments it is sometimes thought to be a product of the late 1640s which was revised during the 1650s. Others feel that the play is an expression of Milton's probable mood under the reign of Charles II. Although Samson triumphs, the play seems bitter and pessimistic; it emphasises rather the element of divine revenge in the Old Testament than New

Testament atonement, salvation and mercy. *Samson Agonistes* is modelled on Greek drama; Milton's introductory preface defends the writing of tragedy on both classical and Christian precedent, and mentions such features of his play as the chorus and the unity of time which are found in Greek drama. Whereas Greek drama was based on well-known public myths, Milton needs to preface his tragedy with 'The Argument' setting out the background of the story, which allows him to compress his play 'within the space of twenty-four hours'.

There is little physical action, the drama takes place in Samson's soul. The various stages of his condition are interpreted and commented upon by the chorus of Hebrews: 'Thou art become (O worst imprisonment!) / The dungeon of thyself'. *Samson Agonistes* is a bare, stark play — 'O dark, dark, dark, amid the blaze of noon' — of pride, suffering and punishment, in which renewal requires a surrender of self to God's purposes and to self-destructive vengeance on God's enemies; it shows 'Just are the ways of God' and concludes 'All is best, though we oft doubt'. Although there are passages of remarkable poetry in the play, its versification and diction are often laboriously awkward. The characterisation of Samson and the treatment of his conversion of will to God's purpose are marred by a self-righteousness which can also be found in Milton's prose but fortunately is less often seen in his poems. The play is a profound treatment of one of Milton's major themes; but Samson is an unattractive hero.

9

The background:
1660–1700

I Charles II

WHILE there was national rejoicing at the return of Charles II, the Restoration left many national problems unsolved. In his Declaration of Breda, Charles promised religious toleration, payment for the Army, and pardon to those who supported the Protectorate, provided that Parliament agreed; unfortunately the new Parliament elected the next year proved less liberal. As a result of harsh laws passed to ensure uniformity, the Presbyterians, Congregationalists and sectarians were once again forced outside the national church and were later to support the Whig opposition to the Court. The Corporation Act (1661), to examine the charters of municipalities, in effect put local power in the hands of Anglicans by excluding all those who refused the sacrament according to the rites of the national church. Attempts by Charles, and later James, to bring in toleration through royal prerogative were challenged by Parliament and distrusted by the Dissenters as a means to reintroduce Catholicism.

The land settlement at the Restoration wrecked many of the old Royalists and contributed to the cynicism which became characteristic of many courtiers. Although royal and church lands were restored, Royalists could only regain their property if it had been confiscated by the Protectorate. Royalists who had been forced to sell their lands to pay the crippling fines levied by Cromwell and Parliament were not recompensed. Part of the older nobility remained impoverished, while the Army officers, lawyers, merchants and traders who become rich and purchased land under the Protectorate retained their wealth and influence. As modern agricultural methods were used more widely, the old relationship between lord and peasant was broken. The national standard of living improved as food became more abundant and famine was no longer a danger. The tenant, however, was no longer seen as a potential soldier of his lord, but as someone who rented land and had to pay its full price.

At the Restoration Charles surrendered most of his inherited feudal rights (such as the prerogative courts and the right to sell peerages and wardships), in return for various taxes which were supposed to pay, but did not, for the expenses of the Court and government. Such reforms resulted in less social mobility. While the peerage was now closed, there were new, expanding wealthy upper and upper-middle classes. The price rise of the earlier part of the century had been brought to a halt and the country seemed to prosper; but prosperity was mostly for those already wealthy. Wage earners were worse off; many were driven from the land into cities. With the breaking of the monopolies of the guilds many trades and crafts were now open, but the result was often a lowering of wages and a loss of protection. A modern class structure was coming into being with the nation divided between the rich landowner, merchant and industrialist, and the poor, landless wage-earner.

There was a great increase in shipping and trade, which now became a government concern, usually at the expense of the Dutch with whom England was at war between 1664 and 1667. For a time there was harmony between the Crown and the London merchants and traders. The increased significance of trade and the Navy reflected the continuing growth of London, which dominated England and contained a tenth of its population. The years 1665 to 1667 were unsettled and saw the beginning of a new opposition to the Court. The Great Plague of 1665—6 was followed by the Great Fire of London, in which within four days more than 13,000 houses were destroyed. In 1667 the Dutch Navy launched a surprise raid up the Thames and towed away the *Royal Charles*, the largest vessel in the fleet. The same year the Earl of Clarendon, the King's main minister and the author of the so-called Clarendon Code which excluded Non-Conformists from government, was impeached.

The secret treaty of Dover with Louis XIV in 1670 was one of the many Stuart attempts to free the monarchy from the constraints of Parliament and form an alliance with France. In return for a French subsidy, Charles promised that he would take part in another war against the Dutch and would, at an opportune time, convert to Roman Catholicism. As rumours of the treaty spread Charles began to lose the confidence of many. Although the war of 1672 was really a land war between the Dutch and France, it contributed to growing distrust between Charles and the merchants, which had begun with the naval disaster of 1667. The Declaration of Indulgence, to Roman Catholics and Dissenters in 1672, raised the issue of the royal prerogative. Parliament replied with the Test Act, affirming Anglican control of religion. Any holder of office had to be Anglican, take various oaths, and declare against Catholic doctrine. The Declaration was originally an idea of Lord Ashley (later Earl of Shaftesbury) and John Locke, who thought it would be limited to Protestant Non-Conformists and thus create a political alliance between the Throne and the Dissenters. When Charles included the Catholics in the Declaration, the Dissenters split and soon the governing cabal of Lord Thomas Clifford, the Earl of Arlington, the Duke of Buckingham, Ashley and the Earl of Lauderdale collapsed. Ashley was dismissed from the Government and became a leader of the Opposition. In 1677 the Duke of York's daughter, Mary, married William of Orange.

The last years of the decade saw the frenzy of the Popish Plot and Exclusion Crisis. In 1678 Titus Oates, who had previously been indicted for perjury, dismissed from a naval chaplaincy, and expelled from a Jesuit college, and who falsely pretended that he held a doctorate of divinity from Salamanca, claimed that there was a Catholic plot to murder the King and massacre Protestants. When Justice Sir Edmund Godfrey, before whom Oates made his charges, was mysteriously found dead, murder was suspected. As Shaftesbury whipped London into hysteria, rumours spread that the French were planning an invasion, and all Catholics were made to leave London. Parliament voted to disband the Army and attempted to impeach Lord Danby, Charles's chief minister, who knew Oates was lying. In 1679 Parliament was dissolved and new elections called. The new Parliament was even more hysterical. A bill was introduced to exclude

James from succession and instead make the heir to the throne the Duke of Monmouth, who was probably Charles's illegitimate son, conceived during the years of his exile, and who may not even have been that. Shaftesbury wanted a weak king with a doubtful title to the throne, who could be controlled by the House of Commons. As the tension grew between those for and against the King, the nation appeared on the verge of a civil war.

In 1680 the House of Commons passed an Exclusion Bill which was defeated in the Lords through the leadership of George Savile, Marquis of Halifax, the famous trimmer who followed a middle course between the Whigs and Tories. After dissolving Parliament, Charles called an election for a new Parliament which met in Oxford to avoid the pressure and danger of the London mobs. Shaftesbury and his supporters arrived expecting complete victory or civil war. Charles offered as a compromise a regency which would allow his brother to succeed to the title of king with little power. When it became clear in 1681 that nothing short of exclusion would satisfy Shaftesbury's followers, Charles dissolved Parliament and had Shaftesbury arrested for treason. Although freed by a London jury, Shaftesbury fled to Holland. A plot by his followers to kill the King, the Rye House Plot, was discovered and contributed to the mood of reaction throughout the country as the Anglican gentry, fearing a Whig revolution, closed ranks behind the Court. City and borough charters were surrendered and remodelled to give the Tories control of local government. Charles never again called Parliament, and was supported by a French subsidy until his death in 1685. During his final illness he declared himself a Catholic.

II James II and William

James II wanted tolerance for Catholics and tried to create an alliance between Dissenters and Catholics against the Anglican establishment. Charles I had lost his head by defending the High Anglicans; James II lost his throne by challenging them — a particularly foolish challenge since the Anglican position was much stronger as a result of the reaction after the Exclusion Crisis. Most Catholics objected to James's policy as likely to lead to terrible repression; but James, influenced by a few Jesuits at the Court, persisted. The beginning of his reign, however, was very unlike its conclusion. The new Parliament was favourable to the King and voted him larger sums than Charles ever had. A foolish attempt by the Duke of Monmouth to raise a revolt was quickly put down and showed that the 'Good Old Cause' was no longer a danger to the throne. Unfortunately James immediately demanded the right to give offices to Catholics, raised a large army which was stationed outside London, put Catholics in charge, enlisted Catholic soldiers and made a Catholic governor of the port of Dover. The 1685 revocation of the Edict of Nantes, which had provided toleration of the Huguenots in France, furthered suspicion, which was intensified when the judges agreed that James could dispense with the Test Acts which had kept Catholics from state offices. In 1686 Catholics were made Lord-Lieutenant of Ireland and put in charge of the fleet. The Privy Council included the Jesuit Edward Petre. There were many conversions, Catholic schools and chapels opened, a Papal Nuncio was received at Court, and Catholics were forced on Oxford and Cambridge. When Magdalen College, Oxford, protested, twenty-five fellows were dismissed.

After the Declaration of Indulgence of 1687 temporarily suspended the Test Act and granted liberty of worship to Catholics and Non-Conformists, James started remodelling city charters to get candidates for Parliament favourable to repealing penal laws. He issued in 1688 another Declaration of Indulgence, and ordered bishops to have it read in churches. Seven bishops who refused were arrested, but declared not guilty by the courts. Many Anglicans and Non-Conformists were on the verge of revolt; but as James had no heir it seemed best not to resist and wait until William of Orange could succeed to the throne. The last straw was when James's Queen gave birth to a son in June 1688. William was invited by leading Anglican lords to save England. He had kept in touch with English lords and radicals over the years, awaiting such a chance, and he soon landed in England with an army. James tried to flee to France, was captured, brought to London, and quietly allowed to escape. After an election was held, Parliament declared the throne vacant, and while the politicians discussed what to do next William announced that if offered the kingship he would accept it; if offered any position less he would immediately return to his own country. Although Mary shared the title to the throne, William made clear that he was the King.

William soon had the usual problems with Parliament which would not vote him the revenues he needed. Even repayment to the Dutch for the cost of transporting William and his troops to England was skimped. Whereas Parliament had voted James a revenue for life, it voted money yearly to the new King. On assuming the throne, he brought England, for the first time during the century, into European power politics. He now governed England, provided leadership in Holland, kept an international alliance intact, and was the main commander and strategist for the forces opposing Louis XIV who declared war on England supposedly to restore James to the throne.

Although William was now the most prominent figure in Europe, the cost of the war made English taxes many times higher than they had ever previously been. There were several attempts at assassinating him, and at times he feared an uprising. By 1697 most of Europe was exhausted with the length and cost of the nine-year war. England was in a serious financial crisis, unable to pay its Army, and some members of the Grand Alliance had made peace with Louis. In the Treaty of Ryswick Louis recognised William as King of Great Britain and promised not to aid his enemies. During the last years of his reign the Old Whigs increasingly became defenders of royal power, while a new generation of Whigs joined with Tories to criticise the throne.

III The arts and society

The Restoration saw the renewed involvement of the Court in the theatre. Charles's expressed preference for French drama contributed towards the writing of rhymed heroic plays; he sometimes saw plays in manuscript and suggested improvements. Such courtiers as Sir Robert Howard, Roger Boyle, Sir Samuel Tuke, the Duke of Newcastle, Etherege, Sedley and Wycherley wrote plays for public performance and saw them into print. Although Dryden's access to the

King is a special case, explained by his marriage into the Howard family, professional writers of the period appear more familiar with their social superiors than previously. Dryden claimed that the supposed refinement of Restoration literature resulted from the example of the King and the returned Court. While serious professional writers still depended upon patronage, they now formed friendships and quarrelled with their patrons.

Although the theatre was still the main literary market-place, such works as *Paradise Lost, Absalom and Achitophel,* Cotton's *Scarronides, The Hind and the Panther,* some plays, and scientific and religious works were reprinted and went through many editions. During the final decades of the century the increasing readership for serious literature began to permit a shift towards professionalisation of writing. Roger L'Estrange's version of Seneca's *Morals* (1678), the translations of *Ovid* published by Tonson (1680), the *Miscellany Poems* (1684, 1685, 1693) that Dryden edited for Tonson, and Tonson's subscription edition of *Paradise Lost* (1688) were signs of an increasing demand for translations and poetry. Both the nobility and professional writers contributed to the books of translations and Tonson's collections. After losing his Poet Laureateship and Court patronage, Dryden only partly turned to the stage for a source of income; his translations of *Juvenal and Persius* (1693), *The Works of Virgil* (1697) and *Fables, Ancient and Modern* (1700) showed that it was now becoming possible to live independently as a writer. As the writer became financially independent, he lost his close association with the Court as a spokesman of the ruling class and instead became its critic. Dryden's stubborn but quiet opposition to William was followed in the next century by the extremely vocal opposition of Swift, Pope, Gay, Fielding and young Samuel Johnson to Walpole and King George. With the rise of the professional writer, literature stopped being a social acquisition and fewer gentlemen in future would write poetry with such ease.

Along with the rise of the professional writer, there was also a new interest in literary lives, literary history and criticism. Literary biographies early in the century are mostly eulogies; modern literary biography in English begins after the Restoration. Beyond Dryden's mixture of biography and criticism in his life of Plutarch, literary biographies include *Theatrum Poetarum: or a Compleat Collection of the Poets* (1675) by Milton's nephew, Edward Phillips (1630–96?) and an *Account of the English Dramatic Poets* (1691) by Gerard Langbaine (1656–92), who also published a catalogue of English plays (1680) and *Momus Triumphans: or the Plagiarisms of the English Stage, exposed in a Catalogue* (1688).

If patronage was becoming less a matter of an artist or writer attaching himself to a noble family or the Court, other channels of support were developing. City and merchant taste had begun to catch up with the Court. By the 1670s the theatre was attended by the city as well as the Court and by the 1680s middle-class and feminine sensibilities began to influence what was performed. Signs of the increasing interest in the arts include Oldham's attempt to live as a professional writer, the emergence of the Grub Street hacks (Grub Street was originally, according to Samuel Johnson, a mean street near Moorfields in London much inhabited by writers of small histories, dictionaries and temporary poems, whence any mean production is called *Grubstreet*), the founding of societies to promote music, and the long line of wealthy who wanted their portraits painted by Kneller, thus allowing him to open a studio for the mass production of paintings. With the spread of wealth among a new upper-middle class, by the 1690s the older Puritan middle-class distrust of the arts as idolatry, falsehood and waste had been transformed into a desire for socially elevating but morally respectable culture. After the coming of William to the Throne, and the symbolic defeat of libertine and High Anglican Court culture, the arts became increasingly moralistic and sentimental.

Beginning in the 1650s with Anne Collins's *Divine Poems* (1653), women increasingly published their writings. While the prolific, eccentric Margaret Cavendish, Duchess of Newcastle (1624–74) and the poet Anne Killigrew (1660–85) and Katherine Philips were minor talents, Aphra Behn was the first professional woman writer who made a career by her pen. She was followed in the 1690s by Mary Pix and other women dramatists. 'The Maidenhead' by

'Ephelia', included in *Female Poems* (1679), is a remarkably witty, skilful poem by an unknown author:

> Men strive to gain it, but the way they choose
> T'obtain their wish, that and the wish doth lose.
> Our thoughts are still uneasy, till we know
> What 'tis, and why it is desired so:
> But th' first unhappy knowledge that we boast,
> Is that we know, the valued trifle's lost.
> Thou dull companion of our active years,
> That chill'st our warm blood with thy frozen fears,
> How is it likely thou shouldst long endure,
> When thought itself thy ruin may procure?

The second half of the century also saw an increase in writings about the inferior status of women in society. Mary Astell (1666–1731) wrote *A Serious Proposal to the Ladies for the advancement of their true and great interest* (1694), *Letters Concerning the Love of God* (1695) and *Some Reflections Upon Marriage* (1700). Although Lady Mary Chudleigh (1656–1710), complained 'Wife and Servants are the same', such authors thought that more education and learning was the solution.

From the mid-century onward there was a proliferation of diaries, memoirs and lives. In the early 1670s the Puritan Lucy Hutchinson (1620–?) wrote for her family the *Memoirs of Colonel Hutchinson* about her husband's public career. Margaret Cavendish, Duchess of Newcastle, published a naïve, exuberant *Life* (1667) of her husband while he was still living. Among the Quakers George Fox (1624–91) kept a journal which was edited for publication (1694) by William Penn (1644–1718). Samuel Pepys's (1633–1703) diaries, written in shorthand, cover his early career, 1660–9, when he was a young man first discovering the possibilities of life. Observant, vivid, rich with private life and public events, the diaries reveal Pepys proud of his beautiful wife, his house and his possessions, desirous of getting ahead, prudent but living every moment fully. He enjoyed the company of prostitutes, attended plays, composed songs and recorded the gossip, scandals and fashions of the first decade of the Restoration. For their human detail the diaries remain popular reading:

July 13th 1667: Mr Pierce tells us what troubles me, that my Lord Buckhurst hath got Nell [Gwyn] away from the King's house, and gives her 100 L a-year, so as she hath sent her parts to the house, and will act no more.

July 14th 1667: To Epsum, by eight o'clock, to the well; where much company. And to the towne to the King's head; and hear that my Lord Buckhurst and Nelly are lodged at the next house, and Sir Charles Sedley with them: and keep a merry house. Poor girl! I pity her; but more the loss of her at the King's house.

John Evelyn (1620—1706) was more sober and serious. His *Diary* is a history of the time; it begins with Evelyn's travels on the Continent during the Commonwealth, where he met Waller, Hobbes and Denham, and continues until 1706, a month before his death. It includes information about Anglican worship under Cromwell, the Royalists in Paris and contemporary sermon styles. Evelyn's style is plain but elegant, as might be expected from someone who had been involved with the Royal Society reform of English prose.

The two volumes of *Athenae Oxonienses* (1691—2) by Antony Wood (1632—95) are an example of the antiquarian interests of the later part of the century. A magpie, obsessively concerned with recording the facts of the past, Wood researched the lives of bishops and writers who had been educated at Oxford from 1500 to 1690. He was helped by John Aubrey (1626—97) whose amusing unpublished *Brief Lives* — notes, anecdotes and gossip about a variety of people, events and things — shows a similar curiosity and obsession with 'searching after Antiquities'.

The Restoration was a new start for English music. The Interregnum had broken the continuity of church music and Charles brought with him a taste for French music. The King's liking for opera influenced the theatre and his attempt to imitate Louis's ensemble of royal violins led to the introduction of church music with long instrumental passages between the declamatory solo vocals which had replaced the older contrapuntal style. The restored Chapel Royal soon produced a new generation, including John Blow (1649—1708) and Henry Purcell (1659—95), with greater understanding of the direction continental music had taken earlier in the century than had the Caroline and Interregnum composers. Purcell, who began to follow the Italian tradition, wrote church, stage and instrumental music in a great range of styles from the rhapsodic to the fugal, but with an emphasis on the declamatory, exalted, ceremonious and public. His florid operatic tendencies are shown by the way his musical settings require words from the poetic text to be continually repeated. The King imported French musicians and made concert-going a social occasion. During the Restoration the first English public concerts began and societies were formed to promote such musical events as St Cecilia's Day performances.

Restoration drama evolved a distinctive acting style. Acting was consciously artificial, stylised and pictorial with gestures exaggerated to suggest the type of character and emotion. Kings and heroes strided across the stage in affected, stately magnificence and struck poses. Often the gestures and poses preceded the words and visually established the meaning of the scene. With perspective scenery and elaborate costumes, the visual effect of such acting would have been like a series of paintings. Artificial stylisation was also characteristic of the way the players delivered their lines. Influenced by Italian opera and French musical spectacles, the new heroic play was performed in a manner similar to the singing voice in recitative. Each emotion had its own delivery. Passionate rants were bellowed, love speeches were made in a whining voice, while the give and take of repartee in dialogue was expressed in cadenced, musical tones. The players trained their voices for a harmonious elocution and gave particular attention to the duration and movement of sounds. Restoration actors were especially concerned with 'tone'. Congreve defined the recitative style as 'improving the natural Accents of Words by more Pathetick or Emphatic Tones', and Colley Cibber compared Thomas Betterton's voice to that of a singer. Recitative music was added to plays and even Shakespearean drama was acted in the new fashion. Despite its many critics this style of acting held the stage until a more natural way of speaking and moving began to prevail towards the end of the century. When Cibber in the 1690s tried to continue the Restoration acting style his audience often laughed and hissed.

While opera influenced Restoration drama, opera did not become naturalised to England during the century. A small number of French operas were performed, but hardly any English operas were written. Shadwell's *Psyche* (1675), with music by Matthew Locke, was more a spectacle play. Blow's *Venus and Adonis* (*c.* 1680) was an experiment at setting a masque to continuous music. Dryden's *Albion and Albanius* (1685), with music by the Frenchman Louis Grabu, was perhaps the first English opera. Purcell followed with *Dido and Aeneas* (1689), *King Arthur* (1691) and *The Fairy Queen* (1692).

The Restoration continued the English emphasis on portraiture. Peter Lely (1618—80) became principal painter to Charles a year after the Restoration and during the next two decades painted hundreds of portraits of the royal family, courtiers, statesmen and other dignitaries. Lely uses the rich colours and textures of draperies, clothing, uniforms or architectural background for compositional purposes. He sometimes uses pastoral settings, but his attempts to capture Van Dyck's languid refinement often result in an appearance of sleepiness. The work of the Bohemian engraver Wenceslaus Hollar (1607—77) and Jan Siberechts from Antwerp (1627—1703), anticipates eighteenth-century topographical landscapes. Although Hollar liked to draw from various viewpoints, Siberechts preferred symmetrical, formal, regular compositions. Antonio Verrio, who came to England from Italy in the 1670s, had a Baroque taste for large allegories and *trompe-l'oeil* effects (trick the eye: giving from a distance the illusion of reality) in the rooms and halls he decorated at Windsor Castle, Whitehall Palace, Chatsworth and Hampton Court, for Charles II, James II and William. Jacob Huysmans from Antwerp was perhaps the painter working in England closest to the European Baroque. Originally associated under Charles II with the circle around Queen Catherine of Braganza, his work is elaborate, allegorical and somewhat confectionery. Francis Barlow whom Evelyn called 'the famous painter of fowls, beasts and birds' is an oddity. 'An Owl Mocked by Small Birds' is Baroque in its turbulent movement, a forerunner of later English animal paintings, and a curious mixture of realism and what seems to modern tastes the surreal. Although Sir Godfrey Kneller (1646?—1723) was the most famous portrait painter of the last decades of the century, his work is often shoddy and reveals the hands of his various assistants who, after he had drawn in the face, were individually specialised in doing the wigs, clothes and background. His repetitive portraits often include allegorical figures, classical costumes and Roman clothing.

The last third of the century saw changes in London architecture, home decorations, and social habits. The return of the courtiers from France, followed by the destruction of the city of London by the Great Fire, the expansion of international trade, the revocation of the Edict of Nantes (which brought many Huguenot workmen to England) and after 1688 the presence of Dutch courtiers, resulted in new fashions, new buildings, new workmanship, new ideas of comfort, and the spread of continental tastes beyond the Court to the wealthy. Coffee, chocolate and tea were first introduced to London by the coffee houses which began opening in the late Interregnum; by the end of the century the new drinks had become fashionable among the upper classes.

Although London still had open sewers and slops continued to be tossed from windows into the streets, housing had become more sophisticated. The Elizabethan great hall had now diminished to a large vestibule, and the ground floor of a large house would include a reception room, parlour, dining-room and a room to which the guests could withdraw after eating. The bedroom, which from the Jacobean period onwards was becoming separated from the upstairs long gallery, now became a distinct room leading off the landing and no longer one of a sequence of rooms in a passage. There was more privacy, comfort, and furniture; mirrors and chests of drawers became normal, while such furnishings as the settee, the dressing-table, the card-table, the day-bed and various cabinets and cupboards were introduced. Walnut, especially walnut veneer and patterned inlays, began to be used in place of oak for the new delicate furniture. Chairs became common and were often upholstered. Parquetry floors, chandeliers, sash windows, glass wall-mirrors, stoneware and Chinese porcelain were among the new fashions. Domestic architecture had become classical; the larger houses had formal gardens with fountains and trimmed hedges and lawns on the European model. Although Christopher Wren's hopes after the Great Fire to redesign the pattern of London streets according to a master plan were defeated by property owners, he and his pupil John Webb (1611–72) rebuilt over fifty of the ninety destroyed churches and were responsible for the use of Portland stone, from the Isle of Portland, in Berkeley, St James and Grosvenor Squares. Wren's elaboration of Jones's sombre classicism into a more Baroque manner, also seen in the wood carvings of Grinling Gibbons (1648–1720), was continued by Nicholas Hawksmoor (1661–1736) and Sir John Vanbrugh in the final decades of the century.

IV Science and Newton

The Restoration saw the triumph of the new approach towards the natural world. Cowley, Dryden and other writers celebrated the new science, seeing in its discoveries an analogy to the restoration of monarchy in England. The King, impressed by the close relationships in France between royalism and an intellectual establishment, was interested in science, as were many members of the Court circle. The Royal Society, which developed out of Wilkins's Oxford Circle, included among its early members several writers, courtiers and Latitudinarian divines. It received its royal charter in 1662. The society's *Philosophical Transactions*, which began publication in 1665, were the first modern scientific papers, the forerunner of the learned journals of today. In the same year Robert Hooke (1635–1703) published the first treatise on microscopy. In the 1660s Henry Power, a disciple of Sir Thomas Browne, also used the microscope to study insects. The Hobbesian view of behaviour and ethics became fashionable among the Court wits, probably because it appeared to give scientific support to their cynical self-interest and hedonism.

The plain prose associated with the Restoration and with the Royal Society can be seen as partly a reaction against the impassioned, enthusiastic, metaphoric language of the Civil War and Interregnum, especially as found in sermons and religiously inspired political writings. Common sense, moderation, prudence and accommodation would prevent the nation returning to the chaos and frenzies of past decades.

Wilkins, a central figure in Interregnum scientific circles, also was an advocate of a new prose style. His *Ecclesiastes* (1646), written in short, pointed sentences, attacks elegant, artificial, witty preaching. In *An Essay towards a Real Character, and a Philosophical Language* (1668), sponsored by the Royal Society, he attempted to lay the foundations for a universal language of communication in a kind of pictorial shorthand referring to 'things'.

Besides influencing the tentative, non-rhetorical, clear prose style of the Restoration the Royal Society popularised the corpuscular, or atomistic view of the natural world. The new atomism was partly a return to the Greek and Roman view of the composition of matter, argued by Democritus (*b. c.* 470 BC), Epicurus (*c.* 341—270 BC) and Lucretius (*c.* 99—55 BC), and advanced again by the Frenchman Pierre Gassendi (1592—1655). As a scientific system it was inadequate (early atomic theory required hooked atoms, glued atoms, or occult sympathies to explain how particles held together), but it laid the foundations upon which Newton was soon to offer a more adequate theory. Robert Boyle (1627—91), the leading Restoration scientist, performed endless experiments of varying usefulness; following Bacon, he assumed that a massive collection of facts necessarily preceded theory. Some of Boyle's best work was on the pressure of atmosphere and properties of a vacuum. He showed that air is a material substance and has weight. His *Sceptical Chymist* (1661) tried to make chemistry into one of the new sciences. Although he cleared the ground by rejecting Aristotle's four elements and other such imaginative notions, he could not proceed beyond description to an understanding of the nature of material transformations. Other Restoration scientists include John Ray (1627—1705), whose classifications began systematic botany, and Richard Lower (1631—91), who conducted some controversial experiments. Lower contributed to the understanding of the relationship of air in the lungs to the blood. He was interested in blood transfusions and after transfusing the blood of a dog into another dog, he transfused the blood of a sheep into a man, who miraculously survived.

If Interregnum and Restoration science was clogged with experiment and fact finding, the great contribution of Isaac

Newton (1642–1727) was to rise above simple empiricism to construct a new mathematical–mechanical system of the world which the discoveries of the astronomers and other scientists had shown but not previously explained. While earlier scientists had argued there was no contradiction between Christian faith and scientific experiment, Newton proposed a universe both created and set in motion by God according to His own laws, laws which bound together all time and space. Newton's particles were not the unexplainable mechanical atoms of the Restoration, but could be studied by the same rules of attraction and repulsion, influenced by such physical forces as gravity, magnetism and electricity, which governed the planetary system.

Professor of mathematics at Cambridge, Newton was primarily a mathematician and theorist. His explanation of planetary motion by mathematics led to *Mathematical Principles of Natural Philosophy* (1687), which formulated three laws of motion and offered a universe of matter in motion in a void of space. The *Principia* explains the movement of the solar system and comets. Newton saw that to calculate gravitational force it was necessary to treat bodies as if all mass were concentrated at the centre; thus bodies can be treated as points for purposes of calculation. The planets are similar to tops, spinning, but attracted by other masses of matter; gravity makes planets orbit in ellipses. Before Newton it was impossible to *prove* the orbit of the sun and earth. The *Principia* also explains the gravitational effect of the moon and sun on the waters of the earth. Under the influence of universal gravitation, every particle of matter attracts every other and the relationships can be explained mathematically. The result is a mechanical, determinist universe, which, although created and set in motion by God, works without spiritual influence. Newton's other great contribution was to optics and it is mostly in his studies of light that he tentatively suggests modern notions of atomic interaction, questioning whether particles might not be governed by the same laws as the planets and large bodies of masses. He made optics a branch of physics, treating light as if it were similar to matter.

10

Restoration literature

I Towards Neo-Classicism

WITH the Restoration, literature adopted a public voice; politics and society replaced the self as the focus of interest while such subjective emotions as 'Enthusiasm', divine inspiration and the inner light were distrusted as causes of the Civil War and the chaos of the Interregnum. The new rationalism and desire for order, which was also influenced by the rise of French Neo-Classicism under Louis XIV, found expression in an unmetaphoric, unpoetic, conversational prose, while the elevating, illustrative simile, with its easy comparisons, replaced the ingenious metaphysical conceit, with its surprising analogies between the dissimilar.

If the poet's imagination descended from the sublime, mystical, fanciful heights of the Interregnum to a new clarity of expression, Restoration Neo-Classicism is more a modification and development of previous styles than a radically new departure in English literature. In keeping with the new rationalism and desire for order it avoids the excesses of previous styles and observes a slightly elevating decorum. A more graceful, poised version of aphoristic Senecan wit is noticeable in the dialogue of Restoration comedy, while the rhymed, balanced couplets of the heroic play give such epigrammatic wit a new elegance and conscious artificiality when used for repartee, argument and heightened emotional speeches. Even the metaphysical conceit survived the Restoration in the verse of Dryden, Cowley, Rochester and Oldham, although its use is more explicit, tentative, amusing, or ironic, especially when compressed and disciplined by the heroic couplet. It was not until a new style, influenced by Boileau, began to take form in the 1680s that an unmetaphoric, conversational verse began to replace the subtly implied analogies which were the basis of early Restoration poetry.

While the panegyric, topical poem, ode, satire and eventually verse epistle flourished during the Restoration, the smaller, more subjective poetic forms were increasingly regarded as trivial games in minor genres. The short Cavalier lyric became a facile exercise in compliment or the pornographic, which only Rochester had the philosophical depth and originality of craft to transform into an expression of the scepticism and cynicism common, despite the optimistic rhetoric of its panegyrists, to the first two decades of the Restoration. Similarly Restoration comedy at its best is ruthless and worldly whereas the heroic play and the sentimental drama which followed, with a few exceptions, are now primarily of historical interest.

II Satire and satirists: Butler, Rochester, Oldham

Although panegyrics and Pindaric odes to the King, the Royal Society and the new science, by Dryden, Waller, Cowley and others, were characteristic of the early years of the Restoration, and were meant to express a new consensus, satire was actually the most significant poetic genre of the last four decades of the century. The generalised satire of types common to the late Elizabethan and Jacobean period had evolved during the Civil War into attacks on particular individuals, topical events and political ideology. With the Restoration, satire on the Parliamentarians, Puritans and Cromwell was continued in such popular works as Robert Wild's (1609—79) *Iter Boreale* ('A Northern March', 1660), a description of General Monck's role in the restoration of Charles II. Easier to follow, less intense than Cleveland, Wild mixes raillery, puns and conceits. While burlesques and travesties were popular, the mock-heroic and other more sophisticated, elevated forms of satire began to develop during the 1660s and 1670s.

While licensing laws effectively prevented the publication of satire directed against the Court, satire of the Government circulated widely in manuscript. Often it imitated and parodied such fashionable genres as the panegyric. The many 'Advice to a Painter' poems parodied Edmund Waller's

Instructions to a Painter (1666), with its idealisation of the Duke of York's supposed victory at sea over the Dutch. In the reaction which followed the nearly revolutionary mood of the Exclusion Crisis, the Government treated even the possession and circulation of satires in manuscript as libellous and treasonable. It was not until 1689, when James II had been replaced by William, that the anti-Stuart satires in *Poems of Affairs of State* could be published.

The most popular poem of the early Restoration was Samuel Butler's (1612–80) mock-heroic *Hudibras* (published in three parts, 1662, 1663, 1677). Influenced by Scarron's travesty of Virgil, it ridicules the heroic and chivalric by using epic and romance formulas to describe the adventures of an absurdly pedantic Presbyterian knight, Hudibras, who attempts to tell time by algebra, and his mystical-Baptist squire, Ralph, who believes he knows the truth by divine inspiration. Writing in an octosyllabic four-stress rhyming couplet, Butler uses earthy language, comic rhymes and clumsy rhythms to deflate pretensions. There is a disproportion between style and sentiments; while trivia are treated in an epic fashion, pretentious ideas are treated in a low diction. *Hudibras* transforms the seventeenth-century genre of humorous, jovial epic romances into a wide-ranging satire; and, as in the best Restoration satire, the figures of mockery become larger than life:

> For *Rhetorick*, he could not ope
> His mouth, but out there flew a Trope:
> And when he hapned to break off
> I'th' middle of his speech, or cough,
> H' had hard works ready, to shew why,
> And tell what Rules he did it by.

Besides attacking the socially disruptive extremism of religious and political fanatics, Butler ridicules the experiments of the new science, the libertine morality of the Restoration and other intellectual, social and literary fashions. He is distrustful of all ideas, sects and philosophies, including the new sciences. The universe is God's work, an example of divine wisdom which can be known only through the senses and by applying reason to be observation of nature. Man, however, deludes himself; his passions and imagination breed fancies and superstitions and convert ignorance into strongly held opinions. Butler wanted a realistic literature; he claimed that heroic verse treated 'the slightest, and most Impertinent Follys in the World in a formall Serious and unnaturall way'. Wars were brawls; romantic love disguised ignoble passions.

Butler's best writing can be found in his two hundred prose *Characters*, where the form concentrated his scepticism on specific topics. Blending the English tradition of social and occupational types with the classical Theophrastan moral and psychological character, and perhaps influenced by Cleveland's satiric prose characters, Butler satisfied both his desire that art should copy real life and his playful sense of language. The characters are written in a clear, rapid, vigorous, sometimes scatological English, based on the unpredictable movements of speech, while using similes, metaphors, allusions, puns and mocking comparisons to make fun of such social types and occupations as 'A Modern Politician', 'A Degenerate Noble', 'A Fantastic', 'A Virtuoso', and such contemporaries as 'A Duke of Bucks', 'A Fifth-Monarchy-Man' and 'A Latitudinarian'.

Early influenced by Hobbes's view of life as matter in motion in pursuit of sensation unless inhibited by fear, John Wilmot, Earl of Rochester (1647–80) epitomises the egocentric individualism, hedonistic Epicureanism and scepticism of the Restoration Court. Such young courtiers as Sedley, Buckhurst, Etherege, Buckingham and Rochester, with their scandalous opinions and conduct, shocked both the citizens and older Royalists. Seeing themselves as heirs to the Cavaliers, aggressively rebelling against Puritanism, asserting their newly re-established aristocratic privileges, influenced by the sexual freedom of the French Court, and encouraged by the King's own promiscuity, they were for more than a decade leaders of fashion, until age and the deepening political crisis of the late 1670s made their libertinism distasteful. The Exclusion Crisis and Rochester's death-bed repentance and conversion, recounted in Gilbert Burnet's *Some Passages in the Life and Death of John, Earl of Rochester* (1680), marked the end of an era.

Rochester began writing Caroline *précieux* poems with a pastoral setting; besides themes of love and honour, constancy and change, there are witty libertine verses in which women turn the satire on men: 'Womankind more joy discovers / Making fools, than keeping lovers'. Such traditional commonplaces as the analogy of love to warfare became revivified by surprising attitudes: 'The victor lives with empty pride, / The vanquished die with pleasure'. While the aggression is often more cruel and less poised than in Carew's verse, the vocabulary is more philosophical and the tone reveals a greater scepticism: 'Live upon modesty and empty fame, / Forgoing sense for a fantastic name'. Ethical issues are punctured as if they were inflated balloons. 'Fair Chloris in a pigsty lay' is remarkable for the comic contrast between its *précieux* pastoral diction, its un-ideal setting, and its psychological ruthlessness. Many of the poems progress from lovely exercises in poetic convention to cynical final stanzas. The *carpe diem* 'Phyllis be gentler, I advise; / Make up for time misspent' concludes:

> Then, if to make your ruin more,
> You'll peevishly be coy,
> Die with the scandal of a whore
> And never know the joy.

The lyrics carry the arguments of earlier Cavalier and *carpe diem* (enjoy the day) verse to their logical conclusion.

The distinction between Rochester's songs and satires is seldom clear. The speaker and the addressee of the love poems are often subject to mockery and irony, the satires have lines of lyric grace. Honorific and low vocabulary rub shoulders when describing a person or event. The direction of a poem is often uncertain. Rochester's distrust of reason and the imagination is part of the attitude towards life which predominated in the early Restoration. The lovely 'Upon Leaving His Mistress' concludes: 'Live up to thy mighty mind, / And be the mistress of mankind'. The magnificent songs, 'Absent from thee, I languish still' and 'All my past life is mine no more' assume a Hobbesian view of the mind. Since 'images are kept in store / By memory alone':

> Whatever is to come is not:
> How can it then be mine?
> The present moment's all my lot,
> And that, as fast as it is got,
> Phyllis, is wholly thine.

Since the senses are all we have and they fail us, there can be
no constancy except in a life of sensation. Man imagines
desires for which he has no appetite and inhibits by ideas the
pursuit of what he wants. By contrast, animals are wiser than
man as they follow their instincts. Rochester is sceptical,
detached and brutal as he views the human condition. He has
no allegiance to any cause.

Rochester improved English satire towards more extended
narrative and a greater sophistication of tone. Although
'Tunbridge Wells' is essentially an improvised sequence of
lampoons on social types in which abuse predominates over
portrayal, it is sustained by its setting and has more unity than
Cleveland's satires. The disorderly movements of the speaker
correspond to the society portrayed, and both the speaker
and those he meets are presented as characters. 'A Letter
from Artemisa', a complex satire within a satire, using two
personae, is far from simple malice and invective. 'The
Disabled Debauchee' uses an ironic impersonation, the mock-
heroic, and an unusual twist in its final stanza to suggest that
debauchery may after all be wisdom. Rochester's contemporary application of Horace's 'Tenth Satyr' was widely
imitated by other poets. In 'Satyr against Reason and
Mankind', influenced by Boileau's clarity, sceptical common
sense and civilised manner in *Satire sur l'Homme*, using the
structure of a moral essay, Rochester laid the foundations
upon which Dryden, Pope and Johnson could build their
verse essays:

> Were I (who to my cost already am
> One of those strange, prodigious creatures, man)
> A spirit free to choose, for my own share,
> What case of flesh and blood I pleased to wear,
> I'd be a dog, a monkey, or a bear,
> Or anything but that vain animal
> Who is so proud of being rational.

Unlike Jacobean invective, Interregnum lampoons, or the
newly fashionable burlesque, the main direction of Augustan
satire after Rochester's and Oldham's imitations of Boileau
is towards an elegant conversational style using a simple
diction in which couplets, rather than being isolated, are
massed into fluent verse paragraphs. While the satirist will use

a variety of tones, the overall impression is that of a man of common sense and experience judging the vanities and follies of contemporary society and of mankind in general.

John Oldham's (1653–83) short career as a writer epitomises the changes which took place in English satire during the 1670s. He began as a follower of Cowley, using the Pindaric ode in 'To the Memory of My Dear Friend, Mr Charles Morwent' (1675). It is with 'A Dithyrambic' (1677), in which he uses the convention of the drunkard's song, that Oldham discovers the uses of an ironic monologue and of purposely bombastic, extravagant speech as a means of satirising Restoration society. For a time the pet poet of Rochester and the rakes, Oldham mockingly uses their speech and sceptical attitudes to portray a drunkard who defends his behaviour through Epicureanism: 'Thus live the gods (if aught above ourselves there be)':

> Drunk we'll march off, and reel into the tomb,
> Nature's convenient dark retiring-room;
> And there, from noise removed, and all tumultuous strife,
> Sleep out the dull fatigue, and long debauch of life.

In 'A Satyr against Vertue' (1679) Oldham's mockery of Rochester by impersonation must have seemed an innovation, since he later had to explain that he meant the opposite of what he appeared to say. While the technique is itself a further development of Rochester's use of an ironic persona, Oldham reverses the mask with the result that the speaker and his values are satirised. Impersonation is also the method of the *Satyrs Upon the Jesuits* (1679–81), where Ignatius Loyola and Henry Garnet, a priest supposedly involved with the Gunpowder Plot, are made to rant evil in couplets. Although Oldham was in advance of most of his contemporaries in exploiting the satiric possibilities of an ironic mask to give his work a structural unity, his manner is crude. Filled with clumsy energy, the verse is harsh, crabbed and abrasive. As is shown by 'Upon the Works of Ben Jonson' and the 'Prologue' to the *Satyrs Upon the Jesuits*, Oldham was a classicist imitating what he understood to be the harshness, accumulated invective, curses and declamation of Persius, Juvenal and the little-known Greek satirist Archilochus.

Oldham, however, began to move towards a finer, more mellow satiric tone. Influenced by Rochester's 'Allusion to Horace', Oldham's 'imitations' of Horace and Juvenal are among the first translations which modernise the classics using contemporary names, settings and events. His imitation of Boileau's *Eighth Satire* (1682) demonstrates the strong influence of the French writer on the evolution of Restoration satire from indignant vituperation to a civilised Horatian manner:

> But sillier man, in his mistaken way,
> By reason, his false guide, is led astray;
> Tossed by a thousand gusts of wavering doubt,
> His restless mind still rolls from thought to thought;
> In each resolve unsteady and unfixed,
> And what he one day loathes, desires the next.

The imitations of the 1680s indicate that before his death Oldham was learning 'the numbers of thy native Tongue' or what Dryden politely, ironically termed 'the dull sweets of Rime'. The influence of imitations and translations on the increasing elegance of Restoration verse can be seen from such versified criticism as the Earl of Roscommon's (1633?–85) translation of Horace's *Art of Poetry* (1680) and his often-praised *An Essay of Translated Verse* (1684), which rejected rugged, sharp satire in favour of smooth raillery and jest using a contemporary setting and names. Besides Oldham's version of Horace, Boileau's *Art Poétique* (1674) was adapted in 1683 by Dryden and Sir William Soames.

III Other poets: Cotton and Traherne

The surviving work of Sir Charles Sedley (1639–1701) is difficult to square with his reputation as a witty debauchee, praised in Rochester's 'Allusion to Horace' for writing 'song and verses, mannerly obscene'. A typical hedonistic libertine of the 1660s, Sedley reformed sometime during the 1670s. While there are poems on drinking and love, many are purely complimentary or reject sexual involvement. Although Sedley reduced the more thoughtful conceits of Carew and the Cavaliers to a facile eloquence, his opening stanzas are excellent. Occasionally capable of such unexpected lines as

'Love still has something of the Sea, / From whence his Mother rose', his usual style is *'Phillis*, you have enough enjoy'd / The Pleasures of Disdain'. The influence of song on Sedley's style is shown by the excellent refrains. His only long poem is *The Happy Pair*, a portrait of a loveless marriage and a satire on ambition; it has those sudden changes in theme and direction noticeable in Rochester's poetry and which make Restoration satire seem an expression of dissatisfied intelligence. Instead of a Restoration plea for libertinism, Sedley contrasts the unhappy marriages of the rich with the 'Bliss' of 'A Rustick Couple'.

His three plays show he had few talents as a dramatist. *The Mulberry-Garden* (1668), set in the months before the Restoration, has Cavaliers, wits, fops, a heroic sub-plot and rhymed verse. Its echoes of and allusions to Lovelace's poetry and life show the Cavalier image that the early Restoration rakes inherited and debauched. *Antony and Cleopatra* (1677) is an example of the drama of the late 1670s moving from the heroic towards Neo-Classicism. *Bellamira* (1687), Sedley's best play, continues the mood of the previous decades with its kept women and deceived keepers, but the wit at times is surprisingly crude.

While similar to Waller and Cowley, Charles Cotton (1630–87) spans both the Interregnum and the Restoration; his main influence was on later burlesque poetry. Scarron's parody of the *Aeneid, Virgile travesti* (1648) and Butler's Hudibrastic tetrameter were models for Cotton's influential *Scarronides* (1664), a burlesque of the first book of Virgil's *Aeneid*, which was followed by a travesty of the fourth book. *A Voyage to Ireland in Burlesque* (1670) is interesting for the casual self-mockery of the narrator. The range of styles in *Poems on Several Occasions* (1689) is extraordinary and includes extreme conceits, Jonsonian plainness and Neo-Classical ornaments. 'Winter Quatrains', an indirect comment on England under Cromwell, is filled with unexpected analogies and topics. Many of the poems, probably from the late 1640s and 1650s, recommend private retirement, friendship and bouts of drinking. Often they echo Lovelace's lyrics. Others have abrupt openings in the fashion of Donne and Suckling and are Caroline exercises in praise of women. In spite of his reputation for simplicity, Cotton sometimes expresses himself in the Interregnum Ovidian manner where poetic ornament and wit are dependent upon the play of words or some jingly effect, with the result that it is difficult to be certain what is meant to be humorous and what is unintentionally comic phrasing. There is the forced wit of 'A Journey into the Peak':

> My flesh was marble, so that, as I went,
> I did appear a walking Monument.
> 'T might have been judg'd, rather than marble, flint,
> Had there been any spark of fier in't.

As a man of letters Cotton has earned a lasting place in English literary history for his continuation into a second book of Walton's *Compleat Angler* (1676).

The vagueness and generality often noticeable in Interregnum mystical writing is also found in the verse and prose of Thomas Traherne (*c*. 1637–74), who wrote *Daily Devotions, Consisting of Thanksgivings, Confessions and Prayers* (1673) and *Christian Ethicks* (1675), which curiously is more concerned with spiritual well-being than with morals or social behaviour. His posthumously published *Hexameron or Meditations on the Six Days of Creation* (1717) is within a tradition that derives from the conclusion of Augustine's *Confessions*, where meditation is mixed with commentary on Genesis. Published anonymously these books received little attention until early in our century when Traherne's prose *Centuries of Meditations* and poems were discovered in manuscript. Recently his *Select Meditations* were identified. The sequential arrangement of Traherne's poems is still a matter of dispute and it is possible that lost manuscripts might provide a more rational coherence to his prose and verse contemplations. Although he refers to the usual steps of mystical contemplative ascent from purgation to illumination towards communion with the divine, Traherne writes from the perspective of someone enjoying continual illumination. There is little reference to sin or guilt. Traherne makes happiness seem easy, a matter of willing it.

The Centuries are to be filled with 'Profitable Wonders' and *'Enriching Truths'*. *Poems of Felicity*, while bringing 'down the highest Mysteries to sense' will be written in 'An easy Stile drawn from a native vein' with

> No curling Metaphors that gild the Sence,
> Nor Pictures here, nor painted Eloquence;
> No florid Streams of Superficial Gems,
> But real Crowns and Thrones and Diadems!

If the rejection of 'idle Fancies, Toys and Words' in favour of the 'naked Truth' belongs to the era of the Royal Society, Traherne's practice is rather Interregnum enthusiasm than rationalist discourse. He writes in a sublime, divinely inspired manner in which thoughts flow into each other as in a reverie; distinctions are blurred, words and themes are reiterated or recast in synonyms, and there is little progression from topic to topic. The prose and verse styles are alike; there is a preponderance of abstract or general nouns and adjectives, with few transitive verbs. The nouns and exclamations are not driven by syntax; they accumulate, pile up, and are held together by conjunctions. Some sentences have no verbs. Thought is associational. There is little feeling of time, event, narrative, temporal space, particularisation, or order. The effect is incantatory, repetitious, rapturous, ecstatic:

> Sweet Infancy!
> O fire of Heaven! O Sacred Light!
> How Fair and Bright!
> How Great am I,
> Whom all the World doth magnifie!

Starting from the Augustinian assumptions that we all were happy once, Traherne, in the magnificent passages of his *Third Century of Meditations*, locates such an unfallen state in childhood. He implies that the pre-existing soul descends into what Vaughan, in 'The Retreate', terms 'my Angell-infancy'; experience brings distraction and loss of the feeling of glory which accompanied intuitive understanding. We pursue a nostalgic notion of happiness until we learn to purify ourselves of the world, recollect the divine image within the mind implanted by God, and begin to recover our original joy through contemplation and experience of divine love. The Augustinian, or 'African', style noted for its associational movement, especially backward and forward in time, and its simultaneity of perspective, becomes in Traherne's hands less disciplined, more affective, and often monotonous, as he communicates his delight in the experience of his illuminated mind.

An eclectic minor writer who still attracts attention is John Norris (1657–1711), author of *Poems and Discourses* (1684) and *A Collection of Miscellanies* (1687). A disciple of the Cambridge Platonist Henry More, touched by the Epicureanism of the last half of the century, but against the natural philosophy of his time, Norris disliked the elegant, polished verse of the Restoration. His poetry ranges from *A Murnival of Knaves: or Whiggism displayed* (1683), a knotty satire in the manner of Cleveland, to the generalised diction of 'The Retirement'. There is also the Cavalier grace of 'The Irreconcilable' and the Cowleyesque humour of 'To his Muse':

> Come Muse, let's cast up our Accounts, and see
>   How much you are in Debt to me:
> You've reigned thus long the Mistress of my Heart,
> You've been the ruling Planet of my Days,
>   In my spare-hours you've had your part,
> Ev'n now my servile Hand your sovereign *Will* obeys.
>   Too great such service to be Free,
> Tell me what I'm to have for being thy Votary.

Although Norris uses a personal, rather than public, voice and prefers the intimate manner of the earlier poets and their stanzaic forms, his ear has become attuned to the couplet; his lines are heavily end-stopped, even when there is no punctuation mark.

While lyric poetry continued to be produced by such minor talents of the period as the late Caroline song writer Alexander Brome (1620?–66) and Philip Ayres (1638–1712), who wrote quatrains to accompany emblems in *Cupids Adresse to the Ladies* (1683) and Petrarchan sonnets in *Lyric Poems* (1687), more interesting were Alexander Radcliffe's (1645?–?) *Ovid Travestie* (1680) and *The Ramble: an Antiheroick Poem Together with some Terrestrial Hymns and Carnal Ejaculations* (1682), which continued the humour, social comment and rakish attitudes of the early Restoration. Thomas Flatman's (1637–88) well-shaped *Poems* (1674, 1676, 1682, 1686) may appear to add little to the range of Caroline feelings, but their moralising and obsession with death show the beginning of a new phase of sensibility. In contrast to Donne's fear of damnation and King's expectation of eternity, Flatman views death as the end of pain: 'In the cold earth the pris'ner lies / Ransom'd from all his miseries'. In Flatman's generalisations, melancholy and touches of pathos there are the seeds of eighteenth-century sentimentalism.

IV Prose: Bunyan, Baxter, Sprat and Glanvill

The decade before the Restoration witnessed an interest in French prose romances throughout high society. The extremely long, complicated, digressive, artificial stories of elegant and heroic behaviour by D'Urfé, Mademoiselle de Scudéry (1608—1701) and La Calprenède (1610—63) were translated into English, although because of their length complete publication sometimes spread over many years. Roger Boyle wrote a romance in the French manner, *Parthenissa* (1654—69), while Walter Charleton (1619—1707) published the anti-romantic *Ephesian Matron* (1659) and *The Cimmerian Matron* (1668). Philosophical and Utopian romances include George MacKenzie's *Aretina* (1660), Margaret Cavendish's imitation of Lucian in *The Blazing World* (1666) and Henry Neville's *Isle of Pines* (1668). After the Restoration fictional autobiographies of criminals, rogues and other notorious characters continued their popularity. Among the still-readable popular fictions are *The English Rogue Described in the Life of Meriton Latroon* (1665—71), written in four parts by Richard Head and Francis Kirkman, Kirkman's *The Counterfeit Lady Unveiled* (1673), and Head's *Life and Death of Mother Shipton* (1667) and *Floating Island* (1673). Later in the century Aphra Behn and Congreve explored the possibilities of narrative techniques. The best prose fiction, however, was written by Bunyan.

English sectarian Puritanism was a product of the seventeenth century and was insufficiently rooted in society to produce a literature until after the 1650s. Whereas the General Baptists evolved from the Dutch Anabaptists and Mennonites and were Arminians who believed that Christ's sacrifice made grace available to all men, the Particular Baptists, to which the tinker John Bunyan (1628—88) belonged, began in England during the 1630s and remained

Calvinists in theology. The Calvinist doctrine of scripture, conversion, faith and particular election was central to Bunyan's beliefs and his works reflect the Calvinist conversion experiences. The natural spiritual blindness of fallen mankind is followed by the awakening to awareness of the sinfulness of one's life. Such consciousness brings humility and despair, fear and trembling. After a long period of terror of reprobation and hell, the sinner discovers his justification through faith. He is one of the elect. (Christian loses his burden at the foot of the cross and is marked and given a roll; in *Grace Abounding* Bunyan is told 'My Grace is sufficient for thee'.) Assurance of spiritual rebirth is followed by a life of spiritual combat and continual temptations to be overcome. Calvinists were encouraged to keep diaries and write autobiographies recording their experience which could be used before the congregation as proof of conversion and which could be followed by others.

Grace Abounding (1666) belongs to this genre of Calvinist spiritual autobiography and differs from now forgotten but similar works primarily in the artistry with which Bunyan treats his conversion. Rather than a record, it is written by a mature man looking back on a crisis in his life. Whereas most spiritual autobiographies do not attempt to describe in detail the emotional turmoil felt before sanctification, Bunyan offers a long history of the fluctuations of despair and hope. The alterations of emotions are reflected in the many words such as 'but' and 'yet' which link antithetical expressions. Many passages and scenes stand out, such as the conviction of sin while playing cat, the year-long obsession to sell Christ, and the vision of the women of Bedford. Bunyan considers himself the greatest sinner, feels possessed by the devil, hears voices, imagines tortures, longs for the innocence of childhood, and is so involved with his condition that the external world hardly exists.

The first part of *The Pilgrim's Progress* (1678), written during Bunyan's first imprisonment (1660–72) for unlicensed preaching, allegorises the Calvinist pattern of conviction of sin, despair, justification and continuing struggle until Christian enters heaven. The need to be vigilant is shown by Christian losing his roll while sleeping, and the continual temptation to despair is represented by the fact that although he has journeyed beyond the Slough of Despond, and lost his burden at the cross, he must face the Valley of Humiliation and the Valley of the Shadow of Death. Even on the Delectable Mountains he is shown the Hill of Error, the Giant Despair, and a door to Hell. *Pilgrim's Progress* turns theology into fiction. It is an allegory of the elect, not Everyman, and its story is a continuous metaphor. From the dramatic opening paragraph with its repetition of 'I' and images ('a man clothed with rags', 'a book in his hand', 'a great burden upon his back') to entry into the heavenly city and the contrasting damnation of Ignorance, the story is filled with detail, events, characterisation, individual habits of speech, conversation, the give and take of personal relations, and social comedy. As fiction *Pilgrim's Progress* is simple but vivid; while often as improbable as previous romances and picaresque tales, it has more feeling of real life and idiomatic language than is usually found in the seventeenth-century novel.

The second part of *Pilgrim's Progress* (1684) is a portrait of a Christian family following the way of the husband. With the companionship of Mercy and later Great-heart, Christiana and the children follow her husband's route. Although the second part includes a similar progression towards justification and sanctification, it has fewer frightening episodes. Great-heart, representative of Christiana's minister, shows her the way and overcomes the dangers. The lighter, more domestic atmosphere is no doubt what Bunyan considered proper for a woman's salvation. Having shown the way to glory, Bunyan said he would illustrate the path to Hell. Told in the form of a dialogue between Mr Wiseman and Mr Attentive, *The Life and Death of Mr Badman* (1680) describes the progress of Badman through his sins, pretended repentance and death. Similar to sensational rogue stories of the time, filled with many digressions and exemplary anecdotes, it is an indication of how the early novel evolved intertwined with Puritan autobiography and exemplary tales. Bunyan's other major fiction *The Holy War* (1682) is an elaborate, confusing allegory. More complex, learned in allusion and elevated in style than Bunyan's other works, it contains numerous glances at Stuart politics and contemporary Court fashions.

The well-known controversialist, Richard Baxter (1615–91) published more than 140 tracts during his lifetime. His devotional classic, *The Saints' Everlasting Rest* (1650), both expresses Puritan assurance in personal salvation and uses meditative techniques. After 1662 Baxter refused to be made bishop and refused to conform, but would not join any sect and was no longer permitted to preach. Friendly with Boyle, Tillotson and Glanvill, he was attracted to the reasonableness and tolerance of the Latitudinarians, but felt that fallen man would remain self-deceived by business and pleasure from an exact understanding of virtue and vice. Repentance, self-examination and despair (the Calvinist scenario for conversion) were necessary to hope. But Baxter could also write 'He that hath the best and rightest Reason, and by consideration makes the most use of it, is the best Christian and doth God best service'. In *Reliquiae Baxterianae: or Mr Richard Baxter's Narrative of the Most Memorable Passages of his Life and Times* (1696), the autobiographical first part, composed in 1665, contains many of the familiar characteristics of Puritan autobiography, including the conviction of sin while stealing fruit in an orchard (imitated from Augustine's *Confessions*) and a description of conversion ('Soul-experiments', 'Heart-Occurrences'); but in keeping with Baxter's moderation, the description of his spiritual education is relatively brief and seen from the outside. Although he has a Calvinist sense of mission, Baxter is similar to the Anglican autobiographers and historians in being concerned with events outside himself and his calling. He can write at length of Cromwell or a Ben Jonson play and of public controversies and debates.

Edward Hyde, the Earl of Clarendon (1609–74) wrote the first major English history and one of the first significant secular, in contrast to spiritual, autobiographies. Chancellor of the Exchequer in 1643, he was appointed guardian of Charles II in 1645 and followed him into exile, where he began his *History of the Rebellion and Civil Wars*. At the Restoration he was made Lord Chancellor and Earl of Clarendon (1661). Unpopular with the younger courtiers and blamed for the war with Holland, he was impeached and fled to France in 1667. Influenced by the French political *mémoire*, usually written in the third person as narrative,

Clarendon in exile began an autobiography, parts of which he used to finish his *History* (published 1702—4). The *History* is classical, elevated and dignified in tone, with long, stately sentences marked by elegant symmetry and antithesis. The manner is impartial but judicial, understated, observant of personalities, but weak on social and economic causes. Clarendon was a conservative who believed in law, religion, tradition and statesmanship; consequently he ascribed the rebellion to individual weakness and ambition. The *History* is notable for the way he has transformed earlier character types into portraits of such real historical figures as Lord Falkland, Charles I and John Hampden. The *Life* (written 1668—70) uses third-person narration and is concerned with historical facts, political judgements, and the characters of friends rather than Clarendon's personal life. Witty, aphoristic, but guarded, Clarendon even writes of himself as a character seen by an amused observer.

The foremost propagandist for the new experimental science and the Royal Society was Thomas Sprat (1635—1713), who, besides *The History of the Royal Society* (1667), wrote Pindaric, conceited verses in the manner of Cowley, and 'An Account of the Life and Writings of Mr Abraham Cowley' (1668). As the society was chartered in 1662, a history might seem premature, but Sprat's purpose is to recommend experimental science for its utility. Besides promoting better knowledge of 'the wonderful contrivance of the Creation', its method of inquiry is contrasted to the attitudes which produce civil and religious turmoil. A 'rational Religion' is more suitable to 'the present Inquiring Temper of the Age'. After blaming 'specious *Tropes* and *Figures*', 'this vicious abundance of *Phrase*, this trick of *Metaphors*, this Volubility of Tongue' for the world's evils, Sprat describes the manner of discourse used by the Royal Society:

They have therefore been most rigorous in putting in execution the only Remedy that can be found for this *extravagance*, and that has been a constant Resolution to reject all amplification, digressions, and swellings of style; to return back to the primitive purity and shortness, when men deliver'd so many *things* almost in an equal number of *words*. They have exacted from all their members a close, naked, natural way of speaking, positive expressions, clear senses,

> a native easiness, bringing all things as near the Mathematical plain-
> ness as they can, and preferring the language of Artizans, Country-
> men, and Merchants, before that of Wits and Scholars.

Sprat was aware that such a style is not appropriate for all occasions. His defence of the Royal Society is written more persuasively than the bare style in which he reviews previous learning. In an appendix to the *History* he suggests to poets that science and inventions can be a source of new images, metaphors and allusions.

The relationship between the rise of modern science, modern prose and new attitudes towards the world after the Restoration can be seen from the writings of Joseph Glanvill (1636—80). Ordained into the Church of England at the Restoration, Glanvill began writing a defence of Henry More's views of the soul which somehow turned into an enthusiastic defence of the new science and a sceptical approach to knowledge. When *The Vanity of Dogmatizing* (1661) was attacked for recommending scepticism, Glanvill replied that he wanted freedom of enquiry, not the radical Greek scepticism of Pyrrho. Dogmatism is 'the raging Plague of our times', destroying the Church and bringing civil turmoil. In *Plus Ultra* (1668) he defends the usefulness of scientific experiments and the religious purposes of the Royal Society and praises Robert Boyle.

The revisions of *The Vanity of Dogmatizing* clearly indicate how style and thought were changing under the influence of the scientific method and the new rational empiricism. The 1661 *Vanity* is a heated, enthusiastic argument for scepticism and the scientific method, written in a Senecan style of loose, asymmetrical and short, antithetical, witty sentences. The language is metaphoric and rhetorical. By 1644 Glanvill was a Fellow of the Royal Society to which the *Scepsis Scientifica* ('Scientific Inquiry', 1665), the second version of *Vanity*, is dedicated. Glanvill praises Sprat and the prose style recommended by the Society. He is against the 'musick and curiosity of fine metaphors and dancing periods'. He wants 'a natural and unaffected eloquence'. He revised his prose to avoid Latin mannerisms and antithetical wit. The third version of *Vanity*, the *Essay Against Confidence in Philosophy* (1676), is written in a bare, abstract, non-metaphoric, non-figurative, unemotional, scientific, objective language, and is very much shorter.

Two popular and influential Restoration divines, Isaac Barrow (1630–77) and John Tillotson (1630–94), were Latitudinarians, members of the Royal Society, and concerned with the reformation of preaching along similar lines to those the Society advocated for conversation and prose. Barrow took a sober, rational approach to religion, arguing the 'Profitability of Godliness' and the 'Fruitlessness of Sin'. He advocated a 'simple manner of speaking to the point'. A master of lucid, logical exposition, but also concerned with correct English grammar, Tillotson was famous for his candid but reasonable and amiable man-to-man tone; Dryden studied his style. In keeping with the ideals of the Royal Society, his approach is utilitarian: men can only be convinced of religion by showing it is to their advantage. There are no flights of fancy, no illuminations; Tillotson's sermons are cultured essays in which he appeals to the best classical writers to prove that Christianity is what the moralists and natural theologians of the past really sought in philosophy.

Although a Tory High Anglican, Robert South (1634–1716) also attacked the elaborate styles of Andrewes and Taylor for their use of metaphors, allegories, similitudes, Greek and Latin, and warned that 'a plausible, insignificant word, in the mouth of an expert demagogue, is a dangerous and dreadful weapon'. While opposed to the Royal Society and the new rationalism, he was very much of his time in his common-sense utilitarianism and satiric sense of humour. He preached a sermon on 'Christianity mysterious and the wisdom of God in making it so'. His style is plain, vigorous, colloquial and wittily urbane.

V From heroic plays to sentimental tragedy: Settle to Otway

At the Restoration, monopolies to form theatrical companies were given to Sir William Davenant and Thomas Killigrew, both Caroline playwrights. Women actresses were permitted to perform in the small playhouses, which made increasing use of scenery and emphasised spectacle. The use of actresses led to plays centred upon young couples who engaged in witty repartee. Repartee was to be a prime interest of both comedy and the heroic play. Besides Caroline *précieux* conventions and topics, there was a French influence brought back by the restored Court. The early heroic play might be said to have begun with Davenant's *The Siege of Rhodes* (1656) and Roger Boyle's *The Generall* (1664), which mixed *précieux* tragicomedy with the rhyme of French classical drama. Another popular type was the humours comedy of Shadwell, influenced by Jonson and the French playwright Molière (1622–73), which offered exaggerated characters; John Lacy and John Caryll adapted Molière in the direction of farce.

Dryden's *Tyrannick Love* (1669) and *The Conquest of Granada* (Part I, 1670; Part II, 1671) provided two models for the rhymed heroic play. Whereas the ranting tyrant Maximin, in the former play, is grotesque and contrasted with the virtuous St Catherine, the latter play combines chivalric romance with the fall of an empire to create an epic-like panorama. In the heroic plays which followed the two elements were brought together as the grotesque and horrific is heightened in Settle's *Cambyses* (1671) and *The Empress of Morocco* (1673). Even after rhymed tragedy went out of fashion, blank-verse heroic plays continued to be written. The heroic plays and Dryden in particular are mocked in Buckingham's *The Rehearsal* (1671) and Joseph Arrowsmith's *The Reformation* (1673). Towards the middle of the 1670s a new direction in drama became apparent when Nathaniel Lee and Dryden turned to blank verse and an emphasis on characterisation, psychology and pathos. With its upper-class characters, refined language and sexual humour, Etherege's *She wou'd if she cou'd* (1668) anticipates such comedies of the 1670s as Wycherley's *The Country Wife* (1675) and his own *The Man of Mode* (1676). From the Exclusion Crisis to the Glorious Revolution drama is notable for political commitment and in tragedy the increasing prominence of pathos. The usual satiric method was to write an historical parallel to contemporary politics; the new affective, pathetic tragedy is represented by Otway's *The Orphan* (1680), Settle's *Fatal Love* (1680) and Banks's *The Unhappy Favourite* (1681).

The early rhymed Restoration heroic play was the product

of a small circle close to the Court. To the extreme stylisation, love—honour debates, idealised heroes and heroines and changeable scenery of Caroline tragicomedy, the Restoration, spurred on by the King's admiration of French drama, added the exotic settings of Davenant's musical entertainments and rhymed verse couplets. Subsequent developments included the return of the Senecan, grotesque, ranting villain of Elizabethan drama, the glory-seeking romantic hero of the French dramatist Pierre Corneille's (1606—84) *Le Cid*, and the patterned, witty artifice of Ariosto's epic *Orlando Furioso*, in which the defence of Christianity provided a setting for the absurd and marvellous.

Although *The Generall* by Roger Boyle, Earl of Orrery (1621—79), brother of the scientist Robert Boyle, was not produced in London until 1664, the manuscript was circulating at Court by 1661, and may have been written in the late 1630s. It probably influenced the rhymed parts of *The Adventures of Five Hours* (1663) by Sir Samuel Tuke (*c*. 1620—74), a play which popularised elaborate, romantic, foreign intrigues. Boyle's innovation was to put into rhyme the set speeches, discourses and repartee concerning such topics as honour, jealousy, revenge and love which were expected in Caroline drama. The almost mechanical opposition of opinions, the artificial patterning of character and verse, and the carrying of casuistry and boasting to extremes is also present in *Mustapha* (1665), which introduces the Restoration heroic play with a villain as the central character.

The influential politician Sir Robert Howard (1626—98) wrote *The Vestal Virgin* (1664) in rhyming couplets with the artificial dialogue and love—honour theme of Boyle's plays. There is a bloody fifth act and an alternative happy ending for those who prefer tragicomedy. It is impossible to know how much of *The Indian Queen* (1664), the first rhymed heroic play produced in London, was Howard's. Dryden only claimed to have written 'part' of it. After the relationship between Howard and Dryden cooled, Howard, in the preface to his collected *Four New Plays* (1665), argues that rhymed drama, *précieux* dialogue, and tragicomedy are unnatural.

Elkanah Settle (1648—1724) significantly figures in the rise and fall of the heroic play. *Cambyses* (1671) made him a rival to Dryden and created a new, influential formula.

Like *Tyrannick Love, Cambyses* uses the Elizabethan convention of a ranting tyrant who out-Herods Herod, but adds a
fantastical illogicality and striving for effect after effect,
which is sensational:

> CAMBYSES: Hold: You're ungrateful. Though you've cruel bin,
> Thus, thus *Cambyses* will your favour win.
> You shall enjoy *Osiris* — Do not start:
> 'Tis he alone that lodges in your heart.
> To win your favour this brave deed I'le do;
> Be cruel to my self, and kind to you.
> Fame shall no longer to the World impart
> That I want pow'r to win a Ladies heart:
> For since all other means successless prove,
> To gain your kindness I'le resign my Love.
> I to my Rival will with Honour yield;
> As the retreating *Parthians* win the field.
> *Osiris*, Madam, is for you decreed,
> He is — I, and the gods have so agreed.
> MANDANA: Oh, now I fear —
> CAMBYSES: Now for his Arms prepare.
> Draw back that Curtain.
> Take your Lover — there.
> [The Scene opens, and on a Table appears the Body of *Osiris*,
> beheaded; & an Executioner, with the suppos'd head in a
> vessel of blood.]

Although Settle's incompetence makes it difficult to distinguish between what is purposely ludicrous bombast and what
is unintended nonsense, Mulgrave and Rochester backed *The
Empress of Morocco* (1673), which after an immense success
was printed with engravings of scenes from the play. In
Empress there is more emphasis on the ludicrous, tyrannical,
grotesque and sensational. Settle also gained a protégé in the
obscure Samuel Pordage (1633—91), whom he helped with
Herod and Mariamne (1673?). Stung by Settle's success,
Dryden, Shadwell and Crowne wrote the quibbling *Notes and
Observations on The Empress of Morocco*. Settle replied in
Notes and Observations on The Empress of Morocco Revised
(1674). Even after Dryden and Lee turned towards a less
artificial drama, Settle continued with the heroic in *The
Conquest of China by the Tartars* (1676) and *Ibraham, the
Illustrious Bassa* (1676), although they also reflect the new

sentimentality. Besides contributing the Whig *The Female Prelate* (1680) to the Exclusion Crisis, Settle's later work includes the amusing *The World in the Moon* (1697), which sets the rehearsal of an opera within a London comedy.

One result of the controversy over *The Empress of Morocco* was Thomas Duffett's (?—?) first burlesque play. His later parody of Shadwell's operatic *Tempest* (1674), itself an adaptation of the Dryden—Davenant version (1667) of Shakespeare's play, and of Shadwell's opera *Psyche* (1675) are more than simple burlesques. Written in prose, they include interesting characters and a vigorous portrait of London low life. They not only parody heroics and opera, but also look forward to the Newgate pastoral of Gay and Fielding.

The absurdities of the rhymed heroic play were mocked in *The Rehearsal* (1671) by George Villiers, Duke of Buckingham (1628—87), which has a 'battle in *recitativo*', laughs at the spectacular use of changeable scenery, and makes fun of the use of epic similes on stage. Buckingham was probably aided by Thomas Sprat, the clergyman Martin Clifford and Samuel Butler, who was his secretary. The mixture of heroic and burlesque, the plotless plot, the satire on artifice, the mockery of epic-romance, the larger-than-life characters and the general disorder have affinities to Butler's *Hudibras*. And as in Butler's poem, the satire is mainly destructive but results in the creation of a world of fantasy. It has been compared to twentieth-century absurdist comedy in its incongruities, lack of plot and mockery of theatrical illusion; there is a dance of dead soldiers and a rebellion of the actors.

Nathaniel Lee (1648?—92) began with the stereotypes of the Restoration rhymed heroic play — a tyrant and a lustful villainness — in *The Tragedy of Nero* (1674). *Sophonisba* (1675) and *Gloriana* (1676) reveal his interest in building plays around usually contrasting female characters. Dryden's announcement that he was tired of rhyme was followed by Lee's *The Rival Queens* (1677), mostly in blank verse, published with a complimentary poem by Dryden. *The Rival Queens*, along with *All for Love*, helped to establish the new dramatic style in which pity for tragic characters replaced admiration of the heroic and wondrous. Although the play is a tragedy of character, in which the focus is rather on the domestic than the heroic, Alexander is a ranting tyrant in the lineage of Marlowe's Tamburlaine and Dryden's Maximin:

> Tear all your Robes — he dies that is not naked
> Down to the waist, all like the Sons of sorrow.
> Burn all the Spires that seem to kiss the skie;
> Beat down the Battlements of every City;
> And for the Monument of this loved Creature,
> Root up those Bowers and pave 'em all with Gold;
> Draw dry the Ganges, make the Indies poor;
> To build her Tomb no Shrines nor Altars spare,
> But strip the shining Gods to make it rare.

While it is often unclear whether or not Lee intends to be ironic, Roxana's amusing boasts sound Drydenesque:

> That to my arm her ruine she must owe,
> Her thankfull head will straight be bended low,
> Her heart shall leap half way to meet the blow.

Dryden and Lee collaborated on *Oedipus* (1678), the first Oedipus play to treat the incest motif as rather psychological than fated.

Writing at a high intensity, Lee is often bombastic despite his attempts at a Shakespearean diction. His taste for melo-dramatic spectacle and Jacobean horrors often tends to the grotesque; in *Caesar Borgia* (1679) there are five stranglings on stage, three poisonings and several other deaths. The puzzling *The Princess of Cleve* (1680) probably should be seen as Lee's sardonic view of the Restoration stage with its heroic ideas and libertine comic heroes. The ruffian rake Nemours who 'if he were dying . . . wou'd call for Wine, Fiddles and Whores' is a portrait of Rochester who, having formerly been Lee's patron, later became his enemy when *The Rival Queens* was dedicated to Mulgrave. Committed to Bedlam in 1684, released in 1688, Lee died of drink four years later.

John Crowne (1640?–1712) followed the changing taste of the age. *The History of Charles the Eighth of France* (1671), a rhymed heroic play, concerns love and honour, the fate of the nation, and has the usual bombast, repartee and witty similes. Through Rochester's influence, Crowne was commissioned to write *Calisto* (1675), a Court masque which includes some amusing comic quarrels in rhyme between Juno and Jupiter. *The Countrey Wit* (1675), a favourite of Charles II, is another instance of Molière's plots being anglicised into a cruder kind of comedy. The two-part, ten-act *The Destruction of Jerusalem* (1677), with its opposing Jews and Romans, lacks the coherent and sustained plot of *The Conquest of Granada*, but shows Crowne's ability to argue in verse and his tendency towards pathos, the sensational and the sentimental. Along with other dramatists Crowne took sides on the Popish Plot and the events that followed. *City Politics* (1682) offers enjoyable farcical satire on Oates, the Whigs and their literary supporters. The Tories have the wit and get the women. *Sir Courtly Nice* (1685) amusingly contrasts the affectations of a delicate, fussy fop with Surly, a morose, ill-mannered brute; in another pair of contrasts there is Testimony, a hypocritical religious fanatic, and Hothead, who opposes such behaviour with an equally zealous fanaticism. Crowne's later work includes an attempt at blending the heroic with pathetic tragedy, *Darius* (1688), a mixture of the heroic with the new chaste classical tragedy in *Regulus* (1692), and a sentimentalised, moralistic comedy, *The Married Beau* (1694). The rhymed, bombastic *Caligula* (1698) is part of the 1690s attempt to revive the heroic play and ranting villains.

Although John Banks (*c*. 1652–1706) made use of such characteristics of the heroic play as great warriors, ranting speeches, idealised love and scenes of horror and gore in *The Rival Kings* (1677), *The Destruction of Troy* (1678) and *Cyrus the Great* (written 1680?, published 1695), his natural direction was towards a more sentimental, tear-jerking, emotional drama. Four plays are based on English history and treat of the sad deaths of the Earl of Essex in *The Favourite* (1681), Ann Boleyn in *Vertue Betrayed* (1682), Jane Grey in *The Innocent Usurper* (published 1694) and Mary Queen of Scots in *The Island Queens* (1684).

Thomas Otway's (1652–85) plays, along with those of Dryden, Lee and Banks, were influential in the transition from rhymed heroic drama to blank-verse sentimental tragedy. The rhymed *Don Carlos* (1676) includes a long final death scene with lots of tears. *Titus and Berenice* (1676), adapted from Racine's *Berenice*, was followed by *Friendship in Fashion* (1678), which mixes farce with extremely bitter satire on Mr Goodville, a thoroughly objectionable libertine. Unlike most Restoration comedies which hold favourable or ambiguous attitudes towards the selfish hedonism of the day, *Friendship* makes the greed and cruelty of Goodville explicit: 'He never made Love but to delude, nor Friendship but for his ends.' The conclusion, in which wife, husband and friend make up their difference, is almost a parody of the cheerful ending of such plays as Dryden's *Marriage à la Mode*:

> Get thee in then and talk to me no more, there's something in thy Face will make a Fool of me, and there's a Devil in this Business which yet I cannot discover. *Truman*, if thou hast enjoyed her, I beg thee keep it close, and if it be possible let us yet be friends.

The History and Fall of Caius Marius (1679) mingles Roman history with *Romeo and Juliet* and is notable for 'O *Marius, Marius*! wherefore art thou *Marius*?' With *The Orphan* (1680), written in blank verse, Otway transformed the libertine of Restoration comedy into a villain who causes tragedy. The plot is as improbable as the psychology of the characters and is an excuse to work up tears for pitiful innocence and to illustrate the noble friendship of Castalio for his wicked younger brother Polydore. When Dryden claimed that the portrayal of masculine friendship in *All for Love* was a worthy subject of tragedy, friendship joined distressed innocence, tears, weak sentimental characters and suicidal concluding scenes as one of the conventions of the new tragedy. *Venice Preserv'd* (1682) is more concerned with the pathos of friendship betrayed and repentance through suicide than with politics. An anti-Whig satire, the play is confusing since the Senate and plotters are equally sordid.

Otway's tragedies have little inner coherence; plot and character are manipulated for effect, to create empathy and to raise admiration or pity. His two final comedies, *The Soldiers Fortune* (1680) and *The Atheist: or, the Second Part of the Soldiers Fortune* (1683), with their bitter cynicism, are of more value. In *The Atheist* the young lovers of the sub-plot of the earlier play are now married, tired of each other, and vicious:

COURTINE: Your humble Servant, my Dearest! I am only glad of this fair opportunity, to be rid of you, my Dearest: henceforth, my Dearest, I shall drink my drink, my Dearest, I shall whore my Dearest; and so long as I can pimp so handsomly for you, my Dearest, I hope if ever we return into the Countrey, you'll wink at a small Fault now and then with the Dairy-Wench, or Chamber-Maid, my Dearest.

Such unpleasantness was objectionable to the new virtuous sensibility which dominated literary tastes for the next century; Otway's sentimental tragedies were praised while his hard-boiled comedies were forgotten.

VI Comedy: Etherege, Wycherley and Shadwell

Given, along with William Davenant, one of the two monopolies to form theatre companies, Thomas Killigrew (1612–83), who had written some Caroline tragicomic romances, was less adventurous in using the new movable scenery. He also had less influence on the direction drama was to take. His *The Parson's Wedding* (probably written 1641 but not acted until 1664) shows the way Jonsonian comedy had developed through the Caroline period into an influence on Restoration drama. A satire on the Platonic love of the Caroline Court and on Puritanism, it also includes two gay young couples and two would-be wits. The young witty gallants are libertines.

While earlier Restoration comedies, notably Cowley's *Cutter of Coleman Street* (1661), make use of roguish Cavaliers, Sir George Etherege's (1634–91) *The Comical Revenge: or Love in a Tub* (1664) significantly contributed towards the new kind of comedy by portraying the manners and attitudes of the Court rakes. Sir Frederick's late-night revels, whores, heavy drinking and fights with constables reflect the world of Rochester, Sedley and the other young wits in rebellion against conventional values. Ironic, self-aware, honest with himself, Sir Frederick is a fashionable satanic hero. Distrusting sentiments, enjoying the battle of the sexes as a game, he can only be conquered by an equal as witty and sceptical as himself. The duel between him and Widow Rich is the main focus of the play and includes an example of the proviso scene which was to be increasingly significant in Restoration comedy. *She wou'd if she cou'd* (1668) is better shaped than previous Restoration comedies. While there are the usual contrasts of such social types as the young and the old, the free and the married, the fashionable and the would-be-in-fashion, and those who live in the city and those who come from the country, the comedy results from the sexual game. Love is, like the play, artifice:

> COURTALL: That which troubles me most is, we lost the hopes of variety, and a single intrigue in Love is as dull as a single Plot in a Play, and will tire a Lover worse, than t'other does an Audience.
> FREEMAN: We cannot be long without some under-plots in this Town; let this be our main design, and if we are any thing fortunate in our contrivance, we shall make it a pleasant Comedy.

Because love must be kept interesting, it requires players who are clever as well as attractive. The proviso scene is part of the sexual game.

The Man of Mode, or, Sir Fopling Flutter (1676) portrays a cold, cynical, but charming Restoration Don Juan who is partly modelled on Rochester; it offers an elegant, but coolly non-committed satiric comedy of fashionable manners and sexual behaviour. During a decade when sexual comedies of promiscuity, seduction and cuckolding were popular, Etherege's play shocked because its two main characters, Dorimant and Harriet, are neither judged nor sentimentalised; they are attractive, witty, engaging, hard and cruel. There is no final reformation of the rake; the play ends inconclusively with Dorimant protesting that he will be faithful, having previously in the same scene promised two women he would continue to see them after his forthcoming marriage. Harriet mocks his claim that he will reform after they are wedded:

> HARRIET: To a great rambling lone house, that looks as it were not inhabited, the family's so small; there you'l find my Mother, an old lame Aunt, and my self, Sir, perch'd up on Chairs at a distance in a large parlour; sitting moping like three or four Melancholy Birds in a spacious vollary — Does not this stagger your Resolution?
> DORIMANT: Not at all, Madam! The first time I saw you, you left me with the pangs of Love upon me, and this day my soul has quite given up her liberty.

HARRIET: This is more dismal than the Country! *Emilia*! pitty me, who am going to that sad place. Methinks I hear the hateful noise of Rooks already — Kaw, Kaw, Kaw — There's musick in the worst Cry in *London*! *My Dill and Cowcumbers to pickle!*

The conclusion is open to speculation; but Harriet, who is as tough-minded as Dorimant, knows what she is doing. The play offers a contrast between those who are wits and those who imitate the 'mode'. While true wit requires an exterior attractiveness, its characteristics are superiority as demonstrated through conquest, power, reputation, cunning, ingenuity and vitality. The Caroline lyric was less concerned with the experience of love than with the strategies of social behaviour within the game of courtship and seduction; *The Man of Mode* goes further in dramatising unethical characters whose morality is to win and to have the inner satisfaction of being superior.

The characteristics of Etherege's poetry are economy, sharp phrasing and control of metaphor. 'To a Lady, Asking Him How Long He Would Love Her' is the most complex of his songs. Several poems begin with Cavalier grace, interestingly complicated by Restoration psychology, but end weakly. Unlike Rochester, Etherege is not a philosophical poet. Whereas Rochester's pornography is both outrageous and reveals the discrepancy between imagination and reality, Etherege is amused at using four-letter words. 'The Imperfect Enjoyment' is more playful than shocking: 'Phillis, let this same comfort ease your care, / You'd been more happy had you been less fair'.

William Wycherley's (1641–1716) *Love in a Wood* (1671) is typical of early Restoration comedy in its multiple plots, exaggerated character types and satire on would-be wits, hypocritical Puritans, lecherous widows and marriages made for money. The assumption is that the young rakish gentlemen are superior to the middle-class citizen. Wycherley's own emphasis, in which love is contrasted to marriage, is shown in Lady Flippant's complaint, 'Not a Husband to be had for mony', and her subsequent remark, 'The Widows Fortune (whether suppos'd, or real) is her chiefest Bait'. Hypocrisy, cunning, the sexual chase and the role of money in marriage are among the themes of his plays. *The Gentleman Dancing-Master* (1672) contrasts the rebellion of the young, who must be cunning if they are to live honestly, with the hypocrisy of those who claim to represent conventional social and moral values.

In *The Country Wife* (1675) we are shown a world of adultery, jealousy, deceit, meanness and cunning, in which appearances of honour, friendship, generosity and love are used to disguise contrary intentions. It is a society in which marriage is treated as a business arrangement, contracted for financial or social reasons. Consequently most wives cuckold their husbands, while the husbands chase whores. Husbands, wives and rakes are, however, concerned with their public reputations. Cleverly exploiting the concern with appearances, Horner spreads a rumour that he is impotent, knowing that women will seize the opportunity to indulge themselves without harming their reputations. *The Country Wife* offers a comic but cruel portrait of Restoration fashionable society in which going to the theatre, drinking, adultery, whoring and card-playing filled the days and nights. It is a brilliant play. The opening exposition is clear and rapid. The 'china' scene in Act Four is famous for its sophisticated sexual wit:

LADY FIDGET: What d'y think if he had had any left, I would not have had it too, for we women of quality never think we have China enough.
HORNER: Do not take it ill, I cannot make China for you all.

Wycherley was most famous during the Restoration for *The Plain Dealer* (1676). Manly, a scornful malcontent of the type found in Jacobean drama, is modelled on Molière's *Misanthrope*. The epigraph on the title page, from Horace ('Ridicule generally decides great matters more forcefully and better than severity'), implies that Manly is excessive in his rejection of society. Although the plot shows Manly's being deceived by those who claim to be sincere, and his consequent learning to deceive others, he is treated sympathetically when betrayed and he remains gruff and surly even when reconciled at the play's conclusion to the way of the world. Fidelia in disguise as a boy faithfully follows Manly and eventually wins his love. She is straight out of romance and her behaviour is as improbable and extreme as Manly's misanthropy. The power of the play derives from its ambivalent perspective and ambiguous resolution.

Aphra Behn (1640–89) shows a strong interest in the problems of forced marriages, the marriage of young women to older men, marriage for money, and prostitutes. *The Dutch Lover* (1673) and *The Rover* (1677, Part II, 1681) are comedies of sexual intrigue. *The Forc'd Marriage* (1670), a tragicomedy, and *The Town-Fop* (1676) show parents trying to force the young into marriage. In *Sir Patient Fancy* (1678) and *The Lucky Chance* (1686), young men of the town cuckold well-to-do London citizens. A Tory, Behn wrote *The Roundheads* (1681) and *The City Heiress* (1682) during the Exclusion Crisis. The latter play satirises Shaftesbury. Her plays have energy, vitality, move rapidly and accept life as a series of sexual chases, a search for money and a game of cheating. For all their complication of intrigue and complex plots, they are racy and, despite some exaggerated situations which border on farce, seem realistic.

Her poetry is similar to her plays in sharing the sensibility of the young rakes. She satirised the Court wits and was satirised in return by them. In many poems she idealises free love:

> Recesses Dark, and Grotto's all conspire,
>   To favour *Love* and soft desire;
>   Shades, Springs and Fountains flowry Beds,
>   To Joys invites, to Pleasure leads,
> To Pleasure which all Humane thought exceeds.

Aphra Behn's prose fiction combines the improbable events and patterned plots of the romances with various techniques meant to create a feeling of realism. These range from an epistolary novel, *Love Letters between a Nobleman and his Sister* (1684) to the psychology of guilt in *The History of the Nun* (1688) to the inconsistent narrator of *The Fair Jilt* (1688), who sometimes is omniscient and at other moments can only guess, or confess ignorance, at what has happened. Although the realism is more in narrative techniques than plot or style, even the telling of the novels is inconsistent judged by later fictional standards and must be seen as the method of a period when the desire for realistic illusion had to be balanced against the reader's expectations of the artificiality of romance. In *Oroonoko* (1688) an African prince is brought to a Surinam slave plantation where he finds his beloved princess. A noble savage he behaves calmly and heroically in contrast to the immoral Christians.

With the success of his first comedy, *The Citizen Turn'd Gentleman* (1672, reissued as *Mamamouchi* in 1675) Edward Ravenscroft (1644–1704) turned from the legal profession to a career as a dramatist. Although his plays have little serious content, they are briskly amusing and often seem to parody the very conventions they employ. The proviso scene of *The Careless Lovers* (1673) includes promises of an adulterous marriage. Adapting his plays from Molière, Pierre Corneille's brother Thomas (1625–1709) and French novels, Ravenscroft added farce, additional characters, disguise, intrigue and explicit conclusions. In *The London Cuckolds* (1681) Ravenscroft took advantage of the identification of the defeated Shaftesbury with the City of London to write a bawdy sexual comedy in which three older citizens marry young wives and are soon given horns.

Thomas Shadwell (1642?–92) was a serious writer who experimented with ways to bring Jonsonian humours, satire and moral purpose to the Restoration stage. As the drama evolved, Shadwell tried to adapt the new themes and conventions to his aims, sometimes with surprising and confusing results. Throughout his development from a writer of humours characters to the sentimental, exemplary comedies with which he concluded his career, he had no sympathy for the hedonistic, libertine morals of the Restoration rakes. One of the few writers to support Shaftesbury and the Whigs during the Exclusion Crisis, Shadwell replaced his rival Dryden as Poet Laureate (1689) under William and Mary.

The Sullen Lovers (1668) is consciously Jonsonian in contrast to the new Restoration comedy of repartee and refined manners. The lovers both satirise others and are themselves humours characters. In his preface to *The Royal Shepherdess* (1669), Shadwell claims that in his play the rules of morality and good manners are strictly observed, with virtue exalted and vice depressed. In *The Miser* (1672), adapted from Molière's *L'Avare*, Theodore tells the supposedly fashionable hedonists, 'No more of your senseless Railing against Marriage, 'tis dull and common.' A better and more comic play is *Epsom Wells* (1672), in which the bustle of social activity at the resort provides a range of follies similar to Rochester's 'Tunbridge Wells'. Shadwell learned that witty repartee is not necessarily opposed to moral satire. *The Libertine* (1675) uses the Don Juan story to satirise libertine, Hobbesian, Restoration assumptions by carrying to a farcical extreme the claim that 'By Natures order, Sense should guide our Reason'. Don Juan and his two henchmen commit violent and sadistic parricide, rape, incest and murder. The repetition of the sensational becomes laughable, even farcical, before the three libertines are carried off to hell. Echoes of Lucretius, Rochester, Hobbes and Milton's Satan link the villainy to the Restoration intellectual milieu. *The Virtuoso* (1676) mocks those who claimed to be experts on a variety of subjects, especially the scientific experiments of the Royal Society. Sir Nicholas Gimcrack, the virtuoso, is obsessed with the study of eels, mites, maggots, frogs, spiders 'and never cares for understanding Mankind'. In the dedication of *A True Widow* (1678) Shadwell criticises the current taste for farce. The marvellous fourth act includes a play within a play during which the characters attend a parody performance of a farce. Theodosia, an especially witty, sceptical young lady parodies the conventional proviso scene of Restoration comedy by refusing to marry Carlus until he makes all her women friends fall in love with him. In *The Lancashire Witches* (1681) the good characters believe there is a Popish Plot.

Shadwell's late plays appear to reflect the values of the Whigs and their Lockean assumptions about human nature and society. He anticipates the concern of dramatists during the last years of the century with education for a proper marriage. *The Squire of Alsatia* (1688), modelled on Terence's *Adelphi*, has a didactic purpose. Humane, liberal tolerant upbringing leads to the reformation of a rake in contrast to the continuing rigid behaviour produced by covetousness and prejudice. *Bury Fair* (1689) mocks older tastes, French manners, the heroic play and the assumptions of the early Restoration. A reformed rake living a Horatian ideal of retirement convinces another rake that 'only Coxcombs persevere to the end of Debauchery'. *The Volunteers* (1692) contrasts the benevolence of the new order with the self-interest of the old. The former serve their country, the latter are only concerned with themselves. Moralists are usually at their best when in opposition; most readers will prefer Shadwell's earlier plays.

I Early poetry

AFTER attending Westminster School under the famous Dr Busby and Trinity College, Cambridge, John Dryden (1631–1700) became a minor employee of the government during the final years of the Protectorate. His *Heroic Stanzas*, influenced by Cowley's wit and by Davenant's use of the quatrain in *Gondibert*, were printed in *Three Poems* (1659) along with elegies by Edmund Waller and Thomas Sprat after Oliver Cromwell's funeral. *Astraea Redux* ('Return of Justice', 1660) celebrates the restoration of Charles II. The final fifty lines addressed to Charles are magnificent with their Virgilian echoes, analogy of the Restoration to Augustan Rome and 'turns' or variations on 'you' and 'your':

> Methinks I see those Crowds on *Dovers* Strand,
> Who in their hast to welcome you to Land . . .
> Oh Happy Age! Oh times like those alone
> By Fate reserv'd for Great *Augustus* Throne!
> When the joint growth of Armes and Arts foreshew
> The World a Monarch, and that Monarch *You*.

Written in vigorous heroic couplets, except for the then controversial innovation of an occasional triplet, *Astraea Redux* reveals what were to become many characteristics of Dryden's style, including the significant modifier ('ambitious *Swede*', 'mortal quarrels', 'designing leaders'), Virgilian phrases ('And Heaven that seem'd regardless of our Fate'), balanced and antithetical phrases often constructed upon zeugmas (figures of speech in which a verb or adjective does duty with two nouns, to one of which it is applicable, while the word appropriate to the other is not used: for instance, 'Madness the Pulpit, Faction seiz'd the Throne' = Madness seized (was prevalent in) the Pulpit, and Faction seized the Throne), sustained analogies to Christian and Roman history ('Thus banish'd *David*'), illustrative similes, compressed wit based on contraries or seeming opposites within a tightly composed couplet line ('Her blowes not shook but riveted his Throne'), single word images implying metaphors ('Of some black Star infecting all the Skies') and the use of contemporary and scholastic ideas ('The Springs of Motion from the Seat of Sense'). The poem reveals Dryden's talents for arguing wittily in verse and for inventing diverse tropes in which to treat contemporary public topics. While many of their characteristics were anticipated by Waller's panegyrics, Dryden's lines are more forceful and energetic.

Dryden's early poems reflect and celebrate the social, political and intellectual changes that came about with the Restoration. The verses complimenting Sir Robert Howard's *Poems* (1660) show that Dryden had moved into the circle of courtier writers (he married Lady Elizabeth Howard in 1663); he alludes to contemporary speculation concerning atoms, contrasts the new classicism in literature with the 'fanatic bays' of the recent past, and implies an analogy between Augustan Rome and the Restoration. The panegyric *To His Sacred Majesty* (1661) is another instance of Dryden celebrating a public occasion, the King's coronation. 'To my Honor'd friend, Dr. Charleton' (1663) reveals Dryden's increasing ability to speak precisely in verse; although the lines are end-stopped there is a continuity to the thought which fuses various topics into a sustained argument. Dryden implies in the poem that, as Columbus's discovery of the New World, the rationalism of Bacon, the scientific research of Boyle, Gilbert and Harvey are part of a restoration of 'Reason' after the tyranny of Aristotle's authority and the scholastic world view, so Charleton's book showing that Stonehenge was, supposedly, used to crown kings is part of the general restoration of England to its true spirit.

The poetry Dryden wrote during the first years of the Restoration was influenced by and helped shape the ideology of the monarchy; analogies are made between the restoration of Charles and the landing of Noah after the Flood, the return of David and the re-establishment of monarchy to Rome by Augustus Caesar. The restoration of Charles is further seen as analogous to the flourishing of the Temple under David and the great period of the arts in Augustan Rome. The style of the poetry accordingly attempts to achieve in English some of the characteristics of Augustan literature; there is respect for such classical genres as the elegy and panegyric, some traits of Latin syntax are adapted to English, echoes of Virgil support Augustan analogies, the tone is elevated, public, reasonable, somewhat witty. The regular pentameter and the end-stopped line of the heroic couplet create a sense of order, control and clarity. Increasingly the verse is organised by a narrative which sets the ideas about the state and society in a temporal and public context, while the imagery suggests that the events be seen within a cosmic or divine scheme. The association of the scientific method, the Royal Society and progress with the Restoration is furthered by linking the disorders of the past with ignorance and errors while implying that the new age is rational and free from fanatical opinions. The precise articulation of Dryden's ideas, his control over his similes and comparisons, the style of address poised between formal and epistolary, and the disciplined movement of the verse and sentences contribute towards expressing the supposedly new attitude towards the world. Dryden was an early member of the Royal Society and was on its committee to improve the English language.

After the Plague, the Great Fire of London and various defeats of the English by the Dutch Navy, it was difficult to sustain the optimism of the first years of the Restoration. *Annus Mirabilis* ('Miraculous Year', 1667) attempts to show that the naval war against the Dutch is going well and that Providence had brought affliction to London so that, like the Phoenix, it will rise from its ashes with renewed vigour. In a long digression, the Great Fire is seen as a test of the English people. The poem shows how the imitation of Virgil had improved Dryden's style; there is more clarity of description and elevation of diction, or what Dryden in the 'Account of the Ensuing Poem', addressed to Sir Robert Howard, calls 'elocution, or the art of clothing and adorning' thoughts 'in apt, significant, and sounding words'. Looking back from the eighteenth century Samuel Johnson said 'There was . . . before the time of Dryden no poetical diction, no system of words at once refined from the grossness of domestic use, and free from the harshness of terms appropriate to particular arts'. While acknowledging the influence of Waller and Denham, Johnson claimed 'the new versification, as it was called, may be considered as owing its establishment to Dryden'. The concept of wit was also changing from the far-fetched ingenuity of the earlier part of the century to appropriate comparisons which, as a test, are translatable into other languages and do not depend upon manipulations of language. Although it is common to speak of its excess of wit, the wit of *Annus Mirabilis* is more the result of ingenious similes than puns, antitheses and other kinds of Caroline and Interregnum Ovidian word play.

II The major poems: 'MacFlecknoe' to 'Religio Laici'

After the death of Davenant, Dryden was made Poet Laureate (1668) and two years later Historiographer Royal. Until 1680 his published writings, except for some translations of Ovid, were mostly for the stage. The songs, prologues and epilogues from his plays include some of the best verse of the period. Addressing the small, intimate theatre audience, Dryden is playfully clever, relaxed, topical, bawdy and like-able, a rather more engaging personality than the Royalist propagandist of the early poems. Having to write clearly and rapidly improved his skills. The similes which begin such prologues and epilogues as *The Wild Gallant* (revised), *The Tempest, An Evening's Love, Sir Martin Mar-all* reveal an ease in bringing comparisons to direct address. There is the famous epilogue to *Tyrannick Love*, where Nell Gwyn steps out of her part as the chaste Valeria and criticises the author: 'O poet, damn'd dull poet, who could prove / So senseless, to make Nelly die for love!' Referring to her notorious private life she mocks her dramatic role by speak-ing her own epitaph: 'Here Nelly lies, who, though she lived a slattern, / Yet died a princess, acting in S Catharine.' The lovely songs from *Tyrannick Love, The Conquest of Granada, Marriage à la Mode*, and *The Assignation* have unexpected sexual meanings which enrich otherwise facile exercises, giving them the libertine, Hobbesian attitudes of Rochester and the Court poets.

As someone whose career as poet and dramatist was linked with the Court, with which he appears to have been temperamentally and ideologically attuned, Dryden in his early writings aimed at expressing a supposed national consensus in favour of the monarchy and the new literary and scientific movements of the Restoration. Although Dryden seemingly ignored until the mid-1670s the new improvements being made by Rochester in satire, his plays and prologues offer many instances of a developing satirical talent. When, because of the Exclusion Crisis, he finally did publish satires he used the skills he had earlier learned as panegyrist to establish the mock-heroic as a significant literary kind. The use of an elevated heroic style for comic purposes was a recent development in European poetry, originating with the French poet and critic Boileau's (1636–1711) *Le Lutrin* (1673). *MacFlecknoe* was circulating in manuscript during 1676 and was printed in 1682 with the subtitle 'A Satyr upon the *True-Blew-Protestant* Poet T. S.'; 'Protestant' was the code word of the time for the anti-monarchical party. Thomas Shadwell, who attacked Dryden in the preface of his *Virtuoso* (1676), was a propagandist for the Whigs who dedicated his adaptation of Shakespeare's *Timon of Athens* (1678) to the Duke of Buckingham, author of *The Rehearsal*, a leader of the opposition to the King, and the Zimri of *Absalom and Achitophel*.

While the occasion for its publication was political, the theme of *MacFlecknoe* is literature. A mock-heroic description of a royal progress and coronation in which the succession to the kingdom of nonsense is passed on from the notoriously unsuccessful dramatist Richard Flecknoe (1620?–78?) to his supposed son (Mac) Shadwell, the satire is an advance in literary sophistication beyond Butler's methods of rough burlesque in *Hudibras*. The elevation of tone, epic manner, polished wit and unity of narrative sustain a superiority of attitude towards a world of literary hacks. The poem abounds in humorous anticlimaxes, puns and innuendoes:

> Sh--------- alone my perfect image bears,
> Mature in dulness from his tender years:
> Sh--------- alone, of all my sons, is he
> Who stands confirm'd in full stupidity.
> The rest to some faint meaning make pretense,
> But Sh--------- never deviates into sense.

The humorous use of Roman analogies and biblical typologies set against the repetition of Sh---------, the references to bad writers, the imagery of fog and false pregnancies, allusions to 'Pissing-Ally' and 'Brothel-houses' create a world of inverted values in which MacFlecknoe is praised for 'inoffensive Satyrs' which 'never bite', laughable tragedies and dull comedies. *MacFlecknoe* is also a mocking survey of past literary fashions ('wings display and Altars raise') and the bad writing of the age.

Absalom and Achitophel (1681), Dryden's greatest work, results from the poet's imagination being fully engaged in what might seem to be unpromising material of the Exclusion Crisis. It consists of a description of David's (Charles II's) illegitimate son Absalom (Monmouth), a survey of English political and religious controversy from the Commonwealth to the beginning of the Popish Plot, a character of Achitophel (Shaftesbury), the temptation and fall of Absalom, character sketches of the opposition, Absalom's progress through the countryside to gain support, the narrator's discussion of the foundation of government, descriptions of David's followers and 'Godlike' David's reassertion of order (Charles's dissolving Parliament at Oxford). The famous character sketches of Achitophel ('Sagacious, Bold, and Turbulent of wit') and Zimri are fine examples of the movement and texture of language supporting meaning:

> Some of their Chiefs were Princes of the Land:
> In the first Rank of these did *Zimri* stand:
> A man so various, that he seem'd to be
> Not one, but all Mankinds Epitome.
> Stiff in Opinions, always in the wrong;
> Was every thing by starts, and nothing long:
> But, in the course of one revolving Moon,
> Was Chymist, Fidler, States-Man, and Buffoon:
> Then all for Women, Painting, Rhiming, Drinking;
> Besides ten thousand freaks that dy'd in thinking.
> Blest Madman, who coud every hour employ,
> With something New to wish, or to enjoy!

The dangerous effect of man's imagination on social and political stability is one of the poem's main concerns.

While the use of the heroic mode for satire is a develop-

ment of the elevated style and of the use of analogy in
Astraea Redux and of the satiric application of an epic
manner to contemporary material in *MacFlecknoe*, the
conception of and characters in *Absalom and Achitophel* are
influenced by *Paradise Lost*. Dryden had adapted Milton's
epic into a rhymed drama, *The State of Innocence* (1674),
and his study of the poem can be seen in the epic-like
structure of his satire, the omniscient narrator, the use of a
multiple historical vision, the setting of the story against
significant moments of Christian history as recorded and
supposedly foretold in the Bible and in passages which both
imitate and are stylistically modelled upon scenes in *Paradise
Lost*: 'Him he attempts with studied arts to please, / And
sheds his venom in such words as these.' Throughout the
poem there is a sustained use of typology creating an implied
analogy between biblical history and seventeenth-century
English politics. The English are '*Adam*-wits, too fortunately
free', 'God's pamper'd people', 'The *Jews*' who 'banish'd
David did from *Hebron* bring'. The temptation and fall of
Absalom brings to mind both the fall of Eve and Satan's
temptation of Christ; the poem's conclusion recalls the
small faithful band of true Christians in Revelation who
withstand the power of the Beast until the Second Coming
when (the phrase comes from a passage in Virgil which had
long been seen as a prophecy of the coming of Christ) 'a
series of new time began'.

The second part of *Absalom and Achitophel* (1682) is
mostly the work of Nahum Tate, although Dryden contributed
the character of Corah (Oates) and the mocking descriptions
of Doeg (Settle) and Og (Shadwell): 'When wine has given
him courage to Blaspheme, / He Curses God, but God before
Curst him.' Although comic there is viciousness in the
humour ('A Monstrous mass of foul corrupted matter') not
found in the earlier poem. Dryden's satire is best when
tolerant and seemingly objective. Although it is packed with
appropriate images to express Dryden's disgust, *The Medal*
(1682), written after a London grand jury refused to indict
Shaftesbury of treason, suffers from its tone of unrelenting
invective and anger: 'A Vermin, wriggling in th' Usurper's
Ear'. After satirically attacking Shaftesbury, the London
mobs and their sects, and the attempt by the extreme Whigs

to replace monarchy with a republic, Dryden offers a vision of the horror which would follow: 'If true Succession from our Isle shou'd fail'. The description of the various sects fighting, of civil war, and of the resulting tyranny until the nation wearied restores monarchy effectively recapitulates in images and events the Interregnum. Whig replies to Dryden's poems include Settle's *Absalom Senior; or, Achitophel Transposed* (1682) and Shadwell's vicious *The Medal of John Bayes* (1682).

The divisions and seriousness brought about in English society by the Exclusion Crisis and the significance of religion at the time explain the writing of *Religio Laici* ('A Layman's Religion', 1682), an essay in verse which, although deriving from the Horatian epistle, was developing as a literary kind in England through the influence of Boileau (who wrote odes, epistles and satires as well as *The Art of Poetry*). Dryden's 'Preface' indicates the contemporary political relevance of scriptural studies:

> Reformation of Church and State has always been the ground of our divisions in England. While we were Papists, our Holy Father rid us, by pretending authority out of the Scriptures to depose princes; when we shook off his authority, the Sectaries furnish'd themselves with the same weapons, and out of the same magazine, the Bible. So that the Scriptures, which are in themselves the greatest security of Governours, as commanding express obedience to them, are now turn'd to their destruction; and never since the Reformation has there wanted a text of their interpreting to authorize a rebel.

From its magnificent opening simile comparing the borrowed light of the 'Moon and Stars' to Reason, through its survey of various contradictory philosophies and matters of religious dispute, the poem tries to persuade that 'The things we *must* believe are *few* and *plain*'. Since human reason is imperfect for understanding divine mysteries, there will always be controversies of biblical interpretation. What the Church of England teaches is sufficient for salvation. Better to curb 'private Reason'

> Than by disputes the publick Peace disturb.
> For points obscure are of small use to learn;
> But *common quiet* is *Mankind's concern.*

Not only does *Religio Laici* advocate the Anglican middle way between Catholic and Dissenter, but also it is an example of the possibilities of the middle style, 'plain and natural, and yet majestick'. The verse is precise, unornamented, and reasonable in tone, yet rhythmic, packed and often imitates the sense, as in 'A Thousand daily Sects rise up, and dye', or in the three stresses of *'To One sole GOD'*. It was perhaps only after 1680, and the assimilation of the new French classical models, that it was possible for the English to write poetry in such a manner. By contrast Dryden's earlier verse, in *Astraea Redux* and *Annus Mirabilis*, is much richer in poetic figures, conceits and word play.

III Later poetry: odes, translations and epistles

Dryden's awareness that the new, unlike the old, satire would be urbane, smooth and polished is alluded to in his 'To the Memory of Mr Oldham', published in *Remains of Mr John Oldham in Verse and Prose* (1684). Imitating the classical elegy with its lack of consolation and its economy, using the fruition imagery often traditional to the elegaic mode, Dryden contrasts his friend's 'harsh cadence of a rugged line' with his own late development towards harmonious, dignified verse. In keeping with the epigrammatic precision of tone, Dryden avoids extravagant tears and praise; instead his praise of Oldham's vigour is tempered with the understated reservation: 'and maturing time / But mellows what we write to the dull sweets of Rime'. A similar honesty can be seen in the ode 'To Anne Killigrew' (1686). A niece of the dramatists Thomas and William Killigrew, Anne was an amateur painter and poet on whose death Dryden wrote a Pindaric ode filled with glorious sentiments concerning the ideals of art, and phrases which subtly qualify his praise of the achievements of the deceased ('May we presume to say', 'Art she had none'). The poem is a playful exercise in the style of Cowley, by a superior artist who humorously imitated earlier literary fashions: 'When ratling Bones together fly / From the four Corners of the Skie'.

In contrast to such cheerful ingenuity is the made-to-order seriousness of *Threnodia Augustalis: A Funeral-Pindaric Poem, Sacred to the Happy Memory of King Charles II*

(1685), *Britannia Rediviva, A Poem on the Prince, Born on the Tenth of June 1688*, and *Eleonora, A Panegyrical Poem Dedicated to the Memory of the Late Countess of Abingdon* (1692). The best moments of *Threnodia* are when Dryden ranges beyond the occasion to speak in his own voice:

> So glorious did our Charles return:
> Th' officious Muses came along,
> A gay harmonious choir, like angels ever young;
> (The Muse that mourns him now, his happy triumph sung.)
> Even *they* could thrive in his auspicious reign;
>   And such a plenteous crop they bore
> Of purest and well-winnow'd grain,
>   As Britain never knew before.
> Tho' little was their hire, and light their gain.
> Yet somewhat to their share he threw;
> Fed from his hand, they sung and flew,
> Like birds of Paradise, that liv'd on morning dew.

Eleonora similarly rises above idealising panegyric at the conclusion when Dryden unexpectedly and wittily begins to satirise 'this bad age', 'So bad, that thou thyself hadst no defense / From vice, but barely by departing hence'.

Soon after the accession of James II to the throne, Dryden, along with many others at Court, became a Roman Catholic. Charges of opportunism can perhaps be answered by Dryden's refusal to return to the Church of England after James fled to France; Dryden was heavily penalised as a Catholic and suspected to be a Jacobite. In 1699 he wrote to his friend Mrs Steward:

> I can neither take the Oaths, nor forsake my Religion, because I know not what Church to go to, if I leave the Catholique; they are all so divided amongst them selves in matters of faith, necessary to Salvation: & yet all assumeing the name of Protestants. May God be pleasd to open your Eyes, as he has opend mine: Truth is but one; & they who have once heard of it, can plead no Excuse, if they do not embrace it.

Despite being a public poet Dryden's inner life was private. He warned 'What I desire the reader should know concerning me, he will find in the body of' *The Hind and the Panther* (1687). The relevant passages are few and tantalising:

O teach me to believe Thee thus conceal'd,
And search no farther than thyself reveal'd;
But her alone for my Directour take,
Whom thou hast promis'd never to forsake!
My thoughtless youth was wing'd with vain desires,
My manhood, long misled by wand'ring fires,
Follow'd false lights; and, when their glimps was gone,
My pride struck out new sparkles of her own.
Such was I, such by nature still I am;
Be thine the glory, and be mine the shame.
Good life be now my task: my doubts are done:
(What more could fright my faith, than Three in One?)

Even the impression given of someone intellectually convinced, but lacking faith, may be misleading, as the verses
which follow mention various paradoxes which have often
been used to show that reason and the senses cannot compre-
hend divine truths. Alluding to *Religio Laici* Dryden says 'let
the moon usurp the rule of day' if he trusts the 'subservient
organs' of sense and reason. While *The Hind and the Panther*
is a puzzling, uneven mixture of controversy, topicality and
apologetics, there are such good satiric lines as 'Never was so
deform'd a beast of Grace'. Dryden claims that Protestantism,
with its reliance on reason and the personal interpretation of
scripture, leads to schism and, eventually, political disobed-
ience. The poem is, however, too long, detailed, digressive
and undramatic; the third part, with its thinly disguised
allusions to divisions among the Catholics, is uninspired.

His translations of passages of Ovid and Theocritus in 1684
were followed by versions of Lucretius and Horace the next
year, the *Satires of Juvenal and Persius* (1692) and *The
Works of Virgil: Containing His Pastorals, Georgics and
Aeneis* (1697). Dryden's paraphrases do not rigidly follow
the original text, which he recasts. Influenced by Boileau's
modernising of classical authors, Dryden, along with
Rochester and Oldham, laid the basis upon which Pope and
Samuel Johnson could build their great satires by imitation
in contrast to Ben Jonson's word-by-word translations.
Besides expanding his source through what are really explanations and the insertion of contemporary political allusions,
Dryden allows his personality free play; the realistic, stark,
grim Tenth Satire of Juvenal, for example, becomes bawdy,
comic, even vulgar as Dryden indulges in play and the mock-

heroic. Whereas Juvenal's sexual passages are clinical warnings, Dryden is amused at sexual incompetence and enjoys comic euphemisms. His translations are seldom dull and offer many instances of his sense of the ludicrous. The translation of Virgil's *Georgics* was prefaced by Addison's influential essay which distinguishes the Georgic from the pastoral. Addison warns against matching the 'lowness' of subject with undignified words and advises an elevated style. Dryden's translation, however, gives humorous emphasis to the mock-heroic qualities of Virgil's *Georgics*:

> When a bull sees a cow
> With two fair Eyes his Mistress burns his breast;
> He looks, and languishes, and leaves his rest;
> Foresakes his Food, and, pining for the Lass,
> Is joyless of the Grove, and spurns the growing grass.
> The soft Seducer, with enticing Looks,
> The bellowing Rivals to the Fight provokes.

Dryden's sophistication of experience can also bring contemporary political implications into his translation, as in the description of the bees in Book Four, where the mock-heroic alludes to recent history: 'The Vulgar in divided Factions jar; / And murm'ring Sounds proclaim the Civil War'.

Among Dryden's best work of the 1690s are poems addressed to artists, in which he is concerned with the relationship of literature to culture. 'To My Dear Friend Mr. Congreve, on his Comedy Call'd the Double-Dealer' (1694) comments upon the arts under Charles II and William. Dryden observes of the increased cultivation of manners after the Restoration: 'what we gain'd in skill we lost in strength'. Congreve is 'the best Vitruvius, come at length', combining the strength of the Jacobeans with the wit of the Restoration. Dryden's confident manner, his sense of place in society and his ease at rapidly making clear analogies as part of a direct, colloquial address, show the virtues of the now triumphant Neo-Classical style. 'To Sir Godfrey Kneller', which appeared in *The Annual Miscellany for the Year 1694*, along with work by the new generation of Addison, Congreve, Dennis and Prior, traces the progress of painting from Ancient Greece through the Renaissance, alluding in passing to the sack of Rome when 'rhyme began t'enervate poetry. /

Thus, in a stupid military state, / The pen and pencil find an equal fate'.

Impressively skilful are the charming and metrically sophisticated 'Ode on the Death of Mr. Henry Purcell' (1696) and two other musical odes, 'A Song of St. Cecilia's Day' (1687) and 'Alexander's Feast' (1697), both celebrations of the feast of St Cecilia. The former uses an implied analogy, also found in Marvell's 'Musick's Empire', between the progress of music and the history of the world from the original chaos, 'When Nature underneath a heap/ Of jarring atoms lay', to the last days, when 'The dead shall live, the living die, / And Music shall untune the sky'. It is notable for the way the rhythm and sound reproduce the local subject-matter as in the seemingly unrhymed metrical chaos of the opening lines, the affective 'soft complaining' description of the flute's 'dying notes' and the triumphant triplet rhyme of the Grand Chorus. In 'Alexander's Feast' Dryden shows in each stanza how music differently affects the conqueror's emotions. The varied Pindaric lines and unexpected metrical effects are impressive. It is noticeable that while Dryden's prosody has become less irregular than in his early writing, he still does not isolate his couplets, fall into smooth verse patterns or rely on antithesis. He varies his caesura and uses enjambement and triplets as means of avoiding excesses of regularity, in contrast to Waller, Garth and others who developed English Neo-Classicism. Although he, along with others, banished conceits after the mid-1670s, he still uses occasional witty analogies.

'To My Honor'd Kinsman, John Driden', published among the translations of Chaucer and Ovid in *Fables, Ancient and Modern* (1700), one of the century's many Horatian poems praising retirement and self-contentment, subtly develops into a satire on the medical profession and an indirect criticism of the government. Dryden's kinsman, John Driden, is used to represent the new opposition to the throne when both the country Whigs and moderate Tories found themselves increasingly against William's foreign wars and authoritarian ways: 'Enough for Europe has our Albion fought: / Let us enjoy the peace our blood has bought'. Dryden's final disillusioned attitude towards the past century is best expressed in *The Secular Masque* (1700):

> All, all of a piece throughout:
> Thy chase had a beast in view;
> Thy wars brought nothing about;
> Thy lovers were all untrue.
> 'T is well an old age is out,
> And time to begin a new.

IV Plays

Dryden was the strongest influence on the theatre of the
second half of the seventeenth century, the last interesting
period of serious drama in England until the end of the nine-
teenth century. The early plays include the crude sexual
buffoonery of *The Wild Gallant* (1663), the popular farce of
the Dryden—Duke of Newcastle *Sir Martin Mar-all* (1667),
the passages of rhymed repartee in the tragicomic *The Rival
Ladies* (1664), and the curious revision, with Davenant, of
Shakespeare's *Tempest* (1667). Whereas Dryden's heroic
plays were formerly judged by naturalistic standards and
dismissed as extravagant silliness, they have increasingly
attracted critical attention for their power, polished artifice,
spectacle, witty verse, ironically comic situations and possible
exemplary significance. *The Indian Emperour* (1665) is one
of the first rhymed dramas in which can be found the
patterned dialogue, intellectual argument, large gestures and
other characteristics of the emerging heroic play. *Tyrannick
Love* (1669), with its theologically well-versed St Catherine,
who besides being a model of piety can rationally prove the
superiority of Christianity to other religions and philosophy,
includes a spectacular torture scene and a witty, outrageous,
argumentative villain, Maximin:

> You must do one, and that without delay;
> Too long already for your death I stay.
> I cannot with your small concerns dispence;
> For deaths of more importance call me hence.

> What! Miracles, the tricks of Heav'n to me?
> I'le try if she be wholly Iron-free.
> If not by Sword, then she shall dye by fire;

And one by one her Miracles I'le tire.
If proof against all kind of death she be,
My Love's immortal, and she's fit for me.

Such amusing bombast brought to the Restoration theatre the ironic distancing found in such earlier dramatists as Marston, Middleton and Webster, while continuing the Roman and Elizabethan tradition of the comic braggart.

The Conquest of Granada, (1670–1), a continuous ten-act spectacle, became, along with *Tyrannick Love*, one of the most imitated heroic plays. Dryden blends the romantic heroism of Corneille's *Le Cid* with the tongue-in-cheek artifice of Ariosto's mannerist, chivalric epic-romance *Orlando Furioso* ('Roland's Madness'), to create a drama in which there are many amusing and ironic touches as the indomitable will of Almanzor, under the conflicting pressures of love and honour, becomes socially responsible. The final victory of the Christians over the Moors, which makes Almanzor's eventual marriage to Almahide possible, reconciles the conflicts of love and honour and heroic individualism and community in the proper tragicomic manner, providentially bringing the rightful heir to the throne. If some of Dryden's Restoration critics saw his hero, Almanzor, as just another version of the ludicrous, bombastic Maximin, others, with perhaps equal justice, felt the play 'so full of ideas that the most refined romance I ever read is not to compare with it; love is made so pure, and valour so nice, that one would imagine it designed for an Utopia rather than our stage'.

Secret Love (1667), the excellent *Marriage à la Mode* (1671), and *The Assignation* (1672) are interesting attempts to elevate English comedy above the crude farce, humours characters, intrigue plots and amusement at trickery which had formed the basis of many plays of the century. By using upper-class or noble characters, a split plot in which the comedy has a thematic relationship to the heroic sub-plot, Dryden succeeded in reshaping the confused multi-plot Caroline tragicomedy into a serious dramatic form. Unfortunately his example was not followed by others. The main theme of *Marriage a la Mode*, dedicated to the Earl of Rochester, is expressed in its opening song with its Hobbesian—Rochesterian assumptions:

> Why should a foolish Marriage Vow
>   Which long ago was made,
> Oblige us to each other now
>   When Passion is decay'd?
> We lov'd, and we lov'd, as long as we cou'd,
>   Till our love was lov'd out in us both:
> But our Marriage is dead, when Pleasure is fled:
>   'Twas Pleasure first made it an Oath.
>
> If I have Pleasures for a Friend,
>   And farther love in store,
> What wrong has he whose joys did end,
>   And who cou'd give no more?
> 'Tis a madness that he should be jealous of me,
>   Or that I shou'd bar him of another:
> For all we can gain, is to give our selves pain,
>   When neither can hinder the other.

The rational approach to sex and marriage is, however, amusingly shown to be irrational as it neglects jealousy, competition, reputation and other enduring human feelings. The heroic sub-plot provides a contrasting picture of idealised love and self-control.

Aureng-Zebe (1675), along with Nathaniel Lee's *The Rival Queens*, was the start of a new direction in English drama, away from the artifice and epic-romance plots of the heroic play, with its emphasis on wonder and admiration, towards a new focus on character, pathos, compassion and sentiment, which found expression in the blank verse tragedy *All for Love* and which with a more explicit moral conclusion was to dominate drama for the next century. Although *Aureng-Zebe*, which shows the new influence of the French dramatic poet Racine (1639—99) on English drama, is less extravagant than the previous rhymed heroic plays, it still contains humorous repartee and comic bombast: 'Hence from my sight without the least reply; / One word, nay one look more, and thou shalt die!' Whereas Almanzor was admirable, if sometimes ludicrous, in his egocentric individualism, Aureng-Zebe is 'by no strong passion swayed', while Morat is 'too insolent, too much a brave'. If Aureng-Zebe and his love, Indamora, temporarily lapse from perfection, Dryden explains in the Dedicatory Epistle it is because he has 'only represented a practicable virtue, mixed with the frailties and imperfections of human life'. Allusions to 'fate' and heaven's justice imply a providential significance to the play's plot and resolution.

Tired of the artifice inherent to the Restoration notion of a rhymed play and influenced by contemporary French Neo-Classical criticism, Dryden turned to blank verse as better able to imitate 'nature' and to raise compassion and pity for his unfortunate hero and heroine. Whereas Corneille's *Le Cid* provided an heroic model for admiration, the new classicism of the 1670s claimed the purpose of tragedy was to raise pity and compassion and provided a more coherent theory in which rules were nature reduced to method. The influence can be seen in *All for Love*. By concentrating on the last stage of the Antony and Cleopatra saga, utilising the psychological intensity that results from the classical unities of time, place and story, and imitating passages from Shakespeare and other dramatists, Dryden creates in *All for Love* (1677) a sympathetic portrait of the lovers which might seem to contrast with the claim in his preface that he wrote the play for 'the excellency of the moral: for the chief persons represented were famous patterns of unlawful love, and their end accordingly was unfortunate'. If the play shows love overwhelming honour as represented in such forms as duty to wife (Octavia), friendship (Dolabella) and soldierly values (Ventidius), the conclusion is of total, unreflecting empathy for the dead lovers.

The shift towards a more affective and classical drama was temporarily diverted by the excitement of the Popish Plot and Exclusion Crisis which resulted in the jibes at Whig demagogy in the Dryden–Lee collaboration *Oedipus* (1678), the topical parallelism of another collaboration with Lee, *The Duke of Guise* (1682), and Dryden's temporary farewell to the stage, *Albion and Albanius* (1685), an operatic masque offering a long allegory of the Restoration. Of the Exclusion Crisis plays only *The Spanish Fryar* (1680) remains interesting.

After the Revolution of 1688, when Dryden lost the Laureateship, he turned once more to writing plays, until the translations of his final years provided an alternative means of financial support. While the extremely classical and often imitated *Cleomenes* (1692), with its single plot, stoicism and compassion, and the operatic *King Arthur* (1691), for which Henry Purcell wrote music, were censored for possible Jacobite significances, the final period saw Dryden's greatest tragedy, *Don Sebastian* (1689), and a now highly regarded, mature, yet disillusioned comedy, *Amphitryon* (1690). In *Don Sebastian* compassion for the main characters and a moral are fused into the design of the plot. A story of unintentional incest, with a revengeful malcontent, *Don Sebastian* adapts Jacobean dramatic conventions in the portrayal of a proud hero and heroine who suffer for the sins of their parents. The speeches show Dryden's late mastery of elevated blank verse, which he fills with allusions to heaven and hell, as a means of enriching the texture and underlining the moral.

V Criticism and prose

Dryden's critical writings are extensive. Each of his plays, many of his longer poems, the *Miscellanies* he edited, and his major translations are prefaced by discussions of literature. Many of the prologues and epilogues of his plays, his dedications, and even some of his letters are concerned with writing. Although his criticism was occasional, and rather reflected his often-changing practice and assumptions than an intellectually developed theory, it introduced to English letters most of the methods which later critics have used in more detail and with more precision, if with less persuasive charm. English literary criticism before Dryden was sporadic and largely a repetition of the Greek philosopher Aristotle (384–322 BC) and rules of rhetoric; with Dryden modern literary criticism began. His *Examen* of Jonson's *Silent Woman* in *Of Dramatic Poesy* (1668) is perhaps the first extended critical analysis in English (it was influenced by the *Examen* or analysis with which Corneille prefaced his own plays) and *The Life of Plutarch* (1683) the earliest sustained mixture of biography and criticism. *A Discourse Concerning the Original and Progress of Satire* (1693), an excellent example of comparative criticism in its discussion of Persius, Horace and Juvenal, and the *Dedication of Aeneis* (1697) contain the first histories of satire and epic in English. Dryden was interested in the history of the genres he practised. *Of Heroic Plays* (1672) traces the origin of such drama from William Davenant's Protectorate musical entertainments, influenced by Italian opera and Corneille, to Dryden's own *Conquest of Granada* for which Ariosto's epic-romance provided a model for the 'design, and variety of characters'. 'An heroic play ought to be an imitation, in little, of an heroic poem; and . . . Love and Valour ought to be the subject.' The heroic poem shows 'the highest pattern of human life'.

Most of Dryden's early criticism is a defence of the artifice of rhymed verse drama against Sir Robert Howard and others who claimed that such speeches were unnatural. But Dryden's aims were rather an elevation than an imitation of nature. The *Preface* to *The Rival Ladies* (1664) defends rhymed repartee where 'the sudden smartness of the answer and the sweetness of the rhyme set off the beauty of each other'. Rhyme also is a means of circumscribing the poet's 'fancy' and emphasising 'judgement'. The 'Letter to Sir Robert Howard' (1667), prefacing *Annus Mirabilis*, claims Ovidian wit 'images more often the movements and affections of the mind, either combating between two contrary passions, or extremely discomposed by one'. Such a stylised picture of 'nature in disorder' is the 'proper wit of dialogue or discourse, and consequently of the drama'. The famous *Of Dramatic Poesy: An Essay* (1668) is a discourse between four characters on such literary topics as the comparative merits of ancient, modern, English, French, Jacobean and Restoration drama. Although his views are represented by Neander, Dryden wrote his essay after the sceptical tentative mode advocated by the Royal Society. Various arguments and examples are presented and tested without reaching any doctrinaire conclusion.

By the mid-1670s Dryden's idea of drama changed under the influence of new French critical theories, which provided alternatives to the artifice of the heroic play and Corneille's 'admiration' of heroic grandeur. Although *Heads of an Answer to Rymer* (1677), which he never published, accepts Neo-Classical rules as a method to imitate nature, Dryden still wants a poet's freedom. Responding to Rymer's *Tragedies of the Last Age* (1677), he quotes the French literary critic Rapin's (1621—87) praise of 'words and discourses' in contrast to plot as the main beauty of tragedy. In *The Grounds of Criticism in Tragedy* (1679) he pays lip service to Aristotle, but subtly transforms the concept of pity and terror from an effect *on the audience* to the emotions the audience feel *for* the tragic characters. Boileau, Le Bossu (1631–80), who wrote *Traité du poème épique*, and Rapin have become his favourite critics, as he somewhat confusedly feels his way towards a less romantic notion of tragedy than the heroic play, while avoiding the rigid interpretation of decorum and moral purpose which Rymer and others derived from recent French theories. Such later criticism as the *Preface to Ovid's Epistles* (1680) and the *Preface to Sylvae* (1685) show Dryden's theory of translation, which is neither as literal minded as the earlier word-for-word translations, nor as far from the original text as Restoration 'imitations'.

Dryden's prose style has the clarity and tentativeness appropriate to a member of the Royal Society, along with a graceful ease of address and an assertion of himself as an interesting person which he probably learned from the Court wits. It avoids the aphoristic and elaborate extremes of the first half of the century and the bare utilitarianism of those who modelled their prose on scientific observation. If Dryden's early manner is at times stiff, his later prose has a vigour and delightful fluency which appear a direct expression of his personality. The sentences are seldom balanced and are varied in shape. The tone is conversational, yet that of a gentleman. Ideas, allusions, digressions, stories and references are introduced without losing the progression of the thought. Dryden's mind was as stocked with ideas and images as those of the Jacobean and Caroline writers, but he expressed himself with greater clarity.

12
Williamite literature

I Neo-Classical criticism and the reformation of manners

BY the late 1680s French Neo-Classicism, as represented especially by Rapin and Boileau, became a pattern for English poetry, drama and criticism. Influenced by French formalistic critics, especially Le Bossu, Thomas Rymer (1641–1713) claimed to judge English drama by the rules derived from Greek and Roman practice and by universal standards common to all nations and ages. In this he was in tune with the evolving Neo-Classicism of the age. Whereas in France, after the controversy over Corneille's play *Le Cid*, Neo-Classicism had triumphed, English drama had little resemblance to accepted critical theory. Rymer muddled the problem by demanding decorum, moral purpose and probability from tragedy. He wanted ideal characters behaving in a manner which would illustrate an educative moral.

His criticism of the plays of Beaumont and Fletcher in *The Tragedies of the Last Age* (1678) brought to light the discrepancy between English drama and critical assumptions; it was, along with Dryden's *All for Love*, part of the reaction against the mixed premises of the heroic play, with its wit, extravagance and claims to portray ideal conduct. *A Short View of Tragedy* (1693), mocking and dictatorial in manner, chaotic in shape, carries to an extreme Rymer's ideas and attacks Ben Jonson, and Shakespeare's *Julius Caesar* and *Othello*:

> Rather may we ask here what unnatural crime *Desdemona*, or her Parents had committed, to bring this Judgment down upon her; to Wed a Black-amoor, and innocent to be thus cruelly murder'd by him. What instruction can we make out of this Catastrophe?

A Whig, Rymer was appointed Historiographer Royal after Shadwell's death (1692).

Rymer's main disciple was Jeremy Collier (1650–1726), an Anglican parson, a non-juror who refused to take the Oath of Allegiance to William and Mary, and a minor essayist whose *A Short View of the Immorality and Prophaneness of the English Stage* (1698) offers a narrow moralistic view of Restoration drama. Imitating Rymer's mocking banter, but with much more sense of the epigrammatic, and assuming the purpose of drama is to instruct, Collier, also influenced by Le Bossu, demanded from comedy ideal types, decorum, poetic justice and moral didacticism. Although his analysis of Vanbrugh's *The Relapse* was modelled on Rymer's criticism of *Othello*, his main barbs were aimed at Congreve and Dryden. Collier's simplified view of literature was unfortunately part of the moralism of an era when the sceptical rationalism, ambiguities and paradoxes of Restoration comedy were replaced by sentimental comedy. 'The reformation of manners', strict morality and social responsibility succeeded the libertinism of the Stuart Court.

II Congreve and drama

Perhaps the clearest indication of the changed sensibility in Williamite England can be seen in the theatre where there was a strong movement towards pure comedy, exemplary characters, sentimentality and the assertion of a moral. The era of the cynical Restoration Court had passed; the new audience was moralistic and objected to smut. Collier's attack on the stage, the founding of societies for the reformation of manners, talk of closing the theatres and prosecuting actors and an attempt to indict Congreve, Durfey and their publishers during the last years of the century were followed in the next decade by the conviction and fining of actors for profanity.

In Shadwell's *The Scowrers* (1690) Eugenia says she will never marry Sir William Rant 'till I see a full Reformation in his Life, and Manners'. While Shadwell, Mrs Manley, Mrs Pix and others wrote reforming comedies, the sceptical, ironic, witty comedy of the Restoration was continued by Thomas Southerne and William Congreve under Dryden's patronage.

Their plays have a detached amusement with sexual comedy, as humorous in itself and as a metaphor for society. Thomas Southerne's (1659–1746) *Sir Anthony Love* (1690) is an energetical, farcical comedy in which a high-spirited young lady dresses as a man of the town; as a libertine rake she is 'above Example, or Imitation'. Religious hypocrisy is satirised through a homosexual priest and a thief who pretends to be a pilgrim. In *The Wives Excuse, or Cuckolds Make Themselves* (1691) changeable scenery is used to make explicit the breakdown of a marriage. The wife is with company when the '*scene* draws' to show the husband on 'a couch' with another woman. Although the play concludes without the wife having yet been seduced and abandoned by her admirer, its sardonic view of society makes such a future seem likely. *The Fatal Marriage, or the Innocent Adultery* (1694) and *Oroonoko, or The Royal Slave* (1696), both adapted from Behn's novels, are in blank verse and have comic sub-plots written in prose which offer another perspective on the main events. Both end with high-flown speeches in the final acts which in their pathos pleased audiences.

Although his novel, *Incognita: or Love and Duty Reconcil'd* (1692) was published under a pseudonym, William Congreve (1670–1729) came to the attention of Dryden and became part of his circle at Will's Coffee House. One of the founding members of the Whig Kit-Cat Club, Congreve was, however, recognised as the heir of Dryden and the sceptical, witty, elegant comedy of the Restoration in contrast to the moralistic, sentimental sensibility which predominated after 1688. *Incognita* was part of the reaction against the long, digressive French romances of the earlier part of the century. While influenced by the novels of Scarron (1610–60) in his urbane, understated, sardonic irony, Congreve, in contrast to most English writers who emphasised Scarron's use of burlesque, seized upon the use of a facetious, self-conscious, engaging manner. Observing the unities of time, place and action of Neo-Classical dramatic theory, Congreve produced an elegant, sophisticated, delightful parody of the mixture of chivalry and *précieux* manners found in the romances. Keeping an amused distance from his narrative he teases the reader with a make-believe world, filled with parallels of characters and events, in which the narrator pretends to be unable to explain what his characters are thinking or feeling, or in which he alludes to the art of story-telling by withholding information. The enjoyment of *Incognita* is less in its purposefully improbable, conventional story than in the worldly, elegant treatment of such absurdities as the sighing contest:

> But there he gave a Sigh, and passionately taking Aurelian by the Hand, cry'd, Ah! my Friend, Love is indeed blind, when it would not suffer me to see you --------- There arose another Sigh: a Sympathy seiz'd Aurelian immediately: (For, by the Way, sighing is as catching among Lovers, as yawning among the Vulgar.) Beside hearing the Name of Love, made him fetch such a Sigh, that Hippolito's were but Fly-blows in Comparison, that was answered with all the Might Hippolito had, Aurelian ply'd him close till they were both out of Breath.
> Thus not a Word pass'd, though each wondred why the t'other sigh'd, at last concluded it to be only Complaisance to one another.

The Old Bachelor (1693), which Dryden helped to revise, epitomises the conventions of Restoration comedy and their relationship to Jonsonian and Roman comedy. Although Congreve approximates unity of place and time, his five plots are related more by similarities of theme than any unity of action. At the centre is Heartwell, a cynical truth-teller who exposes lies but who falls into the same emotional situations and traps as the other characters. By contrast Bellmour is a typical Restoration rake, promiscuous, witty, impudent and pleasure-seeking. Vainlove, who enjoys the game of courtship more than success, is a humours character. There are the usual conventional dupes. The play offers a sense of time passing, of the need to seize the day; wit, pleasure, love, youth, verbal repartee are to be enjoyed. With age, caution, and marriage, pleasure will pass although desires will remain the same.

There is a tough scepticism under an apparent make-believe artificiality in *The Double Dealer* (1693). In design Neo-Classical, with extreme unity of place, scene and action it supposedly is an illustration of divine providence. Instead of Wycherley's Plain-Dealer, there is Maskwell, who manipulates others by playing upon their vanity and greed. On the verge of complete success he, like Volpone, becomes so enamoured with his cunning that he ruins his schemes. The comedy shows an aristocratic society threatened and then restored; but as the upper classes are fools and hypocrites, it is difficult to reconcile the justice of the play's conclusion with the previous events. Collier objected:

> And the *Double Dealer* is particularly remarkable. There are but *Four* Ladys in this Play, and *Three* of the biggest of them are *Whores*. A Great Compliment to Quality, to tell them there is not above a quarter of them Honest.

Poetic justice is asserted but the satire is strong. The conclusion of *Love for Love* (1695) poses similar problems. *The Mourning Bride* (1697) is more clearly a play with a moral in which virtue is rewarded:

> Let us that thro' our Inocence survive,
> Still in the Paths of Honour persevere;
> And not from past or present Ills Despair:
> For Blessings ever wait on vertuous Deeds;
> And tho' a late, a sure Reward succeeds.

Similar to other tragedies of the 1690s, it is a blank verse melodrama blending the heroic and pathetic with Rymer's demand that poetic justice must be seen. Two lines have become famous: 'Musick has Charms to sooth a savage Breast' and 'Heav'n has no Rage, like Love to Hatred turn'd, / Nor Hell a Fury, like a Woman scorn'd'.

The Way of the World (1700) shows Congreve's study of the Roman comic writer Terence (*c.* 190–159 BC) in its theme of a family inheritance endangered by an interloper. That the hero brings together the family in their common interest in contrast to the villain's tyrannical ways can be seen as an expression of Whig principles. If the family is a metaphor for the State, the brilliant proviso scene may be interpreted as Lockean political theory applied to personal and social relationships. *The Way of the World* is, however, at core a tough-minded Restoration comedy in which the promiscuous, witty Mirabel understands the ways of the world better than the clever, villainous Fainall:

> FAINALL: Very likely Sir, What's here? Damnation! (*Reads*) *A deed of Conveyance of the whole Estate real of* Arabella Languish *Widdow in trust to* Edward Mirabel. Confusion!

> MIRABEL: Even so Sir, 'tis *the way of the World*, Sir: of the Widdows of the World. I suppose this Deed may bear an Elder Date than what you have obtain'd from your Lady.

There is a tension between the ironic, detached, observant comedy of the Restoration and the moralising of the last decade of the century in Congreve's plays. His characters are refined, their feelings are understated, their epigrammatic wit has a formal precision similar to the rhymed repartee of the heroic play, the plots are elegant, dynastic order has replaced sexual comedy as the central subject, the relationship of money to marriage is treated significantly, and the hero's and heroine's progress towards marriage implies a maturity of character; but Congreve's plays show a society in which combat is disguised by style and decorum. Perhaps the distinction between such plays and Restoration comedy is the difference between Hobbes and Locke. Whereas Hobbes saw men naturally in a state of warfare, Locke recognised but skirted around the state of war in his social compact in assuming that society is held together by mutual interest.

Nahum Tate (1652–1715) has a representative place in the history of the time. *Brutus of Alba* (1678) has the small cast, Roman subject-matter and blank verse which, under the influence of Dryden and Lee, were common to the late 1670s. *The History of King Richard the Second* (1680), *A History of King Lear* (1681) and *The Ingratitude of a Common-Wealth* (1681), the latter based on *Coriolanus*, were adaptations of Shakespeare's plays in keeping with Tory politics and Restoration taste. *Lear*, which was popular throughout the next century, has a notorious happy ending in which the old king resigns his throne to the happily married Cordelia and Edgar! As there is a moralistic streak in his work, it is not surprising that after the publication of Jeremy Collier's *Short View* Tate made proposals for regulating 'the Stage & Stage-Players'. Within a year King William did and, although mocked by Swift and Pope, Tate gained a reputation for purity and morality.

Tate also wrote pastorals, lyrics about the pains of love, funeral elegies, Cowleyian odes, and moralising, melancholy poems in the manner of his friend Flatman:

From Clime to Clime with restless Toyl we Roam,
But sadly still our old Griefs we retain,
And with us bear beyond the spacious Main
The same unquiet selves we brought from Home.

Although Alexander Pope claimed that nine bad poets 'made a Tate', Tate had some talent at satire and the mock-heroic. 'The Battle of the Bawds in the Theatre Royal' was followed by his continuation of *Absalom and Achitophel* (1682), covering the collapse of the Whig cause and the return of James to England. *Panacea: A Poem Upon Tea: In Two Canto's* (1700) is an example of the new use of the mock-heroic for social trivia. After Shadwell's death (1692) Tate was made Poet Laureate.

Author of verse satires and burlesques and several collections of songs, Thomas Durfey (1653–1723) had a long career as a dramatist which includes an heroic play, *The Siege of Memphis* (1676) and such amusing mixtures of farcical intrigue and sex as *The Fool Turn'd Critick* (1676) and *Madam Fickle* (1676). *A Fond Husband* (1677) concludes with the cuckolded husband doing nothing as the rake coolly departs with the remark, 'I wear a sword, Sir, — and so — Farewel'. Charles II loved it. Durfey wrote the usual Exclusion Crisis comedies, *Sir Barnaby Whigg* (1681) and *The Royalist* (1682), in which clever Tories seduce the wives of hypocritical Whigs and win the witty females. His plays of the 1690s, such as *Love For Money* (1691), *The Marriage Hater Match'd* (1692) and *The Richmond Heiress* (1693) are notable for virtuous characters, exemplary fathers, reformed rakes, poetic justice, pathos and the workings of providence. He was not, however, one of the natural moralists of the period; his love of low comedy found expression in the racy, entertaining, three-part *The Comical History of Don Quixote* (1694, 1695), with its bawdy puppet show and dirty songs set to music by Purcell. Durfey's own instincts are perhaps expressed in *The Campaigners* (1698), a cynical comedy in which the rake reforms for practical, commonsensical reasons; it includes 'New Reformation begins throughout the nation', a song written in reply to Collier. The two-part prose tragedy *The Famous History of the Rise and Fall of Massaniello* (1699) concerns mob rule and the rise of a fisherman to a tyrant.

During the last five years of the century there were interesting attempts to adapt the witty dialogue, character types and situations of Restoration comedy to the new sentimentality and moral earnestness. Whereas the Restoration often treated marriage and libertinism cynically, the comedy of the final years of the century seems sincerely concerned with the problems of marriage, of the sexual double standard, and the position of a wife. George Farquhar (1678–1707) was, in *Love and a Bottle* (1698) indebted to the bawdy talk and libertine attitudes of the earlier comedies; but in *The Constant Couple* (1699), Angelica reforms the rake, Sir Harry Wildair, while the play's sub-plot brings about the romantic reunion of a separated couple. Farquhar's best plays, *The Recruiting Officer* and *The Beaux' Stratagem*, belong to the next century. Although the actor Colley Cibber (1671–1757) attempted to revive the ironic double perspective of the earlier heroic play, his *Love's Last Shift* (1696), one of the first sentimental comedies, blends romantic love with the foppery and libertine attitudes of the Restoration. Loveless, a rake, returns to England where he fails to recognise his virtuous wife whom he left ten years previously. She allows herself to be seduced by him, and after she reveals her identity he is converted to 'chast' and 'Vertuous Love'. Sir John Vanbrugh (1664–1726), the famous architect who combined the classical with the Baroque at Castle Howard and Blenheim Palace, cleverly continued *Love's Last Shift* in *The Relapse* (1696). Vanbrugh wrote witty, tough, colloquial prose in the Restoration manner. Although he answered Collier by claiming that comedy shows people how not to behave, he avoids adultery and seduction in his plays. In *The Relapse*, the supposedly reformed Loveless chases another woman, while his wife is attracted to another man. They stop short of adultery, although the wife's admirer leaves the audience in doubt 'how long this influence may last'. Lord Foppington's extravagant foppish ways have made him a delight to audiences. Vanbrugh's scepticism about social convention is reflected in the extremely ugly marriage of the Brutes in *The Provok'd Wife* (1697), which is contrasted to the romantic love of Belinda and Heartfree. It is noticeable that the comedy of the 1690s, whether moralistic or sceptical, often gives equal consideration to the perspective of the heroine, unlike Restoration drama which usually saw men involved in a battle or game of conquest with women. The new comedy seems concerned with family and the relationships between husband and wife, whereas the earlier comedy treated man as a predatory animal in a competitive society.

The tragedy of the 1690s, such as Settle's *Distress'd Innocence* (1690) and Southerne's *The Fatal Marriage* (1694), tended towards pathos in which a hero acts stoically in distressing circumstances. There was a conscious attempt to revive the heroic play in blank verse with a touch of pathos. Cibber's *Xerxes* (1699) and *The Tragical History of King Richard III* (1700), and Mary Pix's *Ibrahim* (1696) have the inflationary declamations, spectacle and blood of the earlier heroic play without its wit and romantic extravagance. Charles Hopkins experimented with the heroic formula, attempting to make it more classic, stoic, pathetic, and illustrative of justice, but without much success.

III New trends in poetry

In the mock-epic topical satire, the burlesque, the generalised, reflective philosophical lyric, and the ironic urban pastoral, new trends are noticeable in poetry from the 1680s onwards, but no new poets of stature appeared. *Miscellany Poems* (1691) by Thomas Heyrick (1650–94), are at their best amusing and fantastic. *The Dispensary* (1699) by Sir Samuel Garth (1661–1719), a friend of Alexander Pope, is a topical mock-epic satire on those who opposed establishing a dispensary for the poor. Written in balanced, antithetical heroic couplets, *The Dispensary* illustrates how Boileau's manner was taken over by such poets as Matthew Prior, Robert Gould and Pope; even John Crowne adapted *Le Lutrin* for *Daeneids* (1692). Garth's main influence on later Neo-Classicism was the regularity of his medial caesura and use of antithesis in contrast to Dryden's freer, more varied, often enjambed couplets. Sir Richard Blackmore (1652–1729) who, following the critical theories of Le Bossu, published a dull epic *Prince Arthur* (1695) and a *Satire Against Wit* (1700), properly belongs to the early years of the next century as do Matthew Prior (1664–1721) who burlesqued

Dryden in the *Hind and the Panther Travers'd to the Story of the Country Mouse and the City-Mouse* (1689) and John Dennis (1657–1734) author of *Poems in Burlesque* (1692). Dennis was capable of Restoration cynicism, elegance, mockseriousness and appreciation of the sexual game. His 'An English Ballad on the Taking of Namur' (1695), a parody of Boileau's 'Ode sur la prise de Namur', remained popular until early in the twentieth century.

IV Prose: Halifax and Temple

Some of the most enjoyable prose of the last decades of the century was written by George Savile, Marquis of Halifax (1633–95). A rationalist and relativist who knew that forms of government are the result of history, environment and circumstance, Halifax believed that England had a balanced constitution in which the King was theoretically absolute but in practice was restrained by Parliament. A hero of the Court during the Exclusion Crisis, Halifax opposed the Tory reaction. His *Character of a Trimmer* advocated prudence and moderation; *A Letter to a Dissenter* (1687) warned that the Declaration of Indulgence was an attempt by James to bring in Catholicism.

Halifax's writings were published either anonymously, usually in reply to Roger L'Estrange's Royalist propaganda, or after his death. The style has the fluency and apparent naturalness desired by those who wanted to reform English prose, but is more ironic, witty, metaphoric, sophisticated and varied in tone. There are brief, epigrammatic sentences; antithesis and aphorisms occur within lengthy, extended, complex sentences in which the syntax, although not as extreme as Milton's, appears Latinate. There is balance and weight, but also variety and a well-bred colloquial ease. The effect is quiet and sceptical, with the restraint and precision of a man of the world who knows exactly what he wants to say and is speaking from long knowledge of human behaviour. It is an appropriate style for someone whose moderation results from prudence.

Advice to a Daughter (1688) consists of characters and brief essays on Religion, Children, Behaviour, Friendship, Vanity and Diversions. Halifax is ethical and prudent and emphasises caution. *A Character of King Charles II* is a classic of witty, epigrammatic observation. Each of its sections ('Religion', 'Dissimulation', 'Amours', 'Conduct', 'Conversation', 'Temper' and 'Conclusion') moves elegantly through a clear beginning, middle and end:

> It may be said that his Inclinations to Love were the Effects of Health, and a good Constitution, with as little mixture of the *Seraphick* part as ever Man had: And though from that Foundation Men often raise their Passions; I am apt to think his stayed as much as Man's ever did in the *lower Region*. . . . He had more properly, at least in the beginning of his Time, a good Stomach to his Mistresses, than any Great Passion for them.

While recognising Charles's weaknesses, Halifax, without being tolerant, knows they are no worse than those of others:

> Subjects are apt to be as arbitrary in their *Censure*, as the most assuming Kings can be in their Power. . . . If Princes are under the misfortune of being accused to govern ill, their Subjects have the less right to fall hard upon them, since they generally so little deserve to be governed well.

A similar clarity and lack of illusion with 'Corrupted Nature' can be found in his 'Political Thoughts and Reflections':

> When the People contend for their Liberty, they seldom get any thing by their Victory but new Masters.
> Liberty can neither be got, nor kept, but by so much Care, that Mankind generally are unwilling to give the Price for it. And therefore, in the Contest between Ease and Liberty, the first hath generally prevailed.

If Halifax looks back to Restoration wit, poise and self-interest, Sir William Temple (1628—99) is a writer whose concerns influenced later sensibility. Tutored at Emmanuel College by the Cambridge Platonist Ralph Cudworth, Temple left the university for travel on the Continent (1648—51). Early in his travels he fell in love with Dorothy Osborne (1627—95) with whom he surreptitiously corresponded before overcoming the objections of both families to the marriage. The letters she wrote to Temple between 1652 and

1654 are spirited, witty and realistic, both an arch portrait of provincial society and a deep expression of 'friendship' — during an age when expressions of love by young women were necessarily guarded and reserved. After Temple became an adviser to Charles II, he felt betrayed by Charles's pro-French policy, and retired in 1681 to the country where at Moor Park, Surrey, he led a well-bred, intellectual life in keeping with that curious blend of Horatian rural retirement and pleasure-seeking Neo-Epicureanism which was an ideal of the second half of the century (Epicureanism was named after the Greek philosopher Epicurus (c. 341–270 BC): as the senses are the only means of testing truth, the aim of life is pleasure through moderation). A cosmopolitan, sceptical free thinker and a keen observer of human behaviour, Temple was a relativist. He did not believe in absolutes; morals were the result of custom. Sharing the utilitarianism of the new movements of his time, Temple believed that reason could decide what was agreeable to us and to others.

Temple's relativism and utilitarianism led him, as it did Swift, into distrust of scientific experimentation, natural philosophy and the claims then being advanced in England and in France, particularly by Fontenelle's *Conversations on the Plurality of Worlds* (1681), that modern learning was superior to that of the past. In an attempt to synthesise biblical history, theology and the new philosophy, Thomas Burnet (1635?–1715), in *The Sacred Theory of the Earth* (Latin, 1681; English translation, 1684–89), tried to show that the physical irregularities of the world resulted from natural causes set in motion by Adam's fall. In the process of defending scripture Burnet wrote of the advancement of modern learning. Temple, who was even sceptical of the Copernican theory of the universe, replied in *An Essay upon the Ancient and Modern Learning* (1690) that as human nature and endowments are the same in all ages the arts do not necessarily improve. Unfortunately in his sceptical attack on the supposed superiority of the moderns he claimed that the Fables of Aesop and the Epistles of Phalaris are among the oldest books and the best. William Wotton (1666–1727) in *Reflects upon Ancient and Modern Learning* (1694) said Temple was wrong; the second edition of *Reflections* (1697) included Richard Bentley's magisterial 'Dissertation upon the Epistles of Phalaris'. Bentley (1662–1742), author of *The Folly and Unreasonableness of Atheism* (1693) and the greatest classical scholar of the age, proved conclusively that the Fables were not so old and that the Epistles were late forgeries. Swift joined the controversy on the side of the ancients with *The Battle of the Books* and *A Tale of a Tub*. Although not published until 1704, they were written between 1696 and 1698 at Moor Park, while he was secretary to Temple.

The emergence of journalism as part of the world of letters is illustrated by Sir Roger L'Estrange (1616–1704). After the Licensing Act of 1662 he was appointed 'Surveyor of the Imprimery', which put him in a position to censor Whig printers. He edited two periodicals, *The Newes* and *Intelligencer* from 1663 to 1666. Although anti-Catholic and against toleration, L'Estrange was knighted by James II. During the 1680s he edited another periodical, *The Observator* (1681–87), which popularised the convention of publishing a one-sided catalogue on contemporary issues, wrote *An Answer* to Halifax's *Letter to a Dissenter*, lost his position as censor and with the Glorious Revolution was for a time imprisoned. His later publications include translations of *The Fables of Aesop and other Eminent Mythologists* (1692; Part II, 1699) and Terence's *Comedies* (1694). One of the first professional translators, L'Estrange recast the original work into a contemporary English style. He found modern comparisons, and did not hesitate to delete or expand to make the text alive for his readers.

After 1688 the major new periodicals were John Dunton's *The Athenian Gazette: or Casuistical Mercury* (1691–7), with John Norris and Samuel Wesley among the writers, and *The Gentleman's Journal* (1692–4) edited by Peter Motteux (1660–1718), which included Dennis, Southerne, Oldmixon, Tate and Congreve among its contributors. Motteux also completed Sir Thomas Urquhart's (1611–60) Caroline translation of Rabelais's (French humanist *c.* 1494–1553) *Gargantua and Pantagruel* and wrote plays. The *Journal* varied its contents, but had a strong interest in literature, in contrast to Ned Ward's (1667–1731) *London Spy* (1698–1709), with its slangy descriptions of low life. With the lapse of the Licensing Act in 1695, the age of Augustan periodicals and polite essays on society and literature had begun.

V Latitudinarians and Locke

A consequence of the Glorious Revolution was the replacing of High Anglicans with Latitudinarians in positions of church authority. Sympathetic to the Whigs during the Exclusion Crisis, Gilbert Burnet (1643—1715) lived on the Continent during the Tory reaction. He accompanied William's invasion of England and was made Bishop of Salisbury (1689). A member of the Royal Society and influenced by the scientific movement, Burnett was against 'wit and stile' in prose. In *A Discourse on Pastoral Care* (1692), he recommended a plain and clear style of preaching. In 1683 Burnet started a somewhat biased *History of his own Time*, which was published after his death. Although Swift described the style as 'rough', the short, choppy sentences occur mostly in the character sketches where Burnet seems influenced by the Senecan-styled characters of the earlier part of the century. In comparison to the earlier characters, Burnet's are more concerned with the motives of individuals. Exterior details are selectively used to illustrate psychology. His clear, undistinguished, impersonal writing is an example of the modern prose which was consciously developed after the Restoration. The documentation and selection of significant details are part of the development towards modern historiography.

Besides Gilbert Burnet, Edward Stillingfleet (1635—99), author of *A Rational Account of The Grounds of the Protestant Religion* (1665); Simon Patrick (1635—99), author of *A Brief Account of the new Sect of Latitude Men* (1662) and *A Friendly Debate between a Conformist and a Non-Conformist* (1669), and Richard Cumberland were among the more than a dozen Latitudinarians made bishops. John Tillotson became Archbishop of Canterbury. The 1690s might be considered the triumph of the rationalist religious movements associated with the Royal Society, although Stillingfleet kept his distance from the new science.

The increasing rationalist approach to religion is shown by John Locke's *The Reasonableness of Christianity* (1695) and *Christianity Not Mysterious* (1696) by John Toland (1670?–1722). Whereas Locke defined reason as natural revelation whereby God communicates to mankind that portion of truth within the reach of natural faculties, Toland took Locke's ideas further in arguing that 'true religion must necessarily be reasonable and intelligible'. Reason is 'the only foundation of all certitude'. Toland's doctrine was clearly Deist; it made scripture and revelation appear useless.

Although John Locke (1632–1704) did not publish until after 1688, his work was shaped by, and often written during, the political and intellectual turbulence of the reign of Charles II. During the middle 1660s, Locke met Antony Cooper, later Lord Shaftesbury, and became his physician. Throughout the remainder of the century Locke was close to the Whig leadership. In the late 1660s when he wrote drafts of the *Letters Concerning Toleration*, Shaftesbury was urging Charles II to use his royal prerogative to issue an act granting toleration to the Protestant Non-Conformists. The Act of Indulgence, however, also granted rights to Roman Catholics, whom Locke and Shaftesbury viewed as subversives owing their main obedience to the Pope, and had to be withdrawn. Locke felt that as long as a variety of religious doctrines could be asserted as truths which must be enforced, England would remain politically unstable. In *An Essay Concerning Human Understanding* (started in 1671), he used the disciplined, analytical, sceptical methods he had learned from his friend Robert Boyle, the Royal Society and his study of medicine, to show that assumptions about innate ideas could not be defended. In what is essentially a contribution to epistemology, Locke argues that knowledge and understanding derive from the senses and experience, from which the mind creates general ideas. Since such ideas are influenced by each individual's personality, emotions and limited view, it follows that all ideas must be tentative. Men must remain sceptical of supposed truths.

Although Locke, influenced by Hobbes's sensationalism, begins with psychology to create an empirical approach to thinking, his rationalism leads him to a scepticism. Since nothing can be known in its essentials, religious truth is a matter of faith and therefore not subject to the commands of those in temporal power. In the *Essay*, his three *Letters*

(1689, 1690, 1692) and *The Reasonableness of Christianity*, he claims that while God provides through man's reason and through the design of the world evidence of His Being and the means to find a natural religion, men are unable to be certain of the truths of their particular belief, especially as societies differ in their customs, ceremonies and morals. In the *Third Letter* he says that while he believes in the Church of England he cannot '*know*' it is the true religion since he cannot prove it. Governments are wrong to impose what are unprovable matters of religious belief on the governed. Beliefs which do not result in disturbing the peace and liberty of others should be tolerated. While such a distinction between Church and State now is fundamental to western society, Locke was controversial at the time when the nation was still seen as a unified body of belief.

The manner of Locke's prose, modest, easy, unpretentious, intimate, tentative but analytical, often curiously confused in syntax and sloppy in structure, reflects his exploratory attitude, as his mind works towards truth. There is a range of manners from the factual and analytical to the autobiographical and what appears to be an interior monologue; at times he addresses the reader in a dialogue. Although the variety can be explained as reflecting the various times Locke worked upon and revised his manuscripts, the effect reinforces his stance as a man of common sense, experimentally thinking his way towards a clearer understanding of ideas. The use of the first-person speaker, the many qualifications, the often intermittent and repetitious development of the thought show Locke, especially in the *Essay*, treating each problem carefully on its own without concern for the niceties of style and rhetoric.

Two Treatises on Government (1690) were originally written in 1681 during the Exclusion Crisis; but were somewhat revised as a justification of the Revolution of 1688, when Locke returned from exile with Queen Mary. *The First Treatise* is a detailed refutation of Sir Robert Filmer's theory. Locke quibbles with the accuracy of the biblical detail in *Patriarcha* and, more significantly, shows that Filmer could not prove that the supposed rights of fathers have been transferred to the ruler of a state. *The Second Treatise* might be described as Locke's answer to Hobbes. He assumes that most men in the state of nature are reasonable and good, but as there will always be controversy over liberty and property, men form a community investing the government with the right to judge what will most contribute to peace, happiness, liberty and rights of property. This compact, unlike Hobbes's contract, is consensual and derives from the will of the community. Arbitrary power in the Lockean scheme is an aggression by the ruler against the community, dissolves the compact, and justifies a change in government.

Bibliographies

1. *The new Cambridge bibliography of English literature*, 5 vols.
   (Cambridge: Cambridge University Press, 1977) vol 1 and 2, covering
   the periods 600–1660 and 1660–1800 respectively, and edited by
   George Watson, are relevant.
2. POLLARD, ALFRED WILLIAM , compiler, *A short-title catalogue of
   books printed in England, Scotland and Ireland . . . 1475–1640*
   (London: Bibliographical Society, 1926; 2nd edn, revised and
   enlarged, rev. by W. A. Jackson and others, London: Bibliographical
   Society, 1976–; to be completed in 3 vols).
3. WING, DONALD GODDARD, compiler, *Short-title catalogue of
   books printed in England, Scotland, Ireland and Wales . . . 1641–
   1700* (New York: Printed for the Index Society by Columbia University Press, 1945–51) 3 vols; 2nd edn, revised and enlarged (New
   York: The Index Committee, Modern Language Association of
   America, 1972–; to be completed in 3 vols).
4. GREG, SIR W. W., *A bibliography of the English printed drama to
   the Restoration*, 4 vols (London: Bibliographical Society, 1962)
   (1939– 59).
5. BUSH, DOUGLAS, *English literature in the earlier seventeenth
   century, 1600–1660*, 2nd revised edn (Oxford: Clarendon Press,
   1962).
6. STRATMAN, CARL JOSEPH, *Restoration and eighteenth-century
   theatre research; a bibliographical guide, 1900–1968*, ed. by C. J.
   Stratman and others (Carbondale: Southern Illinois University Press,
   1971).
7. SUTHERLAND, JAMES RUNCIEMAN, *English literature of the late
   seventeenth century* (Oxford: Clarendon Press, 1969).

Annual bibliographies

8. Modern Humanities Research Association. *Annual bibliography of
   English language and literature*, VL, (London: The Association,
   1920–).
9. Modern Language Association of America. *MLA international*

bibliography (New York: Modern Language Association of America, 1921–)

10. *Eighteenth century: a current bibliography* (Philadelphia: American Society for Eighteenth Century Studies, n.s.1, 1975–). Includes the period 1660–1700. Continues the series of the same name earlier published in *Philological Quarterly.*

Further reading

ROBERT ADOLPH: *The Rise of Modern Prose Style* (Cambridge, Mass.: MIT Press, 1968)

G. P. V. AKRIGG: *Jacobean Pageant* (London: Hamish Hamilton, 1962)

ALEXANDER WARD ALLISON: *Towards an Augustan Poetic* (Lexington: University of Kentucky Press, 1962)

MAURICE ASHLEY: *Oliver Cromwell and the Puritan Revolution* (London: The English Universities Press Ltd, 1958)

G. E. AYLMER: *The Struggle for the Constitution* (London: Blandford, 1963, 1971)

STEPHEN B. BAXTER: *William III* (London: Longmans, 1966)

ROBIN BRIGGS: *The Scientific Revolution of the Seventeenth Century* (Bristol: Longmans, 1969)

SIR GEORGE CLARK: *The Later Stuarts* (Oxford: Clarendon Press, 1934; 2nd edn, 1955)

GODFREY DAVIES: *The Early Stuarts 1603–1660* (Oxford: Clarendon Press, 1934; reprinted, 1949)

HORTON DAVIES: *Worship and Theology in England*, Vol. II, *From Andrewes to Baxter and Fox, 1603–1690* (Princeton: Princeton University Press, 1975)

PAUL DELANY: *British Autobiography in the Seventeenth Century* (London: Routledge and Kegan Paul, 1969)

E. J. DIJKSTERHUIS: *The Mechanisation of the World Picture*, translated by C. Dikshoorn (Oxford: Clarendon Press, 1961)

KERRY DOWNES: *English Baroque Architecture* (London: A. Zwemmer Ltd, 1966)

DEAN EBNER: *Autobiography in Seventeenth-Century England; Theology and the Self* (The Hague: Mouton, 1971)

PHILIP J. FINKLEPEARL: *John Marston of the Middle Temple: An Elizabethan Dramatist in his Social Setting* (Cambridge, Mass.: Harvard University Press, 1969)

ROSEMARY FREEMAN: *English Emblem Books* (London: Chatto and Windus, 1948)

WILLIAM H. HALEWOOD: *The Poetry of Grace: Reformation Themes and Structures in English Seventeenth-Century Poetry* (New Haven: Yale University Press, 1970)

A. R. HALL: *The Scientific Revolution 1500–1800* (London: Longmans, Green & Co., 1954)

CHRISTOPHER HILL: *The Century of Revolution* (London: Nelson, 1961, 1964)

CHRISTOPHER HILL: *The World Turned Upside Down: Radical Ideas During The English Revolution* (London: Temple Smith, 1972)

ROBERT D. HUME: *The Development of English Drama in the Late Seventeenth Century* (Oxford: Clarendon Press, 1976)

ARTHUR C. KIRSCH: *Jacobean Dramatic Perspectives* (Charlottesville: University Press of Virginia, 1972)

TAI LIU: *Discord in Zion: The Puritan Divines and the Puritan Revolution 1640–1660* (The Hague: Martinus Nijhoff, 1973)

LOUIS L. MARTZ: *The Paradise Within: Studies in Vaughan, Traherne and Milton* (New Haven: Yale University Press, 1964)

LOUIS L. MARTZ: *The Poetry of Meditation: A Study in English Religious Literature of the Seventeenth Century* (New Haven: Yale University Press, 1955)

WILLIAM FRAZER MITCHELL: *English Pulpit Oratory from Andrewes to Tillotson* (London: SPCK, 1932; reprinted New York: Russell and Russell, 1962)

DAVID OGG: *England in the Reigns of James II and William III* (Oxford: Clarendon Press, 1955)

STEPHEN ORGEL: *The Illusion of Power: Political Theatre in the English Renaissance* (Berkeley: University of California Press, 1975)

DAVID PIPER (ed.): *The Genius of British Painting* (London: Weidenfeld and Nicolson, 1975)

ISABEL RIVERS: *Classical and Christian Ideas in English Renaissance Poetry* (London: George Allen & Unwin, 1979)

GEORGE SAINTSBURY (ed.): *Minor Poets of the Caroline Period*, 3 vols (Oxford: Clarendon Press, 1905–21)

RICHARD SOUTHERN: *Changeable Scenery: Its Origins and Development in the British Theatre* (London: Faber and Faber, 1952)

J. E. SPINGARN (ed.): *Critical Essays of the Seventeenth Century*, 3 vols (Oxford: Clarendon Press, 1908–9; reprinted Bloomington: Indiana University Press, 1959)

LAWRENCE STONE: *The Crisis of the Aristocracy 1558–1641* (Oxford: Clarendon Press, 1965)

LAWRENCE STONE: *Social Change and Revolution in England 1540–1640* (London: Longmans, 1965)

JOHN SUMMERSON: *Architecture in Britain 1530–1830* (Harmondsworth: Penguin Books, 1953)

STEPHEN TOULMIN & JUNE GOODFIELD: *The Architecture of Matter* (London: Hutchison, 1962)

W. VAN LENNEP (ed.): *The London Stage 1660–1800*, vol. I: 1660–1700 (Carbondale, Ill.: Southern Illinois University Press, 1965)

ELLIS WATERHOUSE: *Painting in Britain 1530 to 1790* (Harmondsworth: Penguin Books, 1953)

OWEN L. WATKINS: *The Puritan Experience* (London: Routledge and Kegan Paul, 1972)

JOAN WEBBER: *The Eloquent 'I': Styles and Self in Seventeenth Century Prose* (Madison: University of Wisconsin Press, 1968)

CHARLES WEBSTER: *The Great Instauration: Science, Medicine and Reform 1626–1660* (London: Duckworth, 1975)

GEORGE WILLIAMSON: *The Senecan Amble: A Study in Prose Form from Bacon to Collier* (London: Faber and Faber, 1951)

J. H. WILSON: *The Court Wits of the Restoration* (Princeton: Princeton University Press, 1948; reprinted London: Cass, 1967)

DON M. WOLFE (ed.):   *Leveller Manifestoes of the Puritan Revolution* (New York: Thomas Nelson, 1944)

DOREEN YARWOOD: *The English Home* (London: Batsford, 1956)

Chronological table
1600-1700

Abbreviations: (D.) = drama,   (O.) = opera,   (P.) = prose,   (V.) = verse

DATE	AUTHOR	EVENT
1600	Fairfax (*c.* 1580): translation of Tasso's *Jerusalem Delivered* (V.) Jonson (1572): *Cynthia's Revels* (D.)	East India Company founded Richard Hooker (*d.*)
1601	Dekker (1572): *Satiromastix* (D.) Jonson (1572): *Poetaster* (D.) Marston (1576): *What You Will* (D.)	Essex rebels and is executed Queen's right to grant patents of monopoly criticised by Parliament Thomas Nashe (*d.*)
1602	Campion (1567): *Observations in the Art of English Poesy* (P.) Shakespeare (1564): *Troilus and Cressida* (D.)	Sir Thomas Bodley's library at Oxford opens Edward Benlowes (*b.*) William Chillingworth (*b.*)
1603	Daniel (1562): *Defence of Ryme* (P.) Heywood (1574): *A Woman Killed with Kindness* (D.) Jonson (1572): *Sejanus* (D.)	Queen Elizabeth (*d.*) James I crowned Ralegh imprisoned for treason Millenary Petitions urge abolition of sign of cross in baptism, marriage ring and priestly vestments William Gilbert (*d.*)
1604	Chapman (1559): *The Tragedy of Bussy d'Ambois* (D.) Marston (1576): *The Malcontent* (D.)	Conference at Hampton Court on religion Conformity enforced Peace with Spain

DATE	AUTHOR AND TITLE	EVENT
1605	Bacon (1561): *Advancement of Learning* (P.)	Guy Fawkes attempts to blow up Parliament
	Drayton (1563): *Poems* (V.)	Thomas Browne (*b.*)
	Jonson (1572): *The Masque of Blackness* (D.)	William Habington (*b.*)
		Thomas Randolph (*b.*)
	Sylvester (1563): translation of DuBartas, *Divine Weekes* (V.)	
1606	Jonson (1572): *Volpone* (D.)	Oath of Allegiance
	Middleton (1580): *A Mad World, My Masters* (D.)	Courts uphold King's levying of impositions
	Shakespeare (1564): *Macbeth* (D.)	Arthur Golding (*d.*)
		John Lyly (*d.*)
		William Davenant (*b.*)
		Edmund Waller (*b.*)
1607	Beaumont (1584): *The Knight of the Burning Pestle* (D.)	James forces bishops on Scottish Church
	Shakespeare (1564): *Antony and Cleopatra* (D.); *Timon of Athens* (D.)	Coke, Chief Justice of Common Pleas, and Archbishop Bancroft in conflict over Church authority
1608	J. Fletcher (1579): *The Faithful Shepherdess* (D.)	Parliament rejects proposed union with Scotland
	Hall (1574): *Characters of Virtues and Vices* (P.)	John Milton (*b.*)
1609	Beaumont (1584) and J. Fletcher (1579): *Philaster* (D.)	Virginia voyagers shipwrecked in Bermudas
	Jonson (1572): *Epicoene* (D.)	John Suckling (*b.*)
	Shakespeare (1564): *Cymbeline* (D.)	
1610	Chapman (1559): *The Revenge of Bussy d'Ambois* (D.)	House of Commons petitions of Right and Grievances
	G. Fletcher (1585): *Christ's Victorie, and Triumph* (V.)	Archbishop Bancroft (*d.*)
	Jonson (1572): *The Alchemist* (D.)	
1611	King James Bible	Parliament dissolved
	Beaumont (1584) and J. Fletcher (1579): *A King and No King* (D.)	George Abbot made Archbishop of Canterbury

DATE	AUTHOR AND TITLE	EVENT
	Donne (1572): *First Anniversarie* (V.)	William Cartwright (*b.*)
	Jonson (1572): *Catiline* (D.)	James Harrington (*b.*)
	Shakespeare (1564): *The Tempest* (D.)	
1612	Bacon (1561): *Essayes* (P.)	Prince Henry (*d.*)
	Donne (1572): *Second Anniversarie* (V.)	John Harington (*d.*)
		Samuel Butler (*b.*)
	Webster (1580?): *The White Devil* (D.)	Richard Crashaw (*b.*)
		Thomas Killigrew (*b.*)
1613	Drayton (1563): *Poly-Olbion* I (V.)	Marriage of James's daughter, Elizabeth, to Frederick of Palatine
	Jonson (1572): *The Irish Mask* (D.)	Sir Thomas Overbury (*d.*)
		John Cleveland (*b.*)
	Webster (1580?): *The Duchess of Malfi* (D.)	Jeremy Taylor (*b.*)
1614	Jonson (1572): *Bartholomew Fair* (D.)	Proposals to marry Charles to Spanish Infanta
	Overbury (1581): *Characters* (P.)	Parliament dissolved over impositions; does not meet again until 1621
		Henry More (*b.*)
1615	Middleton (1580): *More Dissemblers Besides Women* (D.)	Richard Baxter (*b.*)
		John Denham (*b.*)
1616	Chapman (1559): *Whole Works of Homer* (V.)	King raises money by selling peerages
	Jonson (1572): *Workes*	Coke dismissed as Chief Justice of King's Bench
	Middleton (1580): *The Widow* (D.)	Francis Beaumont (*d.*)
		William Shakespeare (*d.*)
		Roger L'Estrange (*b.*)
1617	J. Fletcher (1579): *The Mad Lover* (D.)	Negotiations for Spanish marriage
	Webster (1580?): *The Devil's Law Case* (D.)	
1618	Chapman (1559): translation of *Georgics* of Hesiod (V.)	Thirty Years War starts on Continent
		Execution of Sir Walter Ralegh

DATE	AUTHOR AND TITLE	EVENT
1618	Jonson (1572): *Pleasure Reconciled to Virtue* (D.)	Declaration of *Book of Sports* Joshua Sylvester (*d.*) Abraham Cowley (*b.*) Richard Lovelace (*b.*)
1619	Drayton (1563): *Poems* (V.) J. Fletcher (1579): *The Bloody Brother* (D.)	Frederick of Palatine accepts crown of Bohemia Samuel Daniel (*d.*)
1620	J. Fletcher (1579) and Massinger (1583): *The Custom of the Country* (D.) Jonson (1572): *News From The New World* (D.); *Pan's Anniversary* (D.)	First English newspapers (in Holland) Thomas Campion (*d.*) John Evelyn (*b.*)
1621	Burton (1577): *The Anatomy of Melancholy* (P.) Massinger (1583): *The Maid of Honour* (D.) Middleton (1580): *Women Beware Women* (D.)	Parliament meets; the Commons claims right to advise King on all subjects Mary Herbert, Countess of Pembroke (*d.*) Roger Boyle (*b.*) Andrew Marvell (*b.*) Henry Vaughan (*b.*)
1622	Drayton (1563): *Poly-Olbion, II* (V.) Middleton (1580) and Rowley (1585): *The Changeling* (D.)	Parliament dissolved James releases from prison Catholic priests and laymen
1623	Felltham (1604?): *Resolves* (P.) Massinger (1583): *The Bondman* (D.) Wither (1588): *Hymns and Songs of the Church* (V.)	Failure of Spanish marriage negotiations William Byrd (*d.*) Giles Fletcher (*d.*)
1624	Donne (1572): *Devotions Upon Emergent Occasions* (P.) Massinger (1583): *The Parliament of Love* (D.)	
1625	J. Fletcher (1579): *The Chances* (D.); *The Elder Brother* (D.)	Act of Revocation re-annexes all Church and Crown lands alienated in Scotland since 1542

DATE	AUTHOR AND TITLE	EVENT
	Massinger (1583): *A New Way to Pay Old Debts* (D.)	James I (*d.*) Charles I king
		Charles marries Henrietta Maria
		John Fletcher (*d.*)
		Thomas Lodge (*d.*)
		Thomas Stanley (*b.*)
1626	Donne (1572): *Five Sermons* (P.)	Parliament declares tonnage and poundage illegal and is dissolved
	Jonson (1572): *The Staple of News* (D.)	Lancelot Andrewes (*d.*)
	Shirley (1596): *The Wedding* (D.); *The Maid's Revenge* (D.)	Francis Bacon (*d.*)
		Cyril Tourneur (*d.*)
		Robert Howard (*b.*)
1627	P. Fletcher (1582): *The Locusts* (V.)	London resists forced loans
		Thomas Middleton (*d.*)
	Massinger (1583): *The Duke of Florence* (D.)	Robert Boyle (*b.*)
		John Hall (*b.*)
1628	Earle (1600?): *Microcosmographie* (P.)	Buckingham murdered
	Ford (1586): *The Lover's Melancholy* (D.)	Parliament's 'Petition of Right' attacks royal prerogative
		Fulke Greville (*d.*)
	Shirley (1596): *The Witty Fair One* (D.)	John Bunyan (*b.*)
		William Temple (*b.*)
1629	Andrewes (1555): *XCVI Sermons* (P.)	Parliament declares anyone enemy who favours Popish or Arminian innovation and who supports King's right to levy duties
	Davenant (1606): *The Siege* (D.)	
	Jonson (1572): *The New Inn* (D.)	Parliament dissolved and does not meet again until 1640
1630	Quarles (1592): *Divine Poems* (V.)	Charles purchases Raphael cartoons
		Charles Cotton (*b.*)
		John Tillotson (*b.*)
1631	Jonson (1572): *Love's Triumph* (D.)	Conformity enforced
		John Donne (*d.*)
	Massinger (1583): *Believe as you List* (D.)	Michael Drayton (*d.*)
		John Dryden (*b.*)

DATE	AUTHOR AND TITLE	EVENT
1632	Donne (1572): *Deaths Duell* (P.)	Van Dyck settles in England
	Jonson (1572): *The Magnetic Lady* (D.)	William Prynne's *Histriomastix* attacks dramatists for immorality
	Massinger (1583): *The City Madam* (D.)	Thomas Dekker (*d.*)
		John Locke (*b.*)
	Shirley (1596): *Hyde Park* (D.)	Katherine Philips (*b.*)
1633	Carew (1594): *Coelum Britannicum* (D.)	Reprinting of *Book of Sports*
		William Laud becomes Archbishop of Canterbury
	Cowley (1618): *Poetical Blossoms* (V.)	George Herbert (*d.*)
	Donne (1572): *Poems* (V.)	Halifax (*b.*)
	P. Fletcher (1582): *The Purple Island* (V.)	Samuel Pepys (*b.*)
	Ford (1586): *'Tis Pity She's a Whore* (D.)	
	Herbert (1593): *The Temple* (V.)	
1634	Donne (1572): *Six Sermons* (P.)	George Chapman (*d.*)
	Habington (1605): *Castara* (V.)	John Marston (*d.*)
	Milton (1608): *Comus* (D.)	George Etherege (*b.*)
		Robert South (*b.*)
1635	Davenant (1606): *The Platonic Lovers* (D.); *The Temple of Love* (D.)	William Laud made Lord High Treasurer
		Edward Fairfax (*d.*)
	Quarles (1592): *Emblemes* (V.)	Thomas Randolph (*d.*)
	Shirley (1596): *The Lady of Pleasure* (D.)	Thomas Sprat (*b.*)
1636	Cartwright (1611): *The Royal Slave* (D.)	William Juxon, Bishop of London, made Lord High Treasurer and Lord High Admiral
	Cowley (1618): *Sylva* (V.)	
		Courts claim King superior to laws
		Joseph Glanvill (*b.*)
1637	Shirley (1596): *The Royal Master* (D.)	Prayer Book made mandatory for Scotland Papal Agent in England
	Suckling (1609): *Aglaura* (D.)	Nicholas Ferrar (*d.*)
		Ben Jonson (*d.*)
		Thomas Flatman (*b.*)
		Thomas Traherne (*b*?)

DATE	AUTHOR AND TITLE	EVENT
1638	Milton (1608): *Lycidas* in *Justa Edouardo King* (V.) Randolph (1605): *Poems* (V.) Quarles (1592): *Hieroglyphikes* (V.)	Scottish Covenant John Lilburne imprisoned John Hoskyns (*d.*)
1639	Fuller (1608): *Holy War* (P.) Shirley (1596): *The Politician* (D.); *The Gentleman of Venice* (D.)	War with Scotland Treaty of Berwick Henry Wotton (*d.*) Charles Sedley (*b.*)
1640	Carew (1594): *Poems* (V.) Donne (1572): *LXXX Sermons* (P.) Jonson (1572): *Timber* (P.); *The Underwood* (V.)	Second war with Scotland Treaty of Ripon acknowledges Scotland's rights and agrees to indemnity Long Parliament until 1648 Parliament impeaches Strafford and Laud Root and Branch petition Robert Burton (*d.*) Thomas Carew (*d?*) Philip Massinger (*d.*) Aphra Behn (*b.*)
1641	Milton (1608): *Reformation touching Church Discipline* (P.) Quarles (1592): *Threnodes* (V.)	Irish uprising Parliament orders arrest and execution of Strafford Thomas Heywood (*d.*) Sir John Suckling (*d.?*) Thomas Rymer (*b.*) William Wycherley (*b?*)
1642	T. Browne (1605): *Religio Medici* (P.) Denham (1615): *Cooper's Hill* (V.) Hobbes (1588): *De Cive* (P.) Milton (1608): *Reason of Church Government* (P.); *Apology for Smectymnuus* (P.)	Charles attempts to arrest five Parliamentary leaders Start of Civil War Theatres closed by law Isaac Newton (*b.*) Thomas Shadwell (*b.*)
1643	Milton (1608): *The Doctrine and Discipline of Divorce* (P.)	Bishops, deans and chapters abolished Parliament and Scotland in alliance

DATE	AUTHOR AND TITLE	EVENT
1643		Solemn League and Covenant
		William Cartwright (*d.*)
		William Chillingworth (*d.*)
1644	Milton (1608): *Areopagitica* (P.); *Of Education* (P.)	Battle of Marston Moor, 2 July
		Celebration of Christmas forbidden
	Quarles (1592): *Shepherd's Oracle* (V.)	Covenant imposed on all adults
		Self Denying Ordinance
		Francis Quarles (*d.*)
		George Sandys (*d.*)
1645	Milton (1608): *Poems* (V.); *Tetrachordon* (P.)	New Model Army formed
		Battle of Naseby, 14 June; Cromwell's horsemen win decisive battle
	Quarles (1592): *Solomon's Recantation* (V.)	
	Waller (1606): *Poems* (V.)	William Laud executed
		Use of Book of Common Prayer and Anglican Church rites forbidden
1646	T. Browne (1605): *Pseudodoxia Epidemica* (P.)	King surrenders to Scots
	Crashaw (1612): *Steps to the Temple* (V.)	Presbyterians and Independents quarrel
	H. Vaughan (1621): *Poems* (V.)	
1647	Cleveland (1613): *Poems* (V.)	Levellers demand religious liberty, 'native rights' and regularly elected Parliament
	Cowley (1618): *The Mistress* (V.)	
	More (1614): *Philosophical Poems* (V.)	Independents gain control of Parliamentary Army
	Stanley (1625): *Poems and Translations* (V.)	Laws against celebration of Easter, Whitsuntide and other festivals
		John Wilmot, Earl of Rochester (*b.*)
1648	Filmer (*c.* 1588): *Anarchy of a Limited or Mixed Monarchy* (P.)	Army seizes King and purges Parliament of Presbyterians and moderates
	Herrick (1591): *Hesperides* (V.); *Noble Numbers* (V.)	Nathaniel Lee (*b*?)
		Elkanah Settle (*b.*)
1649	Gauden (1605): *Eikon Basilike* (P.)	Trial and execution of Charles I, 30 January
	Lovelace (1618): *Lucasta* (V.) Milton (1608): *The Tenure of Kings and Magistrates* (P.); *Eikonoklastes* (P.)	Rump Parliament declares England Commonwealth; abolishes monarchy and House of Lords; declines Army proposal for representative elections and protection of religious conscience
		Richard Crashaw (*d.*)

DATE	AUTHOR AND TITLE	EVENT
1650	Baxter (1615): *The Saints' Everlasting Rest* (P.)	Charles II recognised by Scots
		Cromwell reconquers Ireland
	Davenant (1606) and Hobbes (1588): *Discourse upon Gondibert* (P.)	Adultery made punishable by death; laws against profanity
	J. Taylor (1613): *Holy Living* (P.)	Repeal of penalties for not attending church
		Phineas Fletcher (*d.*)
	H. Vaughan (1621): *Silex Scintillans*, I. (V.)	Jeremy Collier (*b.*)
		Thomas Heyrick (*b.*)
1651	Cleveland (1613): *Poems* (V.)	Navigation Act causes war with Dutch
	Davenant (1606): *Gondibert* (V.)	Charles crowned in Scotland
	Hobbes (1588): *Leviathan* (P.)	Scots beaten at Worcester, 3 September
	Stanley (1625): *Poems* (V.)	Charles escapes
	H. Vaughan (1621): *Olor Iscanus* (V.)	
1652	Benlowes (1602): *Theophila* (V.)	Thomas Otway (*b.*)
	Crashaw (1612): *Carmen Deo Nostro* (V.)	Nahum Tate (*b.*)
	Winstanley (1609): *Law of Freedom* (P.)	
1653	Shirley (1596): *Six New Plays*	Rump Parliament dissolved in April
	Walton (1593): *Compleat Angler* (P.)	Barebones Parliament dissolved in December
		Cromwell made Protector
		Sir Robert Filmer (*d.*)
		John Oldham (*b.*)
1654	Hobbes (1588): *Of Liberty and Necessity* (P.)	William Habington (*d.*)
	Milton (1608): *Second Defense of the People of England* (P.)	
1655	Marvell (1621): *The First Anniversary of . . . The Lord Protector* (V.)	Lifting of laws against residence of Jews in England
	H. Vaughan (1621): *Silex Scintillans*, II (V.)	Military rule by Major-Generals
	Waller (1606): *Panegyric to My Lord Protector* (V.)	

DATE	AUTHOR AND TITLE	EVENT
1656	Cowley (1618): *Poems* (V.) Davenant (1606): *First Day's Entertainment at Rutland House* (O.); *The Siege of Rhodes* (D.) James Harrington (1611): *Oceana* (P.)	After elections, Major-Generals exclude over 100 members from new Parliament John Hall (*d.*) Joseph Hall (*d.*)
1657	King (1592): *Poems* (V.)	Humble Petition and Advice pleads with Cromwell to become King Richard Lovelace (*d.*)
1658	T. Browne (1605): *Hydriotaphia* (P.); *The Garden of Cyrus* (P.) Davenant (1606): *The Cruelty of the Spaniards in Peru* (O.) John Hall (1627): *Emblems* (V.)	Cromwell dies, 3 September Richard Cromwell becomes Protector John Cleveland (*d.*) Henry Purcell (*b.*)
1659	Davenant (1606): *The Siege of Rhodes*, II (D.) Lovelace (1618): *Lucasta: Posthume Poems* (V.) Sprat (1635): *Three Poems upon the Death . . . of Oliver Lord Protector* (V.) Suckling (1609): *Last Remains* (V.)	Parliament meets; Army forces dissolution Richard Cromwell resigns Restored Rump Parliament and Army disagree over form of government Thomas Southerne (*b.*)
1660	Dryden (1631): *Astraea Redux* (V.) Milton (1608): *Readie and Easie Way* (P.)	General Monck recalls excluded members of Long Parliament who proclaim Charles II King Charles's Declaration of Breda and return to England
1661	Robert Boyle (1627): *The Sceptical Chymist* (P.) Dryden (1631): *To His Sacred Majesty* (V.) Glanvill (1636): *The Vanity of Dogmatizing* (P.)	Corporation Act examines charters to keep Parliament Anglican Savoy Conference at which bishops refuse compromise with Presbyterians on Church government Samuel Garth (*b.*)
1662	Butler (1612): *Hudibras*, I (V.) Davenant (1606): *The Playhouse to Be Let* (D.) Dryden (1631): *To My Lord Chancellor* (V.)	Act of Uniformity and authorisation of Prayer Book Charles becomes Patron of Royal Society Parliament refuses Charles the right to dispense with uniformity

DATE	AUTHOR AND TITLE	EVENT
1663	Butler (1612): *Hudibras*, II (V.)	
	Dryden (1631): *The Wild Gallant* (D.)	
1664	Cotton (1630): *Scarronides* (V.)	War with Dutch until 1667
	Etherege (1634): *Love in a Tub* (D.)	Katherine Philips (*d.*)
		Matthew Prior (*b.*)
	R. Howard (1626): *The Vestal Virgin* (D.)	John Vanbrugh (*b.*)
	R. Howard and Dryden (1631): *The Indian Queen* (D.)	
1665	Dryden (1631): *The Indian Emperour* (D.)	The Plague
		Theatres close
		John Earle (*d.*)
1666	Bunyan (1628): *Grace Abounding* (P.)	Great Fire of London
		Theatres reopen in November
	Tillotson (1630): *The Rule of Faith* (P.)	James Shirley (*d.*)
	Waller (1606): *Instructions to a Painter* (V.)	William Wotton (*b.*)
1667	Dryden (1631): *Annus Mirabilis* (V.); *Secret Love* (D.)	Abraham Cowley (*d.*)
		Jeremy Taylor (*d.*)
	Milton (1608): *Paradise Lost* (V.)	George Wither (*d.*)
	Sprat (1635): *History of the Royal Society* (P.)	John Arbuthnot (*b.*)
		John Pomfret (*b.*)
		Jonathan Swift (*b.*)
1668	Dryden (1631): *Of Dramatic Poesy: An Essay* (P.); *An Evening's Love* (D.)	Sir William Davenant, Poet Laureate (*d.*); Dryden new Poet Laureate
		Triple Alliance between England, Netherlands and Sweden
	Etherege (1634): *She wou'd if she cou'd* (D.)	
1669	Dryden (1631): *Tyrannick Love* (D.)	Parliament prorogued
		Sir John Denham (*d.*)
	Shadwell (1642): *The Royal Shepherdess* (D.)	Henry King (*d.*)
1670	Behn (1640): *The Forc'd Marriage* (D.)	Dryden appointed Historiographer Royal

DATE	AUTHOR AND TITLE	EVENT
1670	Dryden (1631): *The Conquest of Granada*, I (D.)	Secret Treaty of Dover
		William Congreve (*b.*)
	Shadwell (1642): *The Humourists* (D.)	Bernard de Mandeville (*b.*)
	Walton (1593): *Lives* (P.)	
1671	Dryden (1631): *The Conquest of Granada*, II (D.); *Marriage à la Mode* (D.)	Colley Cibber (*b.*)
	Milton (1608): *Paradise Regain'd* (V.); *Samson Agonistes* (D.)	
	Villiers (1628): *The Rehearsal* (D.)	
1672	Shadwell (1642): *Epsom Wells* (D.)	Declaration of Indulgence
		Break-up of Triple Alliance
	Wycherley (1641): *The Gentleman Dancing-Master* (D.)	War with Dutch
		Joseph Addison (*b.*)
		Richard Steele (*b.*)
1673	Behn (1640): *The Dutch Lover* (D.)	Revocation of Declaration of Indulgence
	Settle (1648): *The Empress of Morocco* (D.)	Shaftesbury, dismissed from Chancellorship, joins opposition
		John Oldmixon (*b.*)
1674	Lee (1648): *Nero* (D.)	Buckingham joins opposition
	Rymer (1641): Translation of Rapin's *Réflexions sur la poétique d'Aristote* (P.)	Robert Herrick (*d.*)
		John Milton (*d.*)
		Thomas Traherne (*d.*)
		Nicholas Rowe (*b.*)
1675	Dryden (1631): *Aureng-Zebe* (D.)	Wren's St Paul's started
		Enforcement of laws against Non-Conformists
	Lee (1648): *Sophonisba* (D.)	
	Wycherley (1641): *The Country Wife* (D.)	
1676	Etherege (1634): *The Man of Mode* (D.)	Edward Benlowes (*d.*)
		John Philips (*b.*)
	Wycherley (1641): *The Plain Dealer* (D.)	

DATE	AUTHOR AND TITLE	EVENT
1677	Dryden (1631): *All for Love* (D.); *The State of Innocence* (O.)	Shaftesbury, Buckingham and other opposition leaders imprisoned
	Lee (1648): *The Rival Queens* (D.)	James Harrington (*d.*)
1678	Bunyan (1628): *The Pilgrim's Progress*, I (P.)	Titus Oates claims Popish Plot to murder King
	Dryden (1631) and Lee (1648): *Oedipus* (D.)	Danby impeached by the Commons; five Catholic lords imprisoned
	Rymer (1641): *Tragedies of the Last Age Considered* (P.)	Andrew Marvell (*d.*)
		Thomas Stanley (*d.*)
		George Farquhar (*b.*)
1679	Dryden (1631): *Troilus and Cressida* (D.)	Dissolution of Parliament; elections
	South (1634): *Sermons* (P.)	New Parliament dissolved
		Roger Boyle (*d.*)
		Thomas Hobbes (*d.*)
1680	Bunyan (1628): *The Life and Death of Mr Badman* (P.)	Monmouth's Progress through west of England
	Dryden (1631): *The Spanish Fryar* (D.)	Exclusion Bill
	Filmer (1588): *Patriarcha* (P.)	Samuel Butler (*d.*)
	Otway (1652): *The Orphan* (D.)	Joseph Glanvill (*d.*)
	Rochester (1647): *Poems by the E— of R—* (V.)	John Wilmot, Earl of Rochester (*d.*)
1681	Dryden (1631): *Absalom and Achitophel* (V.)	New Parliament meets at Oxford
	Marvell (1621): *Miscellaneous Poems* (V.)	Shaftesbury proposes Monmouth heir to throne
	Oldham (1655): *Satyres Upon the Jesuits* (V.)	Parliament dissolved and does not meet again until after the death of Charles
	Ravenscroft (*c.* 1642): *The London Cuckolds* (D.)	Shaftesbury tried for treason by London jury
1682	Bunyan (1628): *The Holy War* (P.)	Shaftesbury flees to Holland
	Dryden (1631): *The Medal* (V.); *MacFlecknoe* (V.); *Religio Laici* (V.)	Sir Thomas Browne (*d.*)
	Otway (1652): *Venice Preserv'd* (D.)	

DATE	AUTHOR AND TITLE	EVENT
1683	Lee (1648): *Constantine The Great* (D.)	Royalist reaction
		City charters examined and forfeited
	Oldham (1655): *Poems and Translations* (V.)	Monmouth flees to Holland
	Otway (1652): *The Atheist* (D.)	Rye House Plot to kill King
		John Oldham (*d.*)
		Izaak Walton (*d.*)
1684	Bunyan (1628): *The Pilgrim's Progress*, II (P.)	
	Southerne (1659): *The Disappointment* (D.)	
1685	Crowne (1640): *Sir Courtly Nice* (D.)	Charles II dies; James II becomes King
	Dryden (1631): *Albion and Albanius* (D.); *Threnodia Augustalia* (V.); Preface and translations of *Sylvae* (P., V.)	Monmouth's rebellion and execution
		Anne Killigrew (*d.*)
		Thomas Otway (*d.*)
		George Berkeley (*b.*)
		John Gay (*b.*)
1686	Behn (1640): *The Lucky Chance* (D.)	James II appoints Catholics to Army and Privy Council
1687	Dryden (1631): *Song for St Cecilia's Day* (V.); *The Hind and the Panther* (V.)	Charles Cotton (*d.*)
		Henry More (*d.*)
		Edmund Waller (*d.*)
1688	Dryden (1631): *Britannia Rediviva* (V.)	James suspends laws against Catholics and Non-Conformists
	Halifax (1633): *The Character of a Trimmer* (P.); *Advice to a Daughter* (P.)	Trial of seven bishops
		Orange sails for England
	Shadwell (1642): *The Squire of Alsatia* (D.)	James flees to France
		John Bunyan (*d.*)
		Thomas Flatman (*d.*)
		Alexander Pope (*b.*)
1689	Dryden (1631): *Don Sebastian* (D.)	William and Mary crowned
	Locke (1632): *A Letter Concerning Toleration* (P.)	Toleration Act
		The Bill of Rights
	Purcell (1658) and Tate (1652): *Dido and Aeneas* (O.)	War with France
		Shadwell replaces Dryden as Poet Laureate

DATE	AUTHOR AND TITLE	EVENT
	Shadwell (1642): *Bury Fair* (D.)	Aphra Behn (*d.*)
		Samuel Richardson (*b.*)
1690	Dryden (1631): *Amphitryon* (D.)	William defeats James in Ireland at Boyne
	Locke (1632): *An Essay Concerning Human Understanding* (P.); *Two Treatises of Government* (P.)	
	Temple (1628): *An Essay Upon the Ancient and Modern Learning* (P.)	
1691	Dryden (1631): *King Arthur* (O.)	Tillotson appointed Archbishop of Canterbury
	Rochester (1647): *Poems of Several Occasions* (V.)	Richard Baxter (*d.*)
		Robert Boyle (*d.*)
	Southerne (1659): *The Wives Excuse* (D.)	George Etherege (*d.*)
1692	Congreve (1670): *Incognita* (P.)	Nahum Tate appointed Poet Laureate
	Dryden (1631): *Cleomenes* (D.); *Eleanora* (V.)	Thomas Rymer appointed Historiographer Royal
		Nathaniel Lee (*d.*)
		Thomas Shadwell (*d.*)
1693	Congreve (1670): *The Double Dealer* (D.); *The Old Bachelor* (D.)	George Lillo (*b.*)
	Dryden (1631): translation of *Juvenal and Persius* (V.); *Discourse Concerning . . . Satire* (P.)	
	Rymer (1641): *A Short View of Tragedy* (P.)	
1694	Dryden (1631): *Love Triumphant* (D.)	Thomas Heyrick (*d.*)
	Wotton (1666): *Reflections Upon Ancient and Modern Learning* (P.)	Archbishop Tillotson (*d.*)
1695	Congreve (1670): *Love for Love* (D.)	Licensing Act lapses
		Many newspapers start

DATE	AUTHOR AND TITLE	EVENT
1695	Locke (1632): *The Reasonable-ness of Christianity* (P.)	Halifax (*d.*)
	Tillotson (1630): *Works* (P.)	Henry Purcell (*d.*)
		Henry Vaughan (*d.*)
1696	Cibber (1671): *Love's Last Shift* (D.)	Jacobite plot to assassinate William.
	Toland (1670): *Christianity Not Mysterious* (P.)	Matthew Greene (*b.*)
	Vanbrugh (1664): *The Relapse* (D.)	
1697	Congreve (1670): *The Mourning Bride* (D.)	Treaty of Ryswick ends war
	Dryden (1631): *Alexander's Feast* (V.); translation of Virgil (V.)	Parliament demands standing army be disbanded
	Vanbrugh (1664): *The Provok'd Wife* (D.)	
1698	Collier (1650): *A Short View . . . of the English Stage* (P.)	Robert Howard (*d.*)
	Farquhar (1678): *Love and a Bottle* (D.)	
1699	Cibber (1671): *Xerxes* (D.)	Sir William Temple (*d.*)
	Farquhar (1678): *The Constant Couple* (D.)	
1700	Congreve (1670): *The Way of the World* (D.)	John Dryden (*d.*)
	Dryden (1631): *Fables, Ancient and Modern* (V.); *The Secular Mask* (D.)	

Index